Michael Kwa'ioloa is a chief, community activist and cultural expert of the Kwara'ae people of Malaita Island, living in Honiara, the capital of Solomon Islands.

Ben Burt is an anthropologist working at the British Museum who has been researching with Kwa'ioloa and the Kwara'ae chiefs since 1979 to document their culture and history.

They have published books and papers together on land tenure, forest resources, oral history and body ornaments, including Kwa'ioloa's account of his early life, *Living Tradition* (1997).

Other UQ ePress books

God's Gentlemen
A History of the Melanesian Mission, 1849–1942
David Hilliard

Workers in Bondage
The Origins and Bases of Unfree Labour In Queensland
1824–1916
Kay Saunders

The Samoan Tangle
A Study in Anglo-German-American Relations 1878–1900
Paul M. Kennedy

Papua New Guinea
Initiation and Independence
Don Woodford

Race and Politics in Fiji
(Second Edition)
Robert Norton

Tax Havens and Sovereignty in the Pacific Islands
Anthony van Fossen

The Chiefs' Country
Leadership and politics in Honiara, Solomon Islands

Michael Kwa'ioloa and Ben Burt

PACIFIC STUDIES SERIES

An imprint of UQP

First published 2012 by University of Queensland Press
PO Box 6042, St Lucia, Queensland 4067 Australia
This edition published 2012 by UQ ePress,
an imprint of University of Queensland Press

www.uqepress.com.au
www.uqp.com.au

© Michael Kwa'ioloa and Ben Burt 2012

This book is copyright. Except for private study, research, criticism
or reviews, as permitted under the Copyright Act, no part of this
book may be reproduced, stored in a retrieval system, or transmitted
in any form or by any means without prior written permission.
Enquiries should be made to the publisher.

Cover design: Kate Barry
Typeset in 11/15 pt Electra LH by Post Pre-press Group, Brisbane
Printed by Lightning Source

UQ ePress Pacific Studies Series Editorial Committee:
Professor Clive Moore (Chair)
Professor Brij Lal
Cataloguing-in-Publication Data available from the
National Library of Australia
http://catalogue.nla.gov.au/

UQ ePress pacific studies series
978-1-921902-24-6 (pbk)
978-1-921902-26-0 (pdf)
978-1-921902-25-3 (epub)

CONTENTS

ACKNOWLEDGEMENTS vi

LIST OF ILLUSTRATIONS vii

INTRODUCTION BY BEN BURT 1

CHAPTER 1 MY FATHER'S LEGACY 29

CHAPTER 2 RESEARCHING OUR TRADITIONAL CULTURE 37

CHAPTER 3 MAKING A LIVING IN TOWN 63

CHAPTER 4 MARRIAGES AND BRIDEPRICE 85

CHAPTER 5 DEALING WITH SORCERY 119

CHAPTER 6 OUR CLAIMS TO ANCESTRAL LANDS 135

CHAPTER 7 WORKING WITH CHIEFS AND POLITICIANS 163

CHAPTER 8 TROUBLE ON GUADALCANAL 191

CHAPTER 9 MALAITA FIGHTS BACK 213

CHAPTER 10 ENDING THE CONFLICT 235

CHAPTER 11 LEADERSHIP AND POLITICS, TRADITION AND DEVELOPMENT 263

BIBILIOGRAPHY 275

INDEX 277

ACKNOWLEDGEMENTS

For valuable comments on the drafts for this book, we are grateful to Graham Baines for the benefit of his long experience of Solomon Islands history and current affairs, to Clive Moore for his expertise on Solomon Islands history and support as commissioning editor for UQ ePress, and to two anonymous reviewers. Lissant Bolton and her British Museum Melanesian Art project made a vital contribution by supporting Kwa'ioloa's visit to London in 2006 and the British Museum Melanesian Research Seminar contributed constructive discussion to the editing of the book. Moffat Mamu kindly agreed to publication of photographs from the Solomon Star. We are very grateful to Nicholas Coppell and the Regional Assistance Mission to Solomon Islands (RAMSI) for funding the book's publication.

LIST OF ILLUSTRATIONS

Maps: Melanesia, Solomon Islands, Malaita and Guadalcanal.	x
Kwa'ioloa presenting a ten-string money to Ben Burt, 2004.	27
Samuel Alasa'a, Kwa'ioloa's father, 1979.	28
Anofiu, where Alasa'a spent his last years, 1991.	35
Michael Kwa'ioloa at the Museum of Mankind, 1997.	36
Chiefs gathered at Kwasibu to discuss the *Land* book, 1991.	42
A research meeting for *Our Forest of Kwara'ae*, 1993.	45
Kwa'ioloa addressing the British Museum conference, 2006.	60
Honiara Central Market, 2008.	62
Kwa'ioloa and Fanenalua at their house, 1999.	66
Malaitan houses and gardens at Gilbert Camp, 2004.	69
Some of Kwa'ioloa's sons.	74
Kwa'ioloa's youngest son Ben Burtte'e, 1999.	78
Watching television in Kwa'ioloa's house, 2004.	81

Kwa'ioloa's sons appearing in the *Solomon Star*, 2005.	83
Visiting relatives displaying ten-string moneys, 1999.	84
Bizel Fanenalua, 2004.	88
Michael Kwa'ioloa discussing a brideprice, 1999.	92
Michael Kwa'ioloa with his grandson, 1999.	98
A Kwara'ae girl dressed for her wedding.	101
A Langalanga brideprice presentation, 2000s.	108
A family from Langalanga making shell-money.	112
A wedding photo of Kwa'ioloa's daughter, 2009.	114
A *vele* sorcerer's kit.	118
Thompson Atoa, 1987	120
An East Kwara'ae landscape, 1984.	134
Maps: Kwara'ae clan lands.	140
Chart: Genealogies of Latea and Fairu.	143
Rocky Tisa with his cattle, 1991.	145
Paul Daokalia, Alex Rukia, Frank Ete, Rocky Tisa.	162
Silas Sangafanoa, paramount chief, 1987.	174
Kwara'ae chiefs at the launch of *Land in Kwara'ae*, 1994.	183
A view from Mount Austen, 1999.	190
Houses in Kobito Two on the outskirts of Honiara, 1991.	200
Scenes from the reconciliation ceremony, 23 May 1999.	208–209
Maps: Honiara and Guadalcanal.	211
The MEF 'joint operation', June 2000.	214
Members of the MEF at Kakabona, July 2000.	219
The MEF bunker at Alligator Creek, October 2000.	221

Militants celebrating the Townsville Peace
    Agreement, 2000. 236
Kwa'ioloa with MEF militants, 2000. 242
Kwa'ioloa at a RAMSI vehicle check. 245
The Solomon Islands National Parliament, 2008. 264

THE CHIEFS' COUNTRY

Melanesia, Solomon Islands, Malaita and Guadalcanal.

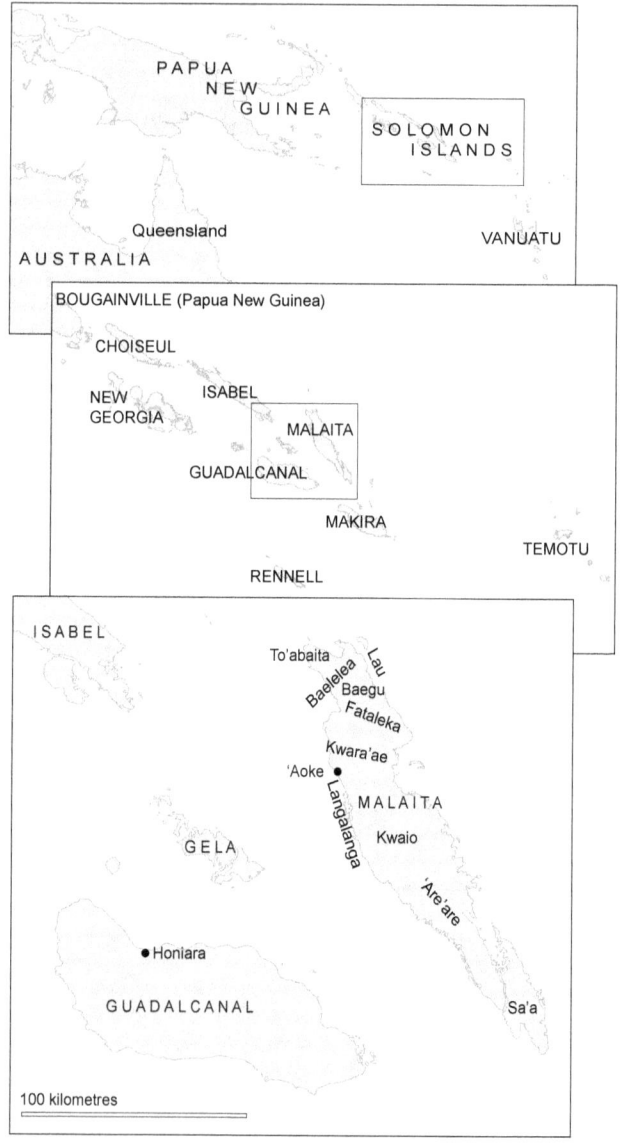

INTRODUCTION
Ben Burt

Michael Kwa'ioloa is already known to many readers of Pacific Islands literature from his first volume of autobiography, *Living Tradition* (Kwa'ioloa & Burt 1997), which I edited for him in the late 1980s. This described his childhood in an old-fashioned community in East Kwara'ae, Malaita, in the 1950s, his first experiences of town life in Honiara, capital of Solomon Islands, in the 1960s, and his early married life back home in Malaita, in the 1970s. He recounted his work for the church, local government and community leaders or 'chiefs', while dealing with the contradictory values and spiritual forces of ancestral tradition and colonial Christianity. For me, Kwa'ioloa's narrative exemplified the experiences of his generation of Kwara'ae men, which they shared with me in the course of my research into *Tradition and Christianity* (Burt 1994a).

The present book continues Kwa'ioloa's autobiography as a series of reflective narratives from Honiara, where he and his wife Bizel Fanenalua have raised their ten children since the 1980s. Life in town has broadened his perspective on the 'tradition' or cultural heritage which pervaded his first book. He now brings its values to bear on issues affecting Solomon Islands as a whole, including urban society and its relations with home, national politics and the civil conflict between Malaitan settlers on Guadalcanal and the indigenous Guales at the turn of the century. Nonetheless, his standpoint and identity remain firmly grounded in his home in Malaita, with an enduring commitment to the local clan communities through which he and his children hold their claims to ancestral lands. In this he represents the experience of townspeople throughout Melanesia, balancing the opportunities and demands of urban and rural life by active involvement in both.

Kwa'ioloa's way of resolving the inevitable contradictions this entails has been to reaffirm the values of his ancestral tradition in the Malaitan communities of Honiara, by continuing the work he began in the 1970s as secretary to the chiefs at home in East Kwara'ae. As local community leaders, Malaita chiefs have been organising to reinstate the values of tradition under their own authority ever since they temporarily supplanted the colonial administration through the island-wide Maasina Rul movement in the 1940s and 1950s. In the Malaitan settlements which have grown up around Honiara since the 1960s, chiefs represent local communities and mediate relations within and between them, as they do at home. Now recognised as a chief himself, Kwa'ioloa has achieved influence by supporting his relatives and neighbours in dealing with their problems and concerns. In this, and in facilitating and co-ordinating the authority of his fellow chiefs, he is enacting the principles of 'leadership' (*fa'ina'ona'o'anga*) as service to the community. Such leadership, which he contrasts with the self-interested 'politics' of elected government officials, is a core theme of this book. For Kwa'ioloa, it is essential to the tradition which the chiefs seek to restore, as a way of life inherited from their ancestors and governed by those who truly represent the interests of their people.

Chapter 1

The values of Kwara'ae tradition were instilled in Kwa'ioloa by his father Samuel Alasa'a, so it is appropriate to begin the book with the old man's handover of inherited authority in 1987, as he was about to die. As a younger son, Kwa'ioloa has not inherited seniority in his clan, now headed by his elder brother's son Samuel Maesatana, but his father gave him the confidential ritual knowledge which, in former times, would have enabled him to become the priest (*fataābu* or tabu-speaker) to their ancestral ghosts. This inheritance conferred the ancestral blessing which gives Kwa'ioloa confidence to exercise leadership within his clan and the wider community, and his father is a continuing presence in his concern for the traditional values of Kwara'ae and Malaita.

Chapter 2

It was our shared interest in this cultural tradition, from very different perspectives, which brought Kwa'ioloa and me together as research partners thirty years ago. For Malaitans, the idea of traditional culture has powerful and complex connotations. As conveyed by the Pijin term *kastom*, its meaning has been much debated, by researchers as well as Malaitans themselves, in relation to local and colonial values, ancestral religion and Christianity. David Akin (2013) has analysed the history of *kastom* as a concept taken by Malaitans from colonial stereotypes of unchanging 'native custom' and adapted to proclaim the distinctive local values which they chose to maintain and develop for the changing times. As such, *kastom*, and for Kwara'ae the equivalent concept of *falafala* or culture, became an ideological focus for the anti-colonial Maasina Rul movement of Kwa'ioloa's parents' generation following the Second World War, and it has continued ever since to have implications of cultural and political autonomy. For Kwa'ioloa and the Kwara'ae chiefs, *kastom* means above all the inherited ancestral values they seek to live by, and their right to do so. *Kastom* will be translated here as 'tradition' to convey the weight of ancestral authority and the negotiable content of this essentialised conception of culture. This echoes the way English-speakers legitimate practices, new as well as old, as 'traditional' to imply a basis in ancient precedent.

I came to Malaita to study both Kwara'ae tradition and their ideas about it, while Kwa'ioloa and the Kwara'ae chiefs were working to reinstate it. Our earlier collaboration is described in Chapter 2, as a background to Kwa'ioloa's work for the chiefs, to our ongoing relationship and to this book. It is Kwa'ioloa who has enabled and supported the continuation of my research beyond my initial 'tradition and Christianity' project, and this is the fifth book we have published together. In the course of this work, we have visited each other's homes and families and shared our life experiences over the years. We speak of each other as 'brothers' (*ngwaefuta* or 'kinsman'), which makes me 'father' to his children, and particularly to his youngest son, my namesake Ben Burtte'e (the *te'e* means 'junior'), who features in this book.

Kwa'ioloa, as secretary to the chiefs of East Kwara'ae, helped authorise my first visit to Malaita, and he explains the chiefs' expectations of anthropology, still only partly realised today. (My own reflections on this relationship are summarised in Burt 2008.) He contributed to my early research and dealt with the suspicions and jealousies which often threatened to obstruct it, even before our first joint project with the chiefs, *The Tradition of Land in Kwara'ae* book on land tenure, which he describes here. The tensions between a popular concern to document and reaffirm traditional knowledge and factional allegations of personal gain against us were acted out most dramatically in disputes over the death in 1984 of the last senior ancestral priest of Kwara'ae, Timi Ko'oliu. The accusation was that Ko'oliu died as a result of his photograph appearing in a booklet I published (Burt 1981), which could have exposed him to defilement by women and thus offended his ancestral ghosts. Kwa'ioloa gives what may (or may not) be the final version of this incident and its interpretation by various interested parties, already referred to in previous publications (Burt 1994:209, Kwa'ioloa & Burt 1997:165-167). In recounting how such debates affected our research, Kwa'ioloa also demonstrates his ability to mediate disputes and facilitate community affairs, in Kwara'ae as he has continued to do in Honiara.

Chapter 3

Honiara, with its large concentrated Malaitan population and eventful political life, seems to suit Kwa'ioloa's talent for community activism and his ambitions for leadership, but he lives there for much the same reasons as everyone else, as he describes in Chapter 3. It is far more difficult in Malaita to earn the cash to buy the kind of things Honiara can provide, including education for the children, health and other public services, let alone the foreign manufactured goods which everyone relies on and the imported luxuries they enjoy. There is employment in Honiara, where the wealth and foreign aid of Solomon Islands has been invested in government and commercial infrastructure, at the expense of the provinces.

As Kwa'ioloa explains, he has developed his own strategies for supporting his family in Honiara's monetary economy, combining work as a special constable with security and building contracts and the various opportunities which arise from community service. The disadvantage of Honiara is that people have to pay for even the most basic material needs, which they can produce for themselves at home. For Kwa'ioloa, this dependence on money, and the business values of the cash economy, lead to selfishness and jealousy, which contrast with the mutual help (*kwaima'anga* or 'reciprocity') and generosity (*alafe'anga*) as crucial values of tradition on which community life depends. The challenge is to maintain these values in town and to educate his children in them, and there are contradictions to be faced. Hospitality to visitors from home, seeking to share the benefits of urban living, can threaten the welfare of his own family and their material aspirations, which include housing for his married sons and the inevitable demand for modern amenities. Kwa'ioloa's debate over providing a video player for his family illustrates the difficulty of bringing up children in town according to the moral values of rural Malaita, and the way tradition must respond to changing times. In bringing in such imported amenities while controlling their moral effects, Kwa'ioloa is consciously fulfilling the responsibilities of both a family head and a community leader.

These relationships extend the values, and the vocabulary, of the family to the broader community. Relatives and even unrelated friends are referred to as 'fathers' and 'mothers', 'sons' and 'daughters', as 'brothers' (same sex) and 'sisters' (opposite sex), including (cross) 'cousins' who are the children of 'aunts' (fathers' sisters) and 'uncles' (mothers' brothers). The same applies to relatives by marriage, distinguishing brothers- and sisters-in-law from parents-in-law. Where necessary, people may say who a relative is actually 'born of', but otherwise they assume that such terms cover moral bonds as well as strictly literal kin relationships. In Kwa'ioloa's account (except in reported speech) these 'extra' (*fafo*) or classificatory relationships have been distinguished by inverted commas, to aid the reader rather than to indicate any distinctions made in his original text.

Chapter 4

In describing his efforts to secure the future for his seven sons and three daughters, Kwa'ioloa goes on in Chapter 4 to show how Malaitan society and the values of its tradition are founded on marriage as a relationship between families legitimated through the payment of brideprice. These payments are made in shell-bead money, mostly made by the Malaita sea people of Langalanga. The standard denomination for Kwara'ae is the ten-string (*tafuli'ae* or 'ten-legs'), although the *bani'au* money made in Kwaio has a similar value, and either are often referred to as 'red money' from the colour of the most valuable beads (for details see Burt 2009:36-38,60-61). Dollars often substitute for part of a shell-money payment according to recognised equivalents, but the progressive devaluation of the Solomon Islands dollar makes the cash values of a ten-string difficult to gauge in a historical account. The Solomon Islands dollar was originally equivalent to the Australian dollar and to half a UK pound, but in 2011 there were more than ten dollars to the pound.

Although the brideprice (*daura'ia*, the 'hanging up' of the shell-money) is said to 'pay for the woman' (*folia kini*), Malaitans are very clear that this is not like paying for goods or property, which is why dollars are generally inappropriate. Through the stories of his children's marriages, Kwa'ioloa explains how the exchange of shell-bead money for a new wife not only unites their families as in-laws but also creates and renews obligations among the relatives and neighbours who contribute and repay this money to help with each other's brideprice payments, one generation after the next. As these stories show, the rules for arranging marriage according to traditional ideals are as often broken as observed. If Malaitans try to uphold the strict moral tradition of their ancestors a few generations ago, who would threaten death for the 'sin' (*usu'a*) of sex outside marriage, they are frustrated by government law, Christian teaching, and the social mixing between men and women which goes on especially in Honiara. Even so, when young men and women become lovers, even if they intend to marry, discovery leads to angry negotiations between families over restitution or brideprice payments, sometimes complicated by cultural differences between their language groups or islands.

For men like Kwa'ioloa, negotiating marriages and contributing to brideprices and wedding feasts have always been opportunities for leadership in the community. Likewise, mediating and contributing to restitution payments to resolve potentially dangerous disputes makes leaders indispensable for maintaining peace and order. Restitution (*fa'aābu'a*, usually translated less accurately as 'compensation') entails restoring the mutual respect which is fundamental to Kwara'ae ideas of sociality, by making a person tabu (see Burt 1998 for a discussion of the concept). You lead others by helping relatives and neighbours in such circumstances out of 'love', a term used by Christians to cover both 'reciprocity' and 'generosity' in Kwara'ae terms. Then they will support you in important ventures by offering and repaying gifts, services and loans. Kwa'ioloa has always provided secretarial services to those less educated than himself, including the Kwara'ae chiefs, helping to mediate disputes within his local community and dealings with officials beyond. He has helped his relatives obtain wives by contributing to their brideprice payments, investing in the relationships which maintain his community at home and create the new Malaitan community in Honiara from people of diverse backgrounds. This is not a matter of accumulating shell-money so much as of channelling the brideprice received from the marriages of 'daughters' to pay for the marriages of 'sons'. Although shell-money can be purchased for dollars, leadership depends on circulating this wealth through exchange to help others, rather than possessing quantities of shell-money.

In this complex of relationships, Kwa'ioloa is adept at balancing his credit against his obligations, but the personal strategy which he describes reveals some contradictions in the politics of exchange. For the sake of his family's independence, Kwa'ioloa has been much less willing to accept help than to give it, paying brideprice for his sons from his own savings rather than accepting the contributions offered by others. He has even provided food for their wedding feasts, which the woman's side normally offers as a partial exchange for the brideprice they receive, implicitly asserting leadership over his new in-laws. How far can a leader avoid incurring the obligations through which others seek to tie him to them in relationships of mutual respect? Perhaps this is an inevitable consequence of life in Honiara, where cash incomes from impersonal relationships make it easier to choose the selfish individualist option of giving without receiving, contra to the ideal of interdependence as practised in Malaita. The fact that Kwa'ioloa has to persuade his sons of the moral imperative to support their relatives reveals the difficulty of maintaining the values of tradition in town, despite good intentions.

Chapter 5

As Kwa'ioloa says, marriage is one of the things which brings people together as a community, and this is when leadership has to be shown. The settlements around Honiara are new communities (*fanoa*, meaning home or habitation) where marriage creates important new ties among families, clans and ethnic groups who might never meet in their homes in Malaita and other islands. But there are corresponding tensions, and besides occasional violent confrontations, people are sometimes suspected of using sorcery to cause sickness and death by secret means, as described in Chapter 5. Sorcery (*kelema*), commonly translated in Pijin as *poison* and often acting through food, is implicitly distinguished from other kinds of spiritual agency (*akalo*, referring particularly to ancestral ghosts) as illegitimate and wrong, in terms of tradition as well as Christianity. As such it is treated much like other unprovoked attacks, the more feared because it is invisible and unpredictable, requiring restitution under threat of violence. Sorcery has no place in Kwara'ae ideals of their own tradition and they tend to attribute its various techniques to other languages and islands, even though it is a common theme in their own local histories (see Burt 2009). While no-one would normally admit to using sorcery, the methods are well understood and there are accepted ways to deal with them.

Nonetheless, there is a certain ambivalence in Kwa'ioloa's attitude to sorcery. As generally agreed, people inflict sickness or death by secret means out of jealousy for their victims' prosperity and success, but some people could be thought to invite attack by being proud and careless of the welfare of others. In this respect, although sorcery is explicitly condemned, it may also represent punishment for anti-social behaviour. This is the implication of some of the old histories, in which sorcerers afflict those who have offended them through selfishness or insult. But Kwa'ioloa also treats sorcery as an attack on the economic development brought about by those who, like him, work to raise their own family's standard of living. This particular contradiction between community expectations and personal ambition seems inherent in leadership in an egalitarian society but it is exacerbated by the opportunities and liabilities provided by life in town. The tensions between a person's ambitions for his own family and his obligations to less successful relatives seeking hospitality on visits from home or help with shell-money payments may well lead to resentments. Kwa'ioloa was himself attacked by sorcery, apparently for helping to bring a sorcerer to account. Sorcery would seem to be a hazard of leadership in Honiara as elsewhere in Melanesia, where the successful may not only suspect others of attacking them from jealousy, but also be accused of using it to advance selfish ambitions.

Chapter 6: Leadership and land

For all his deep involvement in the Malaitan community in Honiara, where his children have grown up and married and his own reputation as a community leader has been established, Kwa'ioloa remains committed to his true ancestral home (*fanoa*) in Malaita as his 'land of origin' (*ano ni fuli*), the foundation of his identity. As shown in Chapter 6, his on-going relationships with relatives there, maintained by mutual help and regular visits, focus on their shared interests in ancestral lands, which represent security for future generations. For the present, however, it is not easy to earn money there and attempts at economic development are continually frustrated by disputes over inherited title to the land. Kwa'ioloa's district of East Kwara'ae is notorious as one of the most disputed areas of Malaita and he has helped repeatedly to defend the land claims of his own Fairu clan, in disputes which go back fifty years.

Kwa'ioloa's account gives a glimpse of the tensions within a local community caused by these competing claims to ancestral lands. Control of a clan's land is vested in men descended from its ancestors in the senior male line, but all descendants have claims, depending on their relationships with these 'leaders' (*fa'ina'ona'o*) for the land. Despite the common English and Pijin translation, these are not 'owners' in the Western sense, and will be referred to as 'land-holders'. The local clans of Kwa'ioloa's home district are long-term neighbours, so intermarried that everyone in the neighbourhood is related to everyone else, often going back ten generations or more. So when it comes to competition for land, men who grew up together as 'fathers' and 'sons', 'brothers' and 'cousins' have found themselves accusing each other in court and even assaulting one another. Kwa'ioloa's father Alasa'a was in dispute with his own sister's husband Ramo'itolo of Latea, whose son married Kwa'ioloa's sister. Kwa'ioloa has been in dispute with his cousin Rocky Tisa, son of his father's clan 'sister' and his own close colleague in work for the Kwara'ae chiefs.

These disputes are a consequence of the way commercial development in Solomon Islands, under government-enforced peace, has encouraged people to seek maximum economic returns from the land. The prevailing land tenure system was designed by ancestors who had less to gain by accumulating resources and wealth than by sharing them to promote group strength and leadership, in defence of local communities which were constantly threatened by feuding with their neighbours. The contradiction between the communal values of the land tenure system and individualistic aspirations for 'development' are among the most intractable issues faced by the chiefs, and government, of Solomon Islands (see Burt 1994).

'Claiming' clan land (*firia*, the term which Kwara'ae translate as 'owning') is also an opportunity for leadership, not necessarily limited to those who are 'senior' (*fa'ina'ona'o*) by birth as nominal leaders of their clans. While acknowledging the seniority of his elder brothers, Kwa'ioloa has assumed leadership in defence of his Fairu clan, including its large number of associates descended from its woman members. His literacy and secretarial experience in dealing with chiefs and government is no doubt an advantage here, especially since people often assume that the courts favour educated people who know how they work. Such leadership at home, while living in Honiara, makes it all the more important for Kwa'ioloa to demonstrate that he still belongs there, unlike the examples he gives of emigrants who have lost their lands through neglect of their obligations to relatives at home.

From Kwa'ioloa's point of view, ancestral lands and their associated traditions remain part of him wherever he lives, and those who lose this relationship lose their own identity. But beyond this, like others in Malaita and Solomon Islands in general, he also hopes that his land may someday yield the kind of wealth enjoyed by more developed countries. Gaining such benefits depends upon establishing historical claims by tracing and linking genealogies, researching ancestral deeds and interpreting the significance of place-names. Kwa'ioloa's researches indicate ancient relationships between his ancestors from Tolinga in the Kwara'ae inland (before they moved to Fairu) and both north Malaita and neighbouring Isabel Island. These histories have encouraged them jointly to claim the island of Anogwa'u, or Ramos, between the two islands. Anogwa'u ('Empty-land') is the Malaitan island of the dead and also the site of a possible oilfield. In a society where even unrelated friends and allies are treated as relatives, evidence of blood relationships enables people to organise around such shared interests to advance land claims, nowadays through formal agreements which can be legitimated by the state. Needless to say, such claims are often contested by those with their own interests in the land concerned.

Chapter 7

As Kwa'ioloa explains in Chapter 7, leadership means being able to 'straighten' (*fa'asagā*) things out between people, to resolve their disputes and grievances. The objective is peace and reconciliation by giving money as restitution, to avoid the injured party seeking restitution by violence, which can still lead to feuding as in pre-colonial times, until the police step in. The disputes which threaten the peace of Malaitan communities in Honiara are less about land, as at home, than rows over offences such as sexual misconduct, swearing, assault or sorcery. As in Malaita, people usually prefer to deal with such matters within the community rather than involving the police and government courts. This is the role of leaders as chiefs, who are trusted to judge the issues according to local values, in more or less formal meetings. Kwa'ioloa grew up under this kind of chiefly authority, organised throughout Malaita under the Maasina Rul movement from the 1940s and maintained as a central feature of the Kwara'ae chiefs' tradition movement since that time (see Burt 1994 Ch.8). Unlike the state system of criminal law, the chiefs act as mediators between civil parties, and in Honiara their authority to do so has been supported by the Magistrates Court.

Kwa'ioloa contrasts the chiefs, as supporters of traditional authority and values, with self-serving politicians who fail to advance the interests of those they persuade to elect them. Politicians represent the political system imposed on Solomon

Islands to create a nation state from diverse local communities. In most of Malaita these communities were no more than loose networks of local clans, from which Malaitans themselves developed unifying institutions, incorporating mission church organisation and inspired by the colonial administration, most successfully through Maasina Rul. The chiefs of Kwara'ae, Malaita and Honiara are the heirs to this movement, but, as Kwa'ioloa complains, their authority has not been recognised as it should under the national constitution. This is the rationale for his own activism, particularly as founder-member of an activist group, the Solomon Islands Traditional Culture and Environmental Conservation Foundation (SITCECF), which supports the chiefs in promoting the values of tradition.

The failure of the Solomon Islands system of government as it stands is manifest in the notorious corruption of elected politicians, which itself raises difficult issues. While there is no doubt that many politicians are resented for enriching themselves, they are also expected to gain support from their electorate by generosity in the distribution of government funds. Insofar as Malaitans have always granted authority to those who support them in need, they also expect the leaders they elect to help them personally in ways which the Solomon Islands constitution and legal system might treat as corrupt. Kwa'ioloa criticises politicians both for failing to help with cash the humble constituents who elect them, and for using the constituency development fund controlled by each member of parliament to buy their votes. His underlying point is that leaders should serve their community rather than themselves, but of course community service is also self-interested. The problem is that the government fails to constrain the selfishness of politicians in the way that local communities expect to constrain their leaders, making elected officials less representative and accountable than chiefs.

The political assumption implicit in Kwa'ioloa's account is a very Malaitan one: that people confer power on their leaders (as on spiritual beings) by treating them with respect ('making them tabu', *fa'aābua*) and 'making them true' and 'real' (*fa'amamana*). Although this power can be used against the followers (or worshippers) as well as for them, it depends ultimately on their assent (see Burt 1994 Ch.3). Just as Malaitans changed their allegiance from ancestral ghosts to God and acknowledged colonial government before rejecting it under the Maasina Rul movement, so they now seek to empower their community leaders as chiefs as they question the legitimacy of their politicians.

Chapters 8 to 10: The Malaita–Guadalcanal conflict

For Kwa'ioloa the vital role of chiefs in the governance of Solomon Islands is demonstrated above all by the conflict between Malaitan settlers of Guadalcanal and that island's indigenous people from 1998 to 2003, which he sees as a failure of the government in becoming increasingly divorced from the population at large. Solomon Islanders commonly refer to the episode as 'the ethnic tension', although it is better described as a civil conflict, brought on by the inequitable economic policies which have promoted immigration by developing Honiara and the north coast of Guadalcanal at the expense of the rest of the island and of other provinces like Malaita. Chapters 8, 9 and 10 deal with the cause of this conflict, its course and its aftermath, expanding upon a version we have already published

(Kwa'ioloa & Burt 2007), which is here set in the broader context of Honiara life and politics.

Kwa'ioloa attributes the conflict to a failure of the national government to deal with Guadalcanal grievances against Malaitan immigrants or to recognise Malaitan claims to land on Guadalcanal; grievances confirmed by Matthew Allen's research among the militants of both sides (2013). Kwa'ioloa regards the question of land claims as an issue of traditional law, to be dealt with by the chiefs of both parties. He recounts how Malaitan settlers, drawn by employment opportunities, were granted land by Guadalcanal land-holders according to apparently traditional agreements which the government ignored. Their claims to these lands, inherited by their sons and grandsons, are enhanced from the Malaitan perspective by their forefathers' labour developing the plantation economy of Guadalcanal, working and fighting with the Americans in the Second World War, and building the infrastructure of Honiara afterwards. In Malaita, working with and defending the land-holders gives a claim to live on and from their land. Kwa'ioloa gives a Malaitan perspective on the issue, but acknowledges the Guadalcanal grievances over competition for land and jobs which led them to drive Malaitans from the rural areas and attack them in Honiara. Perhaps his most controversial points are references to ancestral histories, which imply more ancient Malaita claims to settlement on Guadalcanal. Guadalcanal people, many of whom have long harboured resentments against Malaitans as overbearing trespassers, will certainly dispute this, although it is not actually the basis of specific Malaita land claims.

Kwa'ioloa experienced the Malaita–Guadalcanal conflict as a chief supporting and attempting to regulate the Malaita militants defending Honiara, as a special constable in the police confronting them to maintain public order, and as a private security contractor protecting various politicians and officials from the lawless situation. He was personally acquainted with many senior protagonists, from government ministers to militant commanders, and heard first-hand accounts, as well as rumours, of many events he did not witness himself. What distinguishes his account of the conflict from official and journalistic reports, well summarised in books on the conflict by Clive Moore (2004) and Jon Fraenkel (2004), is his local perspective, representing the interests and values of the Malaitan settlers of Honiara. This is corroborated by Allen (2013) on the basis of accounts by the militants themselves, for which Kwa'ioloa provides the broader social context of life in Honiara before and after the conflict.

The way the militants legitimated their claims and campaigns also raises issues around the interpretation of traditional values. Although compensation claims arising from the conflict have been much criticised as extortionate abuses of traditional practices, for instance as 'the manipulation of custom' (Fraenkel 2004, and see Moore 2004:160-163), they have also resolved grievances by negotiation to avert the threat of violence. The government may indeed have paid off the militants rather than facing up to them and dealing with their grievances, but demanding restitution under at least the implicit threat of violence is actually how Solomon Islands dispute settlement always operated. However, many claims against the government were made for grievances caused by known individuals and groups, which indicates a problematic attitude to government and the state.

The relationship between Malaitans and the state is full of contradictions. At the same time that politicians are expected to behave as generous leaders, 'government' itself, like its colonial predecessor, tends to be regarded as a group or institution outside of society. Malaitans originally used the term 'government' (*gafamanu*) to mean 'colonial officer', and people still tend to personalise government in opposition to themselves. They do not seem to identify with the national government as their own, as they do with a body of leaders like their chiefs or even their local and provincial government authorities. When they feel that government is responsible for a grievance, people feel justified in exacting payments proportionate to its means, as they would with a rival community. Apart from the many fictitious claims made during the conflict, which amounted to outright blackmail under force of arms, much of the 'manipulation of custom' could also be seen as unresolved negotiations on the relationship between local communities and the government of Solomon Islands.

Kwa'ioloa and his colleagues in SITCECF became involved in one such negotiation on behalf of ten Kwaio men who were killed in an attempt to assassinate the Guadalcanal rebel leader Harold Keke in 2002. The popular allegation that the government had sent them made it responsible for their deaths, according to Malaitan tradition, implying that Keke was an enemy of the government rather than of the victims. Their relatives' compensation claim against the government was not so much a 'manipulation of custom' as a confrontation between two legal systems, which was mediated by Kwa'ioloa and his fellow chiefs in the absence of a constitutional settlement between the values of tradition and of the state. As Akin has described (1999), the contradiction has a history reaching back far into the colonial period, when the government often refused to recognise the principles involved, especially for Malaitan grievances against itself, and notably in Kwaio claims for deaths caused by government retaliation for the killing of District Officer William Bell in 1927. The conflict with Guadalcanal has enabled some Malaitans, at least, to enforce their legal values upon a government which has for so long imposed its own laws upon them.

This was one of the issues addressed by Kwa'ioloa and the SITCECF chiefs when they responded to the conflict and its aftermath by engaging in debates on the future of Solomon Islands. They were involved in consultations on traditional law for the United Nations High Commission for Human Rights, in the formation of the Malaita Ma'asina Forum pressure-group for devolved government, and in land agreements to facilitate development at home. However, as observers of Solomon Islands may agree, the underlying causes of the Malaita–Guadalcanal dispute have yet to be resolved. In 2006 a commission of inquiry into rioting in Honiara which led to the burning of Chinatown, identified as underlying causes poverty resulting from government failure to promote development, particularly of the infrastructure serving the outlying settlements of Honiara. Its recommendations included increasing participation by local communities and the redistribution of power from central to local institutions, as advocated by SITCECF and the chiefs (Solomon Islands Parliament 2009).

Chapter 11

The government did not endorse this report, but Kwa'ioloa's conclusions in Chapter 11 concur with it. His last chapter is comprised of several statements about the moral and political issues facing Solomon Islands society today. For Kwa'ioloa, the inequitable economic development under a corrupt political elite represents an abandonment of the traditional values of sharing and co-operation, as the wealthy become selfish and the poor become resentful. He objects to imported Western solutions based on 'rights' for women and children as different sections within society, as contradicting traditional values. Kwa'ioloa's answer, shared in various forms by many other Malaitans in Honiara and at home, is to reinstate the authority of the chiefs as leaders who care for their people by giving them a role in the national constitution of Solomon Islands. A 'house of chiefs', as in Vanuatu and Fiji, would advise the elected parliament on matters of tradition. Some Malaitans with experience of government and administration question how chiefs would be selected to avoid the self-interested misuse of power which has discredited the parliamentary system. This could be a problem for several parts of Solomon Islands, including areas of Malaita, like Kwara'ae, which have no tradition of powerful inherited leadership. But Kwa'ioloa and the chiefs have identified the contradictions between local and state systems of political and legal authority, which the government has as yet failed to resolve.

Writing Kwa'ioloa's story

This book should be explicitly declared for what it is, to avoid it being misunderstood as something it is not. It expresses Kwa'ioloa's personal experience and culture and my academic research, but as a product of the relationship between us it also represents our separate as well as shared values and interests. It is Kwa'ioloa's book, but I have helped to write it because I agree that he has important things to say about life in Honiara and politics in Solomon Islands, which few others have the opportunity to publish. This is his political agenda as an activist in the longstanding Malaitan movement to reconstitute local culture within the Solomon Islands state. Accordingly, Kwa'ioloa seeks to demonstrate and promote the values of tradition under the authority of the chiefs. He wants to put his personal experiences on record to this end, for the benefit of his country, his community, his family and his own personal reputation. Without doubting Kwa'ioloa's integrity, the reader should recognise that he has a particular perspective which may not represent all sections of his community, let alone his country. He speaks as the head of a large family, as a chief, a pastor, police officer and mediator of relationships within and beyond his community. But he is no longer a young man, he does not speak for women, and he is a Kwara'ae and a Malaitan, not simply a Solomon Islander.

My task has been to help Kwa'ioloa communicate to an audience far wider than the community which shares his experience, and in this I have my own interests. As an anthropologist it is a rare privilege to be entrusted with personal information of such cultural and historical interest as Kwa'ioloa's narratives. If I were not sympathetic to his cause the opportunity would not have arisen, so I am also his advocate, with an interest in producing an account which is coherent, clear and persuasive. This is not to say that I endorse all Kwa'ioloa's opinions or claims for, as an anthropologist and a Whiteman (*ara'ikwao*, as Malaitans call us), I seek to understand his world-view rather than to share it. I make no judgements on his claims to land or the disputes he has taken part in or mediated for others, including the conflict between Malaita and Guadalcanal, but I do have sympathy for his underlying political values, and so I am pleased to have my name appear on his book. We are not presenting an impartial or disinterested analysis of Solomon Islands history and culture, so much as a commentary based on personal experiences which reflect those of a significant section of the community.

Compiling the book has been a joint enterprise. What we have produced between us is neither a spontaneous narrative by Kwa'ioloa nor a composition by me, but a collaborative interpretation of his experiences and ideas devised for an audience represented by us both, as Solomon Islander and Whiteman. Most of the book, like its prelude *Living Tradition*, was dictated by Kwa'ioloa in response to my questions and comments. We began in Honiara in 2004 with the Malaita–Guadalcanal conflict and continued during his visit to London in 2006 for the British Museum's *Melanesian Art* research project. I recorded and transcribed his words and translated them from Pijin as I edited the narrative, incorporating some shorter transcripts from recordings we had made previously and a few pages from accounts he wrote subsequently in response to further queries.

This method has allowed Kwa'ioloa to express himself freely and fluently, while leaving me a great deal of discretion as editor. I have tried to convey his style of presentation, which owes much to Malaitan oral literature. There is a certain reticence in speaking of matters which belong to other communities, while emphasising the importance of his own. The names of people and places are listed as fully as possible to give historical substance to the account. Bare facts passed on as hearsay and history are given circumstantial detail, including reported speech. Much of my work has been to reduce the repetition and redundancy which is common to any verbal account and characteristic of Malaitan narrative style, to resolve accidental inconsistencies and interpret idiomatic expressions, while trying to convey something of the distinctive Malaitan style of presentation. Kwa'ioloa's Pijin usually expresses Kwara'ae conceptual categories and his explicit references to key Kwara'ae terms are included in endnotes to each chapter.

While we agreed on the basic agenda of the book, its structure only emerged in the editing, as I arranged passages to illustrate themes which now form the chapters. These themes were not always obvious to me at the outset, but I tried to discern Kwa'ioloa's underlying intentions and he has endorsed them in reading, amending and approving the drafts. One consequence of this process is that Kwa'ioloa may sometimes seem to speak in two different modes or frames of reference, Malaitan and Whiteman. On the one hand he is creating a record for his own community and on the other he is representing his community to the world beyond. This is implicit in his relationship with me, as his audience and editor, but it also reflects his lived experience of mediating local and global culture. Whiteman readers can judge for themselves how well he understands and communicates with them, and the better he succeeds the more sympathetic they may be to his values and attitudes which they find strange. Even so, there are many tensions and contradictions between the local and the global, which neither Kwa'ioloa nor anyone else has yet managed to resolve, and this is one of the things which makes his account so interesting.

Kwa'ioloa is not the first articulate autobiographer who has needed editorial support to communicate his experiences in writing, and there are several other examples from Malaita (e.g. Keesing 1983, Fifi'i 1989, Kenilorea 2008). As mediators, editors like myself enable the authors to share their perspectives not only with their own people but also with strangers who may have an important influence on their lives. Through this book Kwa'ioloa is communicating realities, values and opinions which may not all be shared by readers of other communities and cultural backgrounds. Such people can now learn about a Malaitan world-view and make their own assessments of it through comparison with their own. They may not believe in God, ghosts or sorcery, but Kwa'ioloa can help them understand why Malaitans do, and how the power of such phenomena, for good or ill, depends on this belief. If readers do not understand history in terms of ancestral precedent, he can demonstrate the essential role of genealogy for relationships between Malaitans and their land. Anyone who questions the solidarity of ethnic groups as 'countrymen' (*wantok*, meaning 'same language') and 'brothers' when this seems at odds with the political and economic values of the nation state, may reflect on why mutual help among relatives is so fundamental to Solomon Islands society, and of particular importance in the otherwise fragmented communities of a Melanesian town. Those who regard Malaitans as more troublesome than their opponents in Solomon Islands politics will have a chance to consider the Malaitan point of view and reconsider some popular stereotypes about them.

All this should help readers to appreciate Kwa'ioloa's central theme: the importance of values based on the traditions of Malaita and Solomon Islands, as mediated by local community leaders as chiefs. Whether or not they agree with his traditional values and his analysis of Solomon Islands politics, they can find here a perspective which many Solomon Islanders share but few have an opportunity to present to their country and the world.

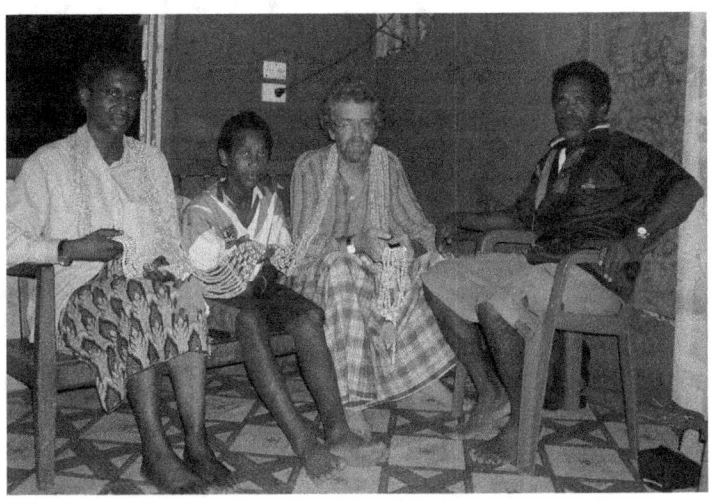

Michael Kwa'ioloa, with his son Ben Burtte'e, presenting a ten-string money from his daughter's brideprice to Ben Burt and his wife Annette Ward in 2004.

Samuel Alasa'a, Michael Kwa'ioloa's father, in 1979. (Ben Burt photo)

1
MY FATHER'S LEGACY

I want to talk about my father's secret knowledge. Before he died he was sick for several years, and it cost me and my elder brother John Maesatana a lot of money to go back home to Anofiu to see our father. Back in 1984 when he was well, his aim was to die in his original home and be buried there, where my mother died. So when he began to be sick, we took him back to stay with Maefatafata, his niece, at home. She cared for him, but that was all; food, rice, kerosene and everything was provided by us, and we would visit him several times a year. Then eventually I wondered why my father was taking so long to die. John Maesatana and others said, 'Father is dying,' and he and our 'brother' Wilson Gua, two chiefs, went and stayed with him for two weeks. Then father said, 'I'm sending you both back to look after the grandchildren and provide for them. I'm a dying man; just send Kwa'ioloa back here.'

My father's eyes had gone blind, so they had tied a vine for him to hold, to lead him to the toilet. That's what we did with father, and I wondered how he had come to be so ill but would not die. One night when I reached home, I said, 'Father, why won't you die? I need you to die, to be at rest.' 'My son, I'll tell you. This oath procedure which is on me, this invocation,[1] if I don't pass it on, it's hard for me to die. I can be here till I rot and still talk, unless I hand it on.' I said, 'Then when will you hand it on, and who will you hand it on to? I love you, I do. Won't you give whatever it is?' Then I explained that Jacob and Esau loved their father Isaac. 'The two fought for their birthright until Jacob took it. Esau sold it for soup. But I want you to give it to me, so you can die, because I'm tired and sorry to see you suffering so long. Father, you are causing problems for my family, because you should be with us in Honiara. That's why you told the other two to go back, because a message came that your grandchildren had no more rice.' I had nothing, because my children were not yet working at that time and I was the only one to support them. 'I have no money. Please hand me the birthright and die now, father,' I cried to him that evening. Then he said, 'It's hard for me to die,' and so on. I said, 'Father, I'm a pastor; I will pray that the Lord gives us the chance and makes it so that nobody visits us this evening. Then by four or five or six o'clock, if nobody comes, that's when we will wait upon the Lord and you will hand on this power of yours, before you die. You must pity me; I don't have knowledge of our lands, I don't have the oaths of invocation. Other people surpass me, and you claim to be the one who remains the principal man. Then why won't you give it to me?' Father said, 'In giving it, if I spew it out in the village, everyone in the village will suffer and die one by one.

Formerly, you had to invoke on a pig first, strike the pig, strangle it, and the pig would die.[2] Then everyone would live, because I had offered it to the ghosts. If I give it for you to hear, then someone must take me to the women's toilet by night.' I said, 'What for?' 'So that I can neutralise it by telling this procedure in the toilet. I'll defile it, or I'll die with it.' I said, 'Father, why?' 'If I tell it directly, you will have the power of invocation. Because it's the invocation of Siale that I'll tell. It's the invocation of 'Aisubu that I'll tell, the invocations of 'Eda'eda, of Baibai, Gwau'ulu and Fiu.[3] It's the invocation of everywhere, the invocation of Timi Ko'oliu's worship at Anomula that I'll tell. I'll tell you, because I am the founder. Timi Ko'oliu was just my younger brother. Before I came to the church, it was me the elders invoked for, and I have done it myself, with pigs; such and such a man, you and you, and so on.' Then I said, 'Father, I desire it. Father, shall I pay you for it? I have a hundred dollars here, father. Please give it to me, in case you give it to someone else in my absence. Please,' I pleaded and cried to my father. Eventually he took a deep breath and thought deeply and said, 'Give me a chance to think about it, because I want to die. The *sisi*-beetle must die within the *di'a* tree.' That meant the invocation procedures would die with him, given to no-one. 'Hey father, you are harming me. Harming me, please give it to me. If you give to me, I'll take over your leadership, and it will help preserve what belongs to Malaita.' Then he said, 'Alright, we'll see over the next few days, but your deadline for going back is Saturday. On Saturday morning you board the ship to return to the grandchildren. If the Lord does not allow me to give it to you before Friday, that means you have no chance. You go back and I die with it. I won't give it to anyone.'

Then I prayed in full, as a pastor, until four o'clock, checking the time and nobody came, although they were interested that I had come for father. I prepared a nice meal that evening, because I had bought tins of Taiyo tuna and things for father. By five o'clock no-one came, six o'clock, seven o'clock and no-one came. I remember it was a Thursday and I had given Maefatafata twenty dollars to buy a big fish at Faumamanu market, and we ate it that evening. Then the two of us slept. We slept until about two o'clock in the morning, when he awoke me. 'Why my son, it may have been the ghosts or God, but they showed me that you are suitable for me to give it to. I dreamed it. I'll give it to you now. Because it is set down that after eight days I will die. If I give it to you, in eight days, day one, two, three, four, five, six, seven; day eight I will die. But don't stay while I die. You must go. Go from me to Honiara, work for your children and forget all about me. But John Tolia, Maesatana's second-born son, must come and take my head and bury me.[4] You understand? If he doesn't come, I'll delay my death until he arrives.' With that, at two o'clock he began to pray. I closed my eyes and held him to me, but I had my cassette recorder ready. He just said, 'Aa . . . aa . . . aa,' he was so weak, but eventually he began to pray, trembling with emotion: 'Oh,' praying loudly, until his voice came out well. That was when I received it, dead-on three o'clock, as he began to speak aloud and give out the invocations.

First he gave out the invocation of Siale, and I was surprised that there were Whiteman words in this invocation. 'Holy Land' was in there, which he pronounced badly as 'olilan', but I know it was true. With that, he trembled and cried and told me all of it. When he finished he came on to Anomula and to all of the tabu-sanctums in Fairu. When he had finished them all he said, 'That's it, dear son. I'm about to die, as you insisted on receiving it.' Then he prayed and had just reached 'Amen' when an earthquake shook us. I held my father as it shook, and the third time he had diarrhoea and everything came out. When my father's life went out he wasn't playing around; the earthquake shook us three times. He didn't die, as he had promised it would be eight days before he died. So I prayed for him to be strong again, and I prayed that the pastors would come for him to dedicate his life to Christ, to be saved on the last day. Then when it was all done, in the morning I washed him with soap, dressed him properly, washed away the shit, then after that I made some good food for him, he ate, and then people came to greet him and talk with him. Eight days after I arrived, John Tolia reached home and when he came up to see him, father was dead. His breath had given out the ghost. John Maesatana's son came and cried and helped to carry the coffin and put him in the grave, as he would have wished.

What he had given me was blessing, honour and power. That's why when I speak people listen to me. I'm only one man, but when I speak the provinces come together: 'Why don't you organise us?' I don't use the invocation, but it gives me blessing and wisdom, so people obey me, and I have power and knowledge. Before father died it was difficult for me to speak about things, but this knowledge makes me speak from the head and everything I say is accurate. When he prayed he had said, 'Give your ear,' and he spoke about everything into my ear. At the time, my body trembled with the power. It gave me the knowledge to write about the country's law, and spiritually, if someone is planning something for me, I know in advance. Father believed in God, and when he died and went directly to Paradise, the spirit of God worked. Sometimes I dream of him saying, 'Oh, somebody's angry with you.' If they are discussing me, I dream I can sit down and listen to them. He advises and guards me, and I believe that is very true of God and our ancestors.

Ever since I was born, during my childhood and youth, until I was married, I lived with my father and always listened to his words. In his old age, I cared for him, until that day when he took pity on me and handed on the invocations of the various sacrificial shrines. He repaid me, the second-to-lastborn of our family, just as Isaac did with his second son Jacob, according to the Scriptures. My prayers and aspirations for my father to hand the power over to me and not my elder brothers followed God's instructions to David, that the man chosen from his many sons to rule Israel after him, his son Solomon, must be just and rule in the fear of God (2 Samuel 2:3).[5] In the same way that David was anointed to take over leadership from Saul, I have been anointed to hold important offices in the church. This has resulted in great blessings from God, so that my sons are all well behaved and obedient and also hold church offices, and their wives are committed members of the church. This is the fulfilment of my father Alasa'a's invocations to ordain me, just as Saul, David and Solomon were blessed with leadership as kings.

Anofiu, the village where Alasa'a spent his last years, in 1991.
(Ben Burt photo)

---

1. *Fiki'a*; the formula for invoking the ancestral ghosts when sacrificing to them.
2. This is how an invocation would be used, in killing a pig to bake as a sacrificial meal for ancestral ghosts to bless the living.
3. These are the tabu-sanctums or sacrificial shrines of their ancestors, as described in Burt & Kwa'ioloa 2001 Ch. 3.
4. Under the ancestral religion, his family would have kept Alasa'a's skull as a focus for praying to him, although as Christians they did not do so.
5. As with the Old Testament Jews, leadership in Kwara'ae and particularly the priesthood of the tabu-speaker, although ideally inherited by the eldest son, may be passed on instead to the most worthy at the discretion of the father and of the ancestral ghosts.

Michael Kwa'ioloa at the Museum of Mankind in 1997, with an exhibition featuring his work with Ben Burt and the Kwara'ae chiefs. (British Museum photo)

2
RESEARCHING OUR TRADITIONAL CULTURE

This book is one of the results of my work with Ben Burt of the British Museum, researching the history and culture of my Kwara'ae people. I have continued this work ever since I came to live in Honiara, but it began long ago when I was at home in Malaita. My work with Ben Burt began in 1979, and I'm very pleased that my 'fathers' approved my working with him. When he came we put him into the hands of Adriel Rofate'e as paramount chief, and he didn't know that I was also to work with him. Then he met me at Faumamanu and that's when Rofate'e and I arranged with my father and the other chiefs for him to stay with me, because I was a man who wrote. The first book he published explained how the first ancestors of Kwara'ae came from overseas and established us where we live.

It was I who had the idea to invite Ben Burt. I remember a meeting in 1973 in which the area council came together with the chiefs at Faumamanu one Thursday. The area council members at that time were Clement O'ogau, Taemana, Ngwasangwane, Fangamae, Marcus Bualimae, Noel Amasia, Samuel Sosoke, Andrew Gwa'italafa and Maefelo. I was their secretary and I did all the writing for the court; registrations, letters, postage, banking. I began by telling them, 'I'm sorry for us all. I myself am quite well off in terms of writing, and I can talk with my father night and day, but some of you don't bother.' Then the son of Le'anafaka, my 'brother' the school teacher Maefolo, said, 'Eh, little brother, I agree with this. How should we tackle this problem? Because the elders will die and when we take over from them everyone will be sorry that we won't be able to speak about the things they spoke about so well.' Maefolo was saying their knowledge would be lost. So I said, 'Alright, I have an idea from when I was at school at Betikama[1] and went into the library and read what men had written in books. Also, when I had to do some research for assignments, I went into the National Library in Honiara, and the library owned by Honiara City Council. I saw the names of men who had written about subjects like Papua New Guinea and Fiji, our so-called 'friends of the Pacific', but where were we, Solomon Islands?' So then the Malaita Council delegate, David Musia, said, 'Michael, I have an idea too. You know how to talk to people of our district; can you do something to obtain a man for us? Or it will be just you sitting down to write everything from the elders.' I said the problem was money: 'Because if we work for free to write things, the time will come when our families, our wives, reject us: "Go and eat the food you've produced in the last week."' Then I said, 'Alright, there is a way. We see from the books that some people have contributed information and others have written it. What about inviting an anthropologist researcher to come and write all about us? He can stay with us, get dirty with us, eat food with us which is strange to him, sleep all around with us. There are men willing to do it.'

I knew about anthropology because I had been to school, up to standard seven, and we had talked about preserving our history. I had heard about that man Maranda who was researching anthropology in north Malaita, and Roger Keesing researching in Kwaio, and I had seen their books in the library.[2] At the time I couldn't read well but I looked through them and knew what they were about. I said, 'Those Kwaio, they can see the photos of their elders, and even when they're dead they will read about them.' Then O'ogau, Sese, Fangamae and the others said, 'So let's look for somebody to work like Roger Keesing does.'

I was a man to write, but all the books I wrote in were lost, due to damp, and people smoking with them.[3] My 'brothers' would come when I wasn't there and ask my wife, 'Bring a paper of Kwa'ioloa's from over there,' and she would bring one which my father had told his genealogy for. Some men, like Bualimae, said, 'But Kwa'ioloa, you write well, so you do the writing.' I said, 'Eh, producing books, writing information and doing it in good English; that I can't do. We use local English, so I can only write court minutes and things like that.' 'But you do know how to.' I said, 'It's more than that. Writing books is difficult.' They got the idea and they said, 'Alright, we must apply for a Whiteman to come and sit down with us and do the work.' So we sent a letter to the Malaita Council, and the council contacted our member of parliament Faneta Sira, who arranged a meeting on another Thursday. He came, we told him and he said, 'Alright. I will call for this man.' So he sent to the Ministry of Education and they sent to England for a man to come and do the work. Ben Burt applied to the Solomon Islands government, but he applied at the right time, and we were church men who prayed for things. When he applied we had already prepared for him and God saw that it was time; that's what we believe. So then we appointed Paramount Chief Adriel Rofate'e, for this man to come and be in his hands to care for him, and for writing I would work with the man. That was our plan and it met Ben Burt's needs in applying, so I think it was no accident but according to God's plan.

The chiefs and elders had high expectations. Osifera, my father Alasa'a, O'ogau, Nole, Tafanga and the others were saying when we met at Tafanga's home at Taba'a in January 1979, 'Oh, let's help Ben Burt so that he can take everything of ours and show it to the Queen of England, then she'll send some money for us to run our own government of chiefs.' Some said, 'So we can build a cultural centre[4] of materials like sheet-iron, because we're tired of building with sago-thatch and having to repair it.' They also said, 'So that he'll send books for our children to learn from, to turn their ideas back towards the things we tell them about respect for people. If we don't give out this knowledge, when we die it will be finished. He must write down the law[5] so that future generations can say, "Oh, formerly with the elders, if a man went with another man's wife, he would be charged so much shell-money or cash to punish him."' So then they could make decisions according to what Ben Burt wrote, and the Queen would authorise this and help us to overcome the government which stole so much money, so a government of our own would stand. That was the thinking of the elders, as I heard them speak at the meeting at Taba'a.

When Ben Burt came, he showed us what we call 'the way'[6] to write books, which is really difficult. We usually think a man raises his name by authoring books, and this made me willing to transcribe recordings and translate from Kwara'ae into English. We had an executive board with a president, secretary, and so on, and when I facilitated programmes with Ben Burt all the chiefs were eager for it.

I contributed to Ben Burt's book *Tradition and Christianity*, but the first book we worked on together was my autobiography, *Living Tradition*, beginning in 1987.[7] For the *Tradition of Land* book, Graham Baines and Ben Burt sent the idea to the World Wide Fund for Nature (WWF).[8] They didn't know about our ways in Kwara'ae but saw that it would be sustainable usage of our true land if we followed a book of what the elders said. So WWF sponsored some meetings and all the chiefs gathered to provide information. They said, 'Let's work on the Kwara'ae law on ways of claiming land so that we and our children will know that if it's truly our land we will know what makes it ours.' That's why the book was so useful and important. In 1991 I got our member of parliament Alfred Maetia to attend a meeting at Kwasibu in East Kwara'ae of about fifty chiefs, Ben Burt and I brought food, which the women cooked for them, and the chiefs listened to us and were willing to help. We worked as a research team, with Frank Ete, Nelson Konai, Rocky Tisa, me and Ben Burt, and Adriel Rofate'e as our consultant. We were knowledgeable about our tradition, but the more I wrote and recorded, the better I understood it. When Ben Burt returned to England, each time he wrote a draft he would send a copy for me to correct in terms of language and the meaning in English. I didn't do this by myself; I went back to the House of

The chiefs gathered at Kwasibu in East Kwara'ae to discuss the *Tradition of Land* book in 1991. Seated, left to right: Samuel Sosoke, Arnon Nwadili, Cornelius Kwasi, Adriel Rofate'e, Alfred Maetia MP, (unknown), Nelson Konabako, Ben Burt, Marcus Bualimae, John Gamu. Michael Kwa'ioloa and Frank Ete are standing behind.

Chiefs at Kwasibu and we sat down to read through the draft, and the chiefs would tell me if something I said was a bit amiss and correct it. Then I would write it for Ben Burt, send it back, and he would send another corrected draft for me to look at and take it to the chiefs again. It was hard work and it cost money, but WWF supported us.

The success of this land book was such that John Naitoro, permanent secretary in the Ministry of Home Affairs, recognised its importance and Alfred Maetia, our MP, launched it in 1994 with the governor-general as guest of honour. The ministry asked me and our SITCECF group to send an estimate for inviting guests and the chiefs from Malaita came to the launch. The High Court of Solomon Islands saw the book and treated it as the first handbook on ways of owning land, not only for Kwara'ae but for Malaita. Some people were a bit cross with me: 'Kwa'ioloa, why do you just say *"The Tradition of Land in Kwara'ae?"* It should be Solomon Islands.' I said, 'Ben Burt is afraid that some ways of claiming land are different from yours, whoever you are. We're not all the same. Only the Kwara'ae chiefs provided information for this.' But in court they used the book as a guide to the ways we can claim land; how an important woman could be given land when she married, how people who fought for us could be offered land for shedding blood and things like that. John Muria, the first Melanesian chief justice, was very pleased with the book because it was the first of its kind in the country. If a man went to the customary land appeal court, John Muria would question him on things in the book and say, 'Very good, but first go back to your area council or house of chiefs to authorise your appeal.' Those who had attacked the elders, or thieves who had used false evidence to contradict them, were afraid to go to the house of chiefs to be questioned on genealogies, landmarks, sacrificial shrines, and so on. The local courts have used it too, because the book shows them straight away when a man wants to rob someone and what the Kwara'ae chiefs declared, and that makes him ashamed.

The book *Our Forest of Kwara'ae*[9] took about three years. Ben Burt and I worked on this book with Frank Ete Tu'aisalo as my advisor and Rocky Tisa and Nelson Konai as my facilitators between Honiara and Malaita, as well as Adriel Rofate'e and other chiefs. For the first draft Mark Merlin from the University of Hawai'i came with us to the cultural centre at Ma'usunga, then Ben Burt sent a second draft to me from

England. When I read it to the chiefs in Kwara'ae language and in English they were so surprised: 'Eh, that's something new! It shows that Ben Burt isn't hiding anything, because the two of you have put our words into English. We are really very pleased.' We made the corrections individually, because I would say, 'You said such-and-such about this tree, its name, its description, where it grows and how we use it.' 'Oh no, there is a mistake, my son, change that tree a bit, that's not its use because it's not tall, its work is so-and-so.' They would tell me what changes to make and it all went back to Ben Burt to correct. For the third draft Ben Burt came back again and for the final draft I came to England in 1997 and we worked in the Museum of Mankind[10] and read it through in Kwara'ae and in English.

Although we had approved the book, Ben Burt still had to find someone to publish it, or it would have remained a draft and we would have just put it aside and smoked with it. The chiefs said, 'Ben Burt must make it into a book, like Roger Keesing.' He was successful in having the British Museum publish the book, but he also applied to the New Zealand high commissioner who fortunately gave some money for publication so that we could receive free copies. When the chiefs saw the book they were so very pleased. We read the first copy to them and they said, 'Even when we die, everything of ours is already in there.' Everyone who saw it was soon asking for copies, and I distributed it also to the high commissioners, the Malaita Province premier and assembly, ministries and even big companies, so they would know about our work.

A research meeting at Kilusakwalo in West Kwara'ae in 1993 for *Our Forest of Kwara'ae*, facilitated by Arnon Nwadili (at far left).

At the same time, we worked on another book, *A Solomon Islands Chronicle*, on the histories of my father Samuel Alasa'a.[11] Although Ben Burt had come to work with us, my father didn't want to release all the secret information about everything belonging to us, because he said Ben would benefit from it to get rich and all those things. Those were his thoughts until I told him, 'Look, Ben Burt has come at the request of our area council, with the approval of the province and the Solomon Islands government. He comes to the market and gives money to Fane to buy fish for us, he buys sugar and things for us, and all this shows he wants your approval to record everything. Father, don't hide anything because you will die, but the books will remain.' That's what convinced my father to share all his knowledge. Working with my father Samuel Alasa'a, sometimes he'd say, 'But you've asked me two or three times!' Ben's way of putting things to the elders always made him cross: 'I've already told you and you say it again! You are really slow in the head!' My father would say that, and I'd say, 'Father, please be patient with me, because you are going to die. I'm taking everything good of ours for Ben Burt and me to compile into a book; your picture will be there and your talk, and it will help me, my sons and grandsons. Everything of yours will remain and even when you're dead we will read about you in years to come.'

I should say that, in terms of traditional knowledge, my father was an important man in the Kwara'ae area, and a father to everyone. He was born before the government arrived and brought up under the old system of leadership. People from all around asked him to tell them their genealogies. He had a good memory and he passed that on to me. I'm proud to say that everyone desires what my father told and they want the book, but myself, I say we should restrict giving it out. It's not that others contradict my father's genealogies, but some are worried because Tolinga is the leading clan in Siale.[12] Tolinga is symbolic; it means 'sharing out' land, persons or goods. Although Daroa, meaning 'divide it up', is the name of another clan, they don't know who it was given to, as we of Tolinga do. But my 'father' David Ofalanga said, 'Michael, I don't want you to give this book to everyone in Kwara'ae. I don't want our genealogies to be public.' I went to see him at Kobito in Honiara in 2005, and he baked a pig worth five hundred dollars for my 'son' Sam Maesatana and me because, he said, 'Before I die I must celebrate with you both. Even when you go back and I die, I forbid this book *A Solomon Islands Chronicle* with all my elder brother's knowledge to be given to lots of people.' Of others who saw the book, Andrew Gwa'italafa, a member of the provincial assembly, was pleased with it and wanted us to write another one for him and his own Ubasi clan. In the library in Honiara lots of people have come to read it and some want us to do the same for their genealogies and the knowledge passed on from their forefathers.

From my own experience, I can say that this anthropological research is not easy and it can cause problems. When I wrote out the cassettes which Ben and I recorded of the elders speaking, it was my first time to do this. Ben gave me cassettes and a recorder, but when I didn't know about research I would just put on the recorder and say, 'Father, speak.' Ben told me to choose the subject, because the elder would say, 'What shall I tell you? Where should I start?' To give an example of what I learned in Biblical terms, someone says, 'Jesus was born of Mary, then he chose his twelve apostles, eventually he was killed and ascended into Heaven.' But from what I learned of anthropological work, you ask the elder to refer back: 'Before he was born, what happened?' 'Oh, the angel Gabriel spoke to Mary and told her she would conceive a child who would be called the Lord Jesus the Saviour.' Then you say to the elder, 'He chose his apostles, but how did he do that?' 'Oh, he told Peter, "I'll make you fishers of men."' You must go back over things to make the elder tell all the details and question him so that the story doesn't jump from one thing to another. That will make the book interesting and easy for readers to understand.

It is important to deal with the chiefs and elders correctly. People expect something in exchange for their knowledge. For example, if my father gave out the genealogy of another clan for a hearing, tracing it so they could win their land because he knew its history from staying with their elders long before, they should give my father some traditional money, or they should buy a bag of rice or some tinned meat or sugar for him to take home. So when Ben Burt and I went to visit the elders, I'd say, 'Give a little cash to the old man,' because he would sit down and give us his valuable knowledge. When we had finished talking he'd give him some money for tobacco or sugar, and he would be very pleased. Sometimes I heard them say that when their photos and information went into a book, they should receive something from the book too. Maybe they were thinking in terms of royalties or something. When they saw the books they were pleased because they were a partial exchange for our work and they would have copies of the books for their children to see: 'Oh, this book transfers our knowledge, so it won't be lost.' Without the books, they would expect help with money, or something for their cultural centre. Otherwise they'd say we had taken their tradition to gain riches from it, and if so we must give something. It's not an exchange or buying and selling, but the information they want to give you is their gift to you, and you must give a gift back to them. It is to help them and if you don't, whatever they tell you, they will be dissatisfied.

There were also some people who opposed our research work from jealousy and suspicion. My 'father' Richard Folota opposed Ben Burt's research in Kwara'ae, at first I think because we didn't let him know. He had no part in the process of asking for an anthropologist because he is from West Kwara'ae. Another reason is because he is of Anomula, with the senior tabu-speaker Timi Ko'oliu, and he thought we might get rich from the research with Timi Ko'oliu and he was jealous of us. So he forbade us to work with Timi Ko'oliu in case we received something from him, such as his invocations (although he had already given the invocations to Folota himself, which made the ghost angry, because he should have sacrificed a pig first). Folota also became an enemy of Rofate'e, although Rofate'e was his brother-in-law, because he led us to work with Timi Ko'oliu. It was jealousy which damaged Folota. When Ben Burt came, in the first book which came out they saw photos of the tabu-speakers and others who had contributed. Then they realised: 'Oh, this is good, our work with Ben Burt is very good.' But in 1984 Timi Ko'oliu died. Then some of the pagans, not those in the church, said, 'Maybe when Ben Burt came and you and Rofate'e straightened it with Timi Ko'oliu to visit his house, take his photo, and put it in the books, then their women walked over it and held it and the ghost killed him.' That's what they thought, and there were accusations against us.[13]

Then in 1992 we were working with WWF, who gave money for the book *The Tradition of Land in Kwara'ae*, and Kath Means of WWF came from Australia. The two of us went to East Kwara'ae to meet the chiefs and discuss the draft for the book which Ben Burt and I had written, working with the chiefs. When they heard about this, they held a meeting two days before at the house of my uncle Di'a at Namosamalua, planning to accuse me and Ben Burt and make us pay compensation for the life of Timi Ko'oliu. Well, my 'younger brother' Thompson Atoa was waiting for me and Kath Means at 'Aoke to bring us in his truck, so we sat in the cabin and came early, arriving about nine o'clock in the morning. As we drove in I realised something was wrong. When we reached Di'a's house everyone there was surprised by the truck and they all ran off into the coconut plantation: 'Oh, Kwa'ioloa has come, who we are planning against!' Kath Means said, 'Why are these men running away?' They were hostile, wanting to accuse me and Ben Burt.

So the people drove to the school and the meeting opened at ten o'clock. My 'father' Bitareo Fini'a had sent my namesake Kwa'i, Kwa'ilalamua: 'Quickly, tell Michael to come here first, before going to the meeting.' Fini'a lived in a nice house down by the taro swamp, and when we arrived he was there with Kwa'i. Kwa'i had killed a Kwaio man and I had got him released from a life sentence.[14] He had sharpened his knife all the way to the handle. Fini'a said, 'My son, watch out; they've been planning since yesterday. All of them; 'Uate'e from the inland and the pagans from 'Ere'ere and Tagero, they slept overnight with Di'a. They are planning that you should give ten shell-moneys on behalf of Ben Burt, today. The woman with you will give it.' I said, 'Not the woman; I'll just give it. What do they want?' Then my father explained everything, and my namesake Kwa'i became emotional. 'You released me from prison. If anyone touches you today, I'll go back to prison for life. Why? I've heard them accusing you over the old man and his photo.' What I said was, 'When I hear all this, I'm not afraid, because they are only my fathers and brothers and I know they'll listen to me. I've known 'Uate'e and the others for a long time, and I've worked with them at their home with Maelekini, the tabu-speaker.' I told my 'father', 'Finia, don't you worry. This is the work the elders asked Ben Burt to come for, and he came according to the proper procedures of the country. If they do this they will be opposing not Ben Burt, Rofate'e and me, but Malaita Province, which granted our research permit. Rather than us, Malaita Province should give compensation.' I came out with this and he said, 'Yes,' and I said, 'I tell you, I'm treating everyone who is complaining like little children who crawl on the ground. They'll take soil and put it in their mouths. Let's go to the meeting quickly so I can take the soil from their hands. I mean what I'm saying, because they're like children, wanting to damage themselves. I'll go and explain so they can express what they're thinking.' Then my 'father' said, 'Thank you my son. If that's the case, I'll let you go to the meeting. Hold that in mind, but don't say as much up there.' So I was happy to go, but I stopped my namesake Kwa'i, because I was a police officer: 'Don't worry, if anyone does something wrong, I'll arrest him. I have my handcuffs and everything with me.' Then Kwa'i was quiet, and I said, 'But leave your knife in O'o's house, Fikumani's son, our son, then go up to the meeting.'

We had brought Ben Burt's books which he had written and we went up. The traditional men of the inland, 'Uate'e and the others, wouldn't come into the ground floor of a two-storey building so they went up a pole directly to the upper floor, to avoid going under women up above. They had opened up two classrooms into one big room, where we met. After we had prayed they said, 'We will deal with the death of that man Timi Ko'oliu first.' Then 'Uate'e said, 'Timi Ko'oliu died because Rofate'e, the paramount chief, and you Michael Kwa'ioloa, our secretary, the two of you enabled Ben Burt to go to 'Ere'ere, then you took his photograph and they defiled it. Because this was a man no woman could go near, no woman could eat of the food he ate, and even the place he sat was very tabu. This was a man the ghosts talked with. He should not have died, but you, you all made him die. Michael, you're my son, but now you must give ten shell-moneys; five *bani'au* and five ten-strings, and five thousand dollars. You must all give it, that's it, we won't be swayed.' He was angry. That was first on the agenda, and secondly they said, 'Oh Michael, we know you have got rich from our tradition. When you work with the Whiteman, Ben Burt, they send money for us but you are all just stealing it. So we want you to stop working on those books.' Then the third issue they raised was, 'You all persist in collecting information to enable Ben Burt to complete his studies so he will receive his large salary and produce his papers, so it's good for him and bad for us.'

Those were the three issues they put to me, so I tried to answer. 'Thank you very much for this; I accept it seems like that, but I don't agree.' Then I took out the Kwara'ae book[15] and said, 'Alright, this is the book you're talking about when you say we destroyed that man, that women sat on it, it was in ships with women sitting above it, women held it, and that's why the man died.' Then I showed the photo of the three priests, Nguta, Maerora and Timi Ko'oliu, and I said, 'My question is this, father 'Uate'e. I don't want to excuse myself and Ben Burt, because we are the main ones doing this work, but Rofate'e is father to all of us and he will be blamed because he wanted us to come. Well, why is it that in the same photo Timi Ko'oliu, Maerora and Nguta are all sitting there and it's only Timi Ko'oliu who has died, not the other two? We have used the book for seven years up to now. Why is it he died the first time the book touched a woman's hand?' David Musia, now a member of the provincial assembly, said, 'What Michael says is very true. If it defiles a man's body so that he dies, Maerora should be dead too, and Nguta, but they are both alive.'[16] Then Ko'oliu's son Fa'ale'a spoke up forcefully: 'It was I who invited my brother Michael Kwa'ioloa and Ben Burt to work with my father, so that our religion would be written about for future generations. Ben Burt gave money to help my father, which none of you did.'

That was that, but then they said, 'Answer the next question. What about you getting rich in cash?' So that was when I told Kath Means; 'Oh, come and brief us on your work,' because the cash Kath Means was giving for the project was what they were complaining about. Rocky Tisa interpreted for her and I stood by to answer questions. She said, 'Alright, before Kwa'ioloa gives the traditional money, I want to ask a question. Under your tradition, formerly, were you ruled by government?' Then Musia answered, 'We were governed, but it was local government in which we just talked with each other, the elders. But government administration, ministries and things; oh no.' 'Alright, my second question is, did your forefathers rule you with cash?' They said, 'No, not cash. Each man worked for himself.' 'Alright, a third question. Have you done any fundraising and won money, which Ete and Michael Kwa'ioloa and Rofate'e then misused?' 'No, we haven't had any money for the work.' 'In that case, who has sent money for you, which they have eaten up?' There! She came to the point. 'Do you know of any man who has sent word to you chiefs saying he's giving millions, or even hundreds of dollars, to you?' They said, 'Oh no.' We had covered everything they were saying. Kath Means said, 'So then, it's I who has given a little money for us to come together like this and eat. I've given it through the project, so that your unwritten ways, which Ben Burt and Kwa'ioloa are helping to write for you, will remain. Even when your elders die, your way of owning land will remain here. I have not come with WWF money for you to eat it up or for salaries or anything, and it's not much money either. It's just to provide the food here for us all, and a little for stationery to complete the work.' So they accepted this: 'Oh, somebody lied to us. They said a lot of money had been given and Ete and Kwa'ioloa had eaten it up.' Kath Means said, 'If you think like that, maybe we should burn all these books, then some of you can try to do it. We Whitemen think you have been lucky; your ancestors from generation to generation have remembered everything and maintained it.' 'No, we won't burn them. We're happy with it. But there were a few questions, that's why we were like this.'

Then I said, 'Alright, let's ask Fa'ale'a. Come brother, because it was you who let us talk to your father Timi Ko'oliu, who slept with us and told us which things in your home were tabu to photograph. How did Timi Ko'oliu, our father, die? Is it true that this is what killed him?' Then Le'a stood up and said, 'My father died from a chill[17] and flu. He was sick and very weak, then a week or two later my mother also got sick, and when she went to the latrine she fell down, very ill. She came up close to the dwelling house and fell down again, so my father lifted her up. He said it should not be a problem because she had come up from the women's area.' The story that Timi Ko'oliu had gone to the women's latrine to help her was just made up to accuse us. 'When my father went to the latrine he got dizzy, so I would support him, but that time he went by himself and he fell down at the fence, and that's how he died.' Le'a said, 'Anyone who says that the ghost killed him because of the books must give me restitution.' He began to cry: 'You must give restitution. They worked hard. None of you gave hundreds of dollars to my father, but this stranger Ben gave him a bit of money, and bought tinned fish for him and kerosene. With us it's just empty talk. This man came as a stranger and my father called him his son. Which of us gave any red shell-money to my father? I don't want empty talk. My father was living in poverty, with no-one to help him.' He was crying. 'Ben Burt helped him. Now Kwa'ioloa, ask them. If it's true it was the books he died from, who should receive the traditional money? Who?' He insisted, and I said, 'Me! It's me! I will receive it. Because my mother Arana and Timi Ko'oliu were born together, my father Alasa'a and Timi Ko'oliu were born together. I have a right to it. And if I made a mistake and Timi Ko'oliu died, I would never give money either. In our tradition, if one man receives the money, that's enough. It kills off all our claims, and we all receive it. Tradition says if it's my father, it rains on everyone. Alright, I'll give it now!' I had brought five ten-string moneys from the brideprice for Gwalota, the daughter of my brother Maniramo, in my bag. 'Here's the money!' I held it up. 'He was my uncle. He loved us, and my sister was married to his son Le'a. Look at him; we are family. Come and talk about it outside; I'm not afraid.'

Then Le'a said, 'See, Kwa'ioloa has the right. Even if he truly did something and my father Timi Ko'oliu died, it's nothing, because he was born with Timi Ko'oliu. It's very good that he brought these books showing my father's head. I can't read or write, but it's good to think that we can read about him and the priesthood he held until he died, so everyone knows that the priesthood came down to Timi Ko'oliu.' That's what Le'a said, and then that man 'Uate'e stood up. 'Oh sorry, Kwa'ioloa, my son, sorry. I'm asking on behalf of all of us pagans. It's in your bag? Can Kath Means provide the five thousand dollars, now?'

Kath Means said, 'Yes, I will provide five thousand dollars, to help Michael and Ben offer this compensation.' But 'Uate'e just said, 'Oh, I'm going. Kwa'ioloa, see me at Gwa'irufa, in Nelson's kitchen, tonight. We'll sleep there. I'm telling us all, we are collecting dust to put in our mouths.' It was what I had told Bitareo. 'All of us here, whether we are good men or senior men, we are like children crawling and taking soil to eat. Kwa'ioloa has come and washed it away. Thank you my son. I withdraw this restitution claim today, and until the time I die.' Then he jumped out of the building and went. That evening Kath Means went to sleep at Nazareth and I crept out and went to 'Uate'e at Gwa'irufa. So that was cleared up, because Le'a himself had ruled it out, I didn't give away my ten-strings, and that was that.

But I have a different explanation for the death of Timi Ko'oliu. I have heard that a while before a certain man was shot down by the ghost in Timi Ko'oliu's shrine at Anomula. He had been asking Timi Ko'oliu for many years to let him go into the most holy place to see the stone with writing on it. Eventually Timi Ko'oliu let him, and he went up to the stone wall and into the place where sacrifices were baked to the ghost, and the ghost shot him in the back. He fell down, incontinent, and they carried him away. He lived, but it came back upon Timi Ko'oliu because he did not take a pig to clear it up: 'The man was defiled, your great-grandchild who came to see you and went into your area. So very sorry, here's a pig.' He forgot to do this, so the ghost killed him for allowing a defiled man to go up there.

The death of Timi Ko'oliu was a very big problem for my research with Ben Burt, but the underlying problem was that many people are suspicious of Whitemen. My father worked with the Whitemen long ago, as you can read in the book we wrote about him,[18] and I am also someone who thinks I know the ways of the Whitemen. I told him that this Whiteman Ben Burt was good and wrote things in full. But lots of people don't like Whitemen. They say the Whitemen come to steal their knowledge to sell it for their own wealth and write to make money from the books. That's what they think.

When I left school I knew nothing about research or anthropology, but working with Ben Burt to research with my own Kwara'ae people has led to where I am today. I have experienced both sides of this work. The good side is documenting all aspects of culture, collecting valuable information and meeting people with different backgrounds. I have worked with other anthropologists and learned from their ideas and experience, improved my written and spoken English, and travelled overseas. I now understand the processes of writing a book, as distinct from secretarial and other kinds of writing, and I know how to transcribe, edit and compile information. The bad side is dealing with the old-fashioned people, climbing high into the hills to reach them and staying in uncomfortable, dirty places with naked men and women, complying with strict rules of a different culture and paying restitution for any mistakes. I had to approach aggressive, jealous people, hold meetings with leaders with strange ideas, and provide money, tobacco and other goods.

From working with anthropologist Ben Burt, I have also travelled via Papua New Guinea, Australia and Singapore to England, and back. My first time to travel internationally was in 1997, when I landed in those countries and discovered what a change it was from life in Honiara and Solomon Islands. I came to London to work with Ben Burt, checking our forest resources draft before it went for publication, because it was written in my own language. I found living in London enjoyable and easy. Millions of people owned houses and worked in innumerable huge beautiful buildings, and transport to work was by underground railway, buses and cars, fast and on time. Very big stores sold thousands of different kinds of goods, but most were very expensive. There was no land or forest to clear for gardens in and around London, where only people with jobs were able to live, for a few without jobs were lying in the streets. We went to pubs to meet friends and listen to music, and attended functions such as a launch ceremony at the Commonwealth Institute and the great Benin centenary.[19] I visited important buildings such as Buckingham Palace, Westminster Abbey, the Houses of Parliament and Saint Paul's Cathedral. On weekends we visited other cities such as Bristol, Hull and Canterbury.

On my second visit in 2006 I attended the Solomon Islands conference at the British Museum, with Kenneth Roga from Western Province, Salome Samou from Temotu and Evelyn Baines from Isabel. We visited the British Museum stores and museums in Oxford and Cambridge to research artefacts from our own areas of Solomon Islands. In the evenings Ben Burt and I enjoyed having drinks in the pub, while I dictated some of the chapters for this book. We also went to a pub where Ben Burt played the accordion with a group playing Irish music. And I cannot forget Pauline and her husband and two lovely children whom I had visited in 1997 when they lived in Hull.

Having visited London twice, I experienced a changed

way of life, taking me to another world of riches and an economic system which it would take Solomon Islands a century to reach. In London, Singapore and Australia there is no comparison with my traditional way of life. People are so busy that they can't even greet anyone when they sit on the same seat in a train, just longing to get off and hurry to work, school or business. They live a Western life with no sign of traditional performances, except for Indian, African and Caribbean dance groups, although the English do play musical instruments.

Solomon Islands tradition must be researched and documented in order to transfer it to future generations. If not it will disappear and we too will cease to respect each other and be too busy to greet our friends, as I have seen in other countries. A hundred years ago our traditional norms were unwritten but transferred orally from our ancestors to our grandparents. Although some of us are knowledgeable in our traditional culture, as time goes on it is slowly being forgotten. When the church arrived, Whitemen began to write about us in general terms, and eventually this resulted in our research with Ben Burt.

Next to documentation is performance, and through panpipe music and chants the elders can continue to teach the young people. Our traditional culture can become familiar to us through action; drumming, singing and dancing. My experience has taught me that my traditional culture must be documented and taught in school for future generations to abide by.

THE CHIEFS' COUNTRY

Michael Kwa'ioloa addressing the British Museum's Solomon Islands conference in 2006, before a portrait of himself demonstrating Malaita ornaments and shell-money. (Elizabeth Bonsheck photo)

---

1. The Seventh Day Adventist school near Honiara.
2. Pierre Maranda researched in Lau Lagoon and Roger Keesing in Kwaio, from the 1960s.
3. Hand-made cigarettes are usually rolled in a strip of exercise-book paper.
4. A *kastom haos* or 'tradition house'.
5. *Taki*, the rules governing relationships.
6. *Ta'itala*.
7. Burt 1994a and Kwa'ioloa & Burt 1997.
8. Burt & Kwa'ioloa 1992.
9. Kwa'ioloa & Burt 2001.

10 The British Museum Ethnography Department, then housed in a separate building.
11 Burt & Kwa'ioloa 2001.
12 Siale is the founding shrine from which many Kwara'ae clans trace their origins, and hence a clan uniting them all, but not everyone agrees on which of the Siale clans is most senior.
13 For an earlier account of the death of Timi Ko'oliu, see Kwa'ioloa & Burt 1997:165-166.
14 For details of this incident, see Kwa'ioloa & Burt 1997:148-152.
15 A sixteen-page booklet; Burt & Kwa'ioloa 1981.
16 Strictly speaking, this argument may have been flawed since not all men would be subject to the same tabus as a senior tabu-speaker like Ko'oliu.
17 *Gwari* or cold/damp.
18 Burt & Kwa'ioloa 2001.
19 A commemoration by Nigerians from Benin of the conquest of their city by the British in 1897.

Honiara Central Market in 2008. (Clive Moore photo)

3
MAKING A LIVING IN TOWN

Although I was born and grew up in the rural area of East Kwara'ae, I have lived in Honiara ever since I moved here with my wife and children in 1980. So I can compare our way of life in town with life at home in Malaita.

If a man comes to work in Honiara, it is completely different from when he stayed in his home district in Malaita. In Malaita everything he eats is free, because he makes gardens, produces taro, feeds pigs, and things like that. To have good things at home, everyone must feed pigs, which can be sold for cash or traditional money. But in Honiara it is more difficult. If a man is employed and works for a company, there is none of this, because there is nowhere to make a garden and no time to work the garden either. So then, the man will live solely by cash, and if there is no cash there is nothing. Living in Honiara is exceedingly expensive, because everything depends on cash, by which I mean you must pay for the kitchen needs of the house, whether rice or vegetables, biscuits, sugar, salt or anything else. You use up these things in a day or two and then buy more. Things like sweet potato you buy in the market, and tapioca, and you also buy firewood in the market, for thirty dollars a bundle. Even leaves for the oven you buy in the market, and greens, all for money, and if you have no cash you look very bad, in Honiara. Honiara is also different because at home building doesn't cost much, as we just use sago-palm leaf and cut raw materials from the forest. In Honiara, first you must have your own land, and then you must have the money to buy materials.

We are still one family with those at home. As I described in *Living Tradition*, it was my brother John Maesatana who founded Kobito and because there were no houses there, families from home came to stay with my brother. Then they started building their own houses until now Kobito is a suburb of Honiara. So my brother was popular and everyone helped him, until he died in 1998. We all provide hospitality for everyone from home, and when we go home everyone loves us too. Some of the relatives who come are not born close to us. They may be from the next clan, but they stay at home until they have nothing and when they come, go straight to whoever they want and treat us as countrymen[1] to stay at your home, and so on. You have a surprise when a man and his wife arrive, and then in a while their children are there too. Suddenly you see them in the evening at the house. It's hard for us to say, 'Eh, go to your brother's house' or something, so we will keep them overnight. If we are too crowded, we do it in such a way that he recognises that he can't stay longer: 'See how many of us there are, maybe a closer brother or a daughter married there, we'll try to . . .' 'Oh, I've tried to find him but I can't.' 'Oh, I'll find them for you.' Then he is adjusted to going to stay with them, and if not he can stay only for a limited time, as a stranger. We call this hospitality,[2] when we keep him and look after his needs. But he mustn't stay too long, unless he is employed and contributes to the food, because we are living by money. With so many adults and children, the wife will feel bad because there are no good things for the families who have arrived. If there is no proper planning there will be problems and shortage of food, and when we Melanesians eat, we must have more than enough. That means an oven for each meal, a big pot of greens, with coconut too, and all this must be paid for. As a result, some families in Honiara feel so bad that they tell their countrymen to their face, 'Eh, go all of you, because we have no cash and no food.'

If someone comes from home, he should remember to bring something for his 'children', but often they don't do that and will not bring any food. When a man comes, sometimes he says, 'Oh, I'm here to do so and so and then go back', but later on he delays his return journey. This is the kind of thing which causes us problems in Honiara. Young boys will come, stay with us all the time, not go back, and not work either. They come because they are too lazy to work in the garden at home and want to run around in Honiara town. We say, 'You all go back home,' but it's hard to make them. They like to stay in town to relax without working, and come back in the evening to eat. Sometimes they bring a lot of other boys to eat in the house too. These are the things which make life difficult in Honiara. Myself, when something like this happens I always budget the cash. If I am taking something like four hundred dollars per fortnight, the day I take the cash I allow one hundred dollars and I buy a bit of rice, sweet potatoes, tapioca and kitchen goods, until eventually I reach the hundred dollars in my pocket. This is so that each evening, when I come home, I can bring some greens, or give some cash to my wife or daughters to go to the market to buy some ferns or something cheap.

The good side of hospitality is that when we go home and come as strangers ourselves, a man will say, 'Eh, your pig is here; have a bit to eat for Christmas.' He'll say, 'Eh, if not for this father of yours, when I was a stranger there I would not have earned money for us. Hey, give father a big pig; he can bake it and take it for our brothers in Honiara.' This is a real continuation of the exchange practices of the past and it connects us back to our original home.

Michael Kwa'ioloa and Bizel Fanenalua at their house at Windy Hill, Gilbert Camp, in 1999. (Ben Burt photo)

Business is one thing which really causes selfishness and greed. When I was small there was an old man called Jonathan Didimae, now dead. He would get tins of fish and corned beef and things like bread, put them in a string bag and come around selling them outside the houses. They called it a hawker licence. My sister Sango'iburi once said, 'Uncle, give it to me, I only have two shillings,' when it was three shillings for a tin of Three-Sevens fish. 'He said, "But for only sixpence less, I make a loss." But he was kind to her and said, 'In that case, I'll have to pay for it' and what he did was take a shilling of his own and add it to my sister's two shillings, and we had a tin of fish. I remember him saying, 'This is business.' This was new to us and we had not seen a store, when I was small. Then he explained, 'Eh, niece, if it was just food from the garden or anything else you asked for; but with this, if sixpence is lost, the business fails.' That's what creates this selfishness in business, as I heard my uncle tell.

When a man comes from the inland to work in urban areas, in 'Aoke, Honiara or overseas, he can become quite rich by earning money and he buys things for himself, such as saucepans, plates and spoons. When he comes back people are surprised: 'Eh, this man is so rich, my word.' When I was a boy I saw relatives who had gone to work for a year on plantations on other islands return and unload their cargos on the beach at Faumamanu, and I was amazed. They brought big boxes, drums of kerosene, tins of biscuits, blocks of stick-tobacco and bags of rice. A number of men and women would carry them to the inland villages and share them out to our families. I know that when my father came with a sack of rice, there was a cupful for each house in the village, until it was finished. My father was very kind, but with some men we would see them bring rice and no-one would taste it. This kind of selfishness comes with all the things we call foreign,[3] meaning everything to do with the Whiteman. Business shows this as soon as people say, 'Oh no, we don't give anything for free, because if we do it will all break down.' They are being proud, and business has changed them.

People like us live well in Honiara because we can make our own gardens inland. Tapioca is the main food which we plant in the outlying settlements, and sweet potato. We live on tapioca because we can replant it in the same place and it will grow over and over again for many years, if we can't extend our gardens because the land belongs to others. Our way is that if it is regrown forest, no-one can work it and if you do they will chase you out, because the area belongs to the man who worked it when it was virgin forest. So on land we were the first to settle we make tapioca gardens, harvest them, and repeat this again and again. When it will no longer grow well, we leave it for the forest to regrow and no-one will come to work it, because it is ours. In this way we worked the whole area of Mount Austen before the ethnic tension. People from Matariu, 'A'ekafo, Namoliki, Fulisango and Kobito settled everywhere, all of them from home on Malaita.

For example, when the wife of my 'father' Peter Finia came in 2005, that was alright because she was my 'mother', and she stayed with me. But I did not have enough money, so my big garden, which I had paid for labour to work, I allowed her and my wife and children to harvest it and take it by truck to market. They sold almost the whole garden, including the bananas, and she must have had a thousand dollars in her pocket. Then I also gave her a hundred dollars each pay-day, for her to use for my 'sisters' at home, who had nothing. After two months, when she went back, she had a big cargo to take, and each of my sons also gave her fifty dollars. All this is good, because she is family and they are very helpful to us at home.

Malaitan houses and gardens at Gilbert Camp, seen from Kwa'ioloa's house at Windy Hill in 2004. (Ben Burt photo)

For me, I won't work in an office where they expect me to work full time, like the 'brothers' who earn wages for years by sitting there. It's not my way to work for someone else, because I see men working for others who rob them of money. That's why I don't like to work for Natives; I have to work for a Whiteman. My way may be rubbish, but I maintain it because many of the 'brothers' who take on contracts despoil the men who work for them. They withdraw money for beer, for girl business, to enrich their families and run businesses. On pay-day they have nothing left and just say, 'Take this amount and I'll make up your wages later.' My way of earning money for my big family is mostly doing private building jobs. I quote a price, for example four hundred dollars to plaster the inside of a house and eight hundred for the outside. I take on men to work with me, and when it is finished I take the cash and pay the men. Whatever remains to me lets me wander about, and the best of it is that in one full year I need to do only two or three months' work. To earn ten thousand dollars I would have to work for a year, but I can gain it in one month from a contract. Then I can do our work for tradition, visiting the chiefs in Malaita and paying for my travel and for food for them at our meetings. That is the purpose of it.

Often people will pay me to do work on their projects. Sometimes when a man wants a loan from the bank they bring the application forms and I fill them in and don't worry. But for appraisals, when they apply to the government for money to run a project, they come and say, 'Eh, maybe you can do it for us.' Then I will sit down with them and take all the information and main points and question them, because I have learned how to do projects. 'What is it you want to do?' 'Oh, this is for chickens.' 'What skills do you have for keeping chickens?' I'll make them tell me everything. 'So what will you build with?' 'Oh, I'll go and buy sago-palm leaf in the market and get second-grade sawn timber.' I help them write the project design, type and print it, and submit it with covering letters. Sometimes they pay me a few hundred or even a thousand dollars. One North Malaita man gave me three pigs for the marriage feast for my son Lawrence Laugere.

Then my nephew, a younger brother of Rocky Tisa, came

and said, 'Eh, a friend of mine, a Guadalcanal man, was working for the Port Authority until they sacked him. He has sixteen thousand dollars in the National Providence Fund but it's impossible for him to withdraw it.' Under the law you can't withdraw from the NPF if you are terminated from your job. He said, 'If he gets it he will go fifty-fifty with anyone who can do it: eight thousand for each of them. He and his wife have been going hungry for two months. They tried it ten years ago, but it was impossible then too.' So I said, 'Oh, go and find him.' He brought him and the two of us sat down under a mango tree at the office of the Diocese of Melanesia in Honiara. I interviewed him and his story was that they had sacked him for nothing. He had worked in Honiara for ten years, but when his brother, who had a house in Honiara, moved to Aruligo, he went to live there and came every day by truck for four dollars a time and back. Eventually he missed some days at work and they sacked him. I went with him to the manager, a man from To'abaita in Malaita, and said, 'Look, this man has a history of ten years faithful work while he lived in Honiara, but what happened when his brother no longer had the house? Did the company give him a house? Did the Port Authority give him married quarters in the labour lines?' 'No.' 'Why?' 'Oh, well.' 'That's what was wrong. When he was living down at Aruligo, did you give him a travel allowance? So why did you terminate him for not attending work? It was because he had no money and was living far away.' But he didn't want to help the man, so I went back and wrote a letter to the manager of the NPF to explain the case: 'This man is innocent. It's a case of unlawful dismissal. Please, I ask and the chiefs ask, help this man, because he has no house and is in trouble with his wife, since he lost his job. If you don't reverse this man's termination, I'm telling you, tomorrow he will take back his NPF fund.' On reaching the NPF, they had an interview and the man took his sixteen thousand dollars. I said, 'Just give me a thousand; it's your money.' He said, 'No, we'll share it, eight each, because I've been trying for almost ten years and it was impossible.' So in the end I took two thousand dollars.

Those are the things I have some talent for, as extra work to gain some money for my family. That's why I wanted to be not a regular police officer but a special constable, so that I could take on extra work whenever I wanted. When I look at my relatives, if they have no work they are in a bad state, and during the time of the ethnic tension everything was hard. We special constables maintained law and order, and they paid us allowances. Twenty-one thousand dollars was the highest I received, as danger allowance for bomb disposal and such things. Then I received my regular payment, from one thousand five hundred rising to twelve thousand. So during the ethnic tension we received good pay.

While we are living in Honiara, one way we get money is by building houses to rent. The rent meets extra costs and we men who work for tradition, going home and coming back, don't have money, so it pays for our children because the money comes in regularly every month. I built my house at Kobito Two in the 1980s and then, when I moved further up in the 1990s, I rented it out and built another house for all the children, then built another house again. Eventually I gave the house to my firstborn son Lawrence Laugere, because he had children ready for school, then he rented it out too and I moved him back with me again. 'You stay here, so you can receive the money, because I can manage for myself.' It will be passed on to the children that when they build a house they should build another one to rent out. When I did this, I advised my younger sister Ivery Arana to build two houses, one at Vura and one at Kofiloko. My idea was that if you go back home you must have houses to rent because without money you will look stupid, because school fees and other expenses are high at home. When a bag of rice in Honiara was eighty-five dollars, at home it was a hundred and twenty, so a man who works for money pays less and one who does not pays more. During the five years she has lived at home, she has had five hundred dollars from each house and has more money than people who have stayed at home for longer. She does well at home and runs a hawker store. There are not many people who do this, just some of us, because building houses costs too much in Honiara, for all the materials. But we have managed to do it by using what little money we have, including my salary as a special constable, which was formerly only two dollars a day.

From all the private jobs I mentioned, I have built a house for each of my sons. We always aim high, not to follow anyone else, but to achieve a good standard of living for our children. Many people try this but can't, and are surprised at how we do it. They say, 'We live alongside the road and the electric power goes above our house, but we don't have it. How is it you live on top of the hill and you have it, but everywhere else is dark?' All this shows the results of my jobs, even though I don't work for anyone else.

My sons aim high too. My fourth son Michael Lili's house was completed, all with permanent materials, and because he was fully committed to his work with the church, the Lord spoke to the heart of the Australian woman he worked for as security, and she paid for thirty sheets of masonite board for him, at sixty dollars each. Every Friday she gave my son Lili fifty dollars, because she saw he was very faithful, neat, and didn't smoke or drink liquor. My second son Wilson Maelaua's house was also a permanent building, and my third, Haman Namua's. My sixth son Alden Afu's house was finished, and Michael junior Maesua's two-bedroom house, which I planned. My firstborn son Lawrence Laugere moved into my original house at Kobito. Then there is my 'son' Sam Maesatana, born of our elder brother who died, who has a good house of expensive materials with furniture and electronic equipment inside, and his younger brother Kwasi has a five-bedroom house, which Sam paid for, near Lawrence's house in Kobito. We have raised our standards, and as a man with sons I have their houses around my house until now we have a big settlement. We have our own church where we come together as a family, authorised to have a pastor in the Missionary Baptist Church; my firstborn son Lawrence Laugere, whom they came and tested with questions from the Bible, and anointed to look after us all.

Some of Kwa'ioloa's sons, with friends. (Michael Kwa'ioloa photo)

When my sons married, I planned everything for them. They must be sure to have a job and, if not, they must make gardens to be self-reliant and turn garden food into money by marketing, using the money to help the family. As we live in Honiara, it is best to have employment. They have specialised trades, but if government can't provide contracts and no companies are coming into the country, I have a licence to work in security, so I can provide employment. They also work for City Security Services, owned by my 'son' Chris Maefani, and they continue to do their own work as self-employed. For instance, Haman Namosia Kwa'i cannot read or write, even to school standard one, but he was in charge of a security post for RAMSI,[5] and his rate of pay was at government level six; almost seven hundred dollars per fortnight. I knew that God the creator, whom I live for, provided a job for him, so he has his own big house.

I also bought electronic equipment for my children at home, to stop them from leaving my house and disobeying my instructions to go out and watch videos. When I was small I didn't see anything electrical. When I went to 'Aoke I heard recordings of Chinese music in the stores,[5] but I didn't know about radio. When I came to Honiara my brother John Maesatana was a man who liked the radio and owned big speakers, and I began to follow such things, but I didn't know about movies. Me and my 'brothers' Fakaisia and Nelson Konai used to go to the Lena Cinema to see movies, where they put up a big cloth and projected it. Eventually the time came when I saw a gramophone, which they wound up and put a record on to and it cried out until it weakened, and they wound it again. Then later there was a tape recorder, which my 'brother' Sampson, who married my younger sister Ivery Arana, bought – a big reel-to-reel. Then more recently I saw the one which they put slides in to project onto a wall, and I was surprised by that: 'That's me, that's my picture!' That's when I began to understand these things, and later, when we were living at Kobito, some people with money had them.

Well, my rule was that every evening my children must be in the house. We prayed, we ate, and took care of ourselves, because my father had said that in the evening his grandchildren must stay in the house. If they went out and someone made trouble, they might say, 'It was you who did that.' My children obeyed me, but eventually in the evenings they would ask, 'One dollar father, one dollar father. We are going to see the video.' What could I say? It was hard to avoid it, because my children wanted to watch the video, and they started to break my rules. In the evenings they would slip out to watch somebody's video, and earn money for them. So I thought, until the time came when I had five thousand dollars in my pocket, and I asked my 'father' David Ofalanga, because I couldn't act without a 'father'.

One evening in his house, we ate and I said, 'Father, your grandchildren are disobeying me, but I sympathise with them in wanting to watch videos. But only yesterday as I came back from police duty at two o'clock at night, I saw Alden Afu with Ben Burtte'e on his shoulders, standing in the rain so that Ben Burtte'e could look into a house and see the video screen. Afu couldn't see but he held his little brother up to watch. When I saw it, tears fell from my eyes. Standing outside the house in the rain because his brother so wanted to watch the movie.' It was Robert Dafe's house at New Valley. So seeing that, next day

I said to my 'father', 'Eh, I think the movies are encouraging my children to watch men stealing and criminals doing wrong. In some of these films soldiers are doing wrong things. So we should screen these films first during the day and a man who has seen it should stand by so that when he cries out we can stop it and fast forward it, and start it again. We should control it.'

So from that I said, 'Father, would you allow me to buy a video screen and a deck?' 'Eh, if you have it, how will you pay for the, what is it, on top of the hill?' 'Father, I have enough money for the electric power to reach us. Let's discuss it.' Then he said, 'No, the children will imitate the stealing, doing wrong with women, cheating; imitate them and forget you, and imitate killing people.' 'Father, the world is going into a time of decline; we cannot escape it. But I think that if it is put into the children's blood, they cannot do wrong things. I believe it.' He said, 'Do you trust yourself?' I said, 'I trust myself. My children are religious people. Since they were small they did not eat betelnut or smoke or drink beer. None of this; they are becoming church leaders.' He said, 'So then?' 'They disobey me and they pester me for money, then I feel sorry for them, because I live for my children. Ben Burtte'e and Afu, if I won't give them two dollars for the evening, they sit down and won't speak, then suddenly Ben Burtte'e will say, "They are watching it now, Afu, this man's films which they advertised." I hear and then I feel sorry for them both and give them two dollars. "We'll go, but the first half is already finished." I have failed, but I believe if I get a screen and deck, they won't go anywhere; they'll sit quietly in the house. They won't adopt Western ways there, because they believe and trust me.' Then 'father' approved it.

Kwa'ioloa's youngest son Ben Burtte'e ready for school in 1999. (Ben Burtdoe photo)

This was in 2001. David Ofalanga was the only elder of the Tolinga-Fairu clan still alive, with old Peter Finia back home. He replaced my father, so I had to ask him first. He said, 'Try it, but how will you do it? How much will a video cost? How much do you have in your pocket?' 'I have five thousand dollars.' 'Hey, with that you should buy chickens, or pigs, or you should buy a store.' I said, 'Father, my children are not capable of running businesses and I don't have time. From the love in their hearts they would give away all the chickens for nothing. The love from my father has spoiled us all, and if we ran a store and a man who wanted something worth fifteen dollars said, "I've only got ten," we'd say, "Take it then," and the store would fail. I know about business because I have studied it and received certificates, father; we are not capable.' That's what I said to David Ofalanga. 'I'll just get it so my children will stay home and obey me.' Then he said, 'They'll do this all the time and get lazy.' I said, 'At the beginning they'll be interested, but eventually they'll get bored and not need it. But my children are in charge, and the electricity is up to me and mother.' 'Oh, for that you pay a deposit to the Solomon Islands Electricity Authority, they put you on a list and it takes years and years.' 'What I'll do', I said, 'I'll make a deal with the bosses, pay them, and the team will come and do the work immediately. I'll budget three thousand dollars for them, even though I've already paid the SIEA, and treat them so they'll do it quickly, privately in their own time.' 'Father' said, 'Try it.' 'When I went to look for things it was two thousand six hundred dollars for a screen, one thousand one hundred and fifty for a deck, and connections and things will cost me another five hundred dollars. It's all under five thousand.' He accepted it.

First of all I dealt with the electricity. I talked to a man at the main road, for me to bring it by cable, and he said, 'A hundred and fifty per month.' Then I hired him for six months, went to deal with the others and gave three hundred dollars to their boss and one hundred dollars to each of the five men in the team. I paid for this from my three thousand six hundred dollars police allowance. I bought two water pipes for a hundred dollars each from boys who were selling them during the ethnic tension, and made posts to connect up with Michael Anitalo's house lower down, drilled the posts according to the advice of my nephew the SIEA inspector and bought cement for my sons to set them in the ground in concrete. Within three days the SIEA connected up to the house and when the inspector arrived he just checked it. As he was my nephew he brought a meter of his own, which I had free without paying for. I gave him a hundred dollars, just for refreshments.

Then, having looked into things first, it went quite well. When I had the video and the power reached the house, we became members of a video shop where you paid a hundred dollars, took your card and then took out a video cassette for six dollars for three nights, and returned it again. Then my children watched them privately and I restricted it so they could not watch during the day: 'You do your work, and at night when we have eaten and prayed, then you can watch it. But you must be sure to get good cassettes, and you must run it through before we watch it, because there will be the women, my daughters-in-laws, my grandchildren, and all us men there. It would be shameful for us to see someone doing wrong with someone before our own eyes. And we will allow only two of you to look after the electronics; Michael junior Maeisua and Alden Afutana only.' These two kept things well under control. They bought big speakers and other equipment, and in the evenings my boys would not go out, but stayed in the house. In 2005, when my son Michael Maeisua went to Australia and then Fiji for the Oceania taekwondo championships, I gave him money to buy CDs and DVDs. Whatever the cassette, we would put it in and enjoy watching, but especially cassettes of the birth and death of Christ.

Everything which happens in the whole world, today we can watch it on television. The intelligence from America about terrorists on planes, the explosives they use and how a person cannot take a bag abroad. That's the good thing about TV. I told my children to take it outside so that other people could come and watch. Eventually those on the other side of the village,

Making a living in town

Watching television in Kwa'ioloa's house in 2004. (Ben Burt photo)

old man Kwa'ite'e and others, told them, 'Eh, you hire some more cassettes and maybe we can throw in two or three dollars when we watch to pay the costs.' The first time they did that, after the people had gone, I almost hit my two sons: 'Why are you selling this?' 'Hey father, it's killing us all to hire these cassettes, with the electricity bill and everything. The fathers say they must give us a bit of money when they watch.' I said, 'But you are undermining my leadership. I bought these things for all of you in the community to watch.' I was treating it in terms of tradition. I wanted everyone to watch for free because of my leadership. Otherwise, when I speak people might not listen to me: 'Oh, that man just goes after money.' If I was to run as a politician they would say, 'Eh, if we support him he will take everything for his family and not for us.' We argued and the two of them went and reported to their fathers in the next settlement. Then three chiefs came and said, 'Michael, what did you say? Why did you tell them to get out? They say you chased them with a stick, to hit them. Hey, they came crying to us,' and so on. I said, 'I won't have it. I will pay for everything.' 'No, give a bit of money to these two, because they've earned it.' So then I just allowed it: 'Oh, if that's what you're worried about.' So now they could raise a hundred or a hundred and fifty dollars for a show, to help themselves out, and I could see that was good.

The other good thing was that the children stayed quietly at home and learned things. Sometimes I and my son would go somewhere and people would say, 'What happened was this,' and so forth, and the boy would say, 'Hey, you don't know anything. I saw it on the TV.' Then: 'Hey, you talk about it then.' I don't want second-hand information, I want my children to know things, and I do know they are very wise. When I say, 'You all be careful', they already know, and the wrong things they see people do, they learn from them. They guard their belongings because they have seen in the movies how men steal things, and when they go out one of them will stay in the house all day. But they don't imitate, and they don't like it when a man steals a girl. 'Oh, this man's way goes against what father and grandfather say, so we'll avoid it. If we want a girl, we don't ask her, we must ask her father, and our father, and after that, marry.' All my sons have married correctly.

Lastly, I also have an office where Ben Burtte'e and Rosie Ri'o study after school, where I have a computer, which the New Zealand High Commission provided for our SITCECF organisation. A retired professor from Scotland, George Scott, who died in 2005, taught us to use the computer and trained Ben Burtte'e to be a skilled operator. But now Ben Burtte'e wants a mobile phone with a screen you can see things in.

Solomon Star, Friday 22 July, 2005

Weekend Magazine

From humble start comes a silver title

By PRIESTLEY HABRU

JUNIOR Michael Mae is an ordinary boy residing with his parents in Honiara.

He does not go to school, although he attended some formal education at the Baptist Mission School in Honiara.

He is not working, but sometimes work for his uncle's security firm in town.

But this 23-year-old from Pongomanu village, east Kwara'ae in Malaita Province loves taekwondo - a modern martial art from Korea that is characterised by its fast, high and spinning kicks.

Junior realised his potential in taekwondo in his mid teenage years.

Residing with his parents at Windy Hill in Gilbert Camp, life was quite hard for this young lad.

But he followed in the footsteps of his elder brother Lawrence who also plays taekwondo.

The interest developed and he joins Jona Club - which is a club formed

Silver boy Michael Junior Mae, centre, with his brothers Haman, left, and Lawrence, right.

are committed Christians always make sure they do not fall into any kind of trouble.

"My father is a very hard man and wants to see his sons and daughters be-

cal sponsors whose support enabled them to attend the Oceania championship in Sydney.

The achievement of this entire team and that of Junior was well received by

pionship but dates are yet to be decided by the OTU committee.

With 81 and its Oceania neighbours embarking on running their own competition through OTU, it will

For now, Junior and his many team-mates who are training with various clubs in town will be hoping to do their best for all if they are again selected to attend any competition outside of the country

example for other taekwondo athletes who wish to become like him one fine day.

He had shown that discipline, hard work and simplicity are some recipes

Kwa'ioloa's sons Haman Namusia, Michael Maeisua and Lawrence Laugere appearing in the *Solomon Star* after Maeisua won the silver medal at the Oceania taekwondo tournament in Sydney in July 2005. (*Solomon Star* 22-7-2005)

---

1 'Countrymen' here translates the Pijin *wantok*, meaning 'same language'.
2 *Goningwae'a* or 'caring for a person'.
3 *Rū 'a'e asi* or 'overseas things'.
4 The Regional Assistance Mission to Solomon Islands, which came to stabilise the country in 2003, after the civil conflict or 'ethnic tension' describe in later chapters.
5 Most stores in 'Aoke and Honiara are Chinese businesses.

Visiting relatives at Kwa'ioloa's house displaying ten-string shell-moneys in 1999. (Ben Burt photo)

4
MARRIAGES AND BRIDEPRICE

Something which is very important in the community of Honiara is weddings,[1] including brideprice and marriage feasts and ceremonies, as well as funerals. Sometimes people of different languages are involved, because our area of southeast Honiara is one village community,[2] and one thing which brings them together, to see each other's faces and unite them, is marriage.[3] Even if people don't pay for the girl, when there is an announcement of the feast we make an appeal for them to attend the wedding and bring something. If I invite fifty guests, a man from Lau or To'abaita comes bringing a plateful, with his wife and children. They line up, shake hands with the couple, put what they have brought in the big dish, are served and go to the place to eat. During the feast, an old woman can just bring one or two dollars and a few sweet potatoes or cassavas for us to bake and share for people to eat, saying, 'Oh, sorry my son, I only have two dollars.' We respect that and when we share out the pig-flesh there is a piece for her. Then the master of ceremonies speaks cheerfully to them, the man whose son is married speaks to them, and the chief says, 'This is the way to do things.' As we Kwara'ae say, 'A single rattle-seed makes no sound.' It takes you and me and the next man to rattle together. This is what happens in Honiara; he is not my brother or my relative, but I invite him so that we can eat together.

Leadership in brideprice and marriage is extremely important. In Honiara we are all different kinds of people, and the girls we pay for come from To'abaita, Fataleka and Kwaio. Brideprice is really important in helping people to join hand in hand, when they gather the money to help a man pay for one girl and then, when the time comes, he returns it to help pay for another one. Even unrelated people will help. For example, when my son Willie Maelaua was married, a Kwaio man who lives at Kofiloko, John Dofe, brought a *bani'au* shell-money and paid it for him. He gave it because when he first arrived I went to his house and talked to him, he was kind to me, and I ordered two bales of second-hand clothes for him from Australia, which he sold to earn some money. I helped him as my friend and his family was like my family. That's marriage in Honiara. It is a very important way for people to help each other.

If you want to help someone, you don't do it casually, at any time. To gain recognition you must give it at the brideprice presentation,[4] when everyone can see that you are helping your 'brother'. Even if you are gone they will say, 'Oh, the son has come and although his father is dead we can see him helping that father of his. So you will have to help him too.' It's not returning it, but mutuality. It is called 'giving on account',[5] meaning he must give it back when a son of yours marries. He can't give it for any other purpose, only for brideprice at a wedding. If a man asks it to be returned just to eat from the money, they say he is rubbish and really poor. For myself, if a man helps me today, I have money ready tomorrow.[6] A 'son' or a 'brother' might be married at any time.

Father told me that marriage is life-long, and so I was afraid of it when I was young. But even so, while I was still a teenager my father and elder brother John Maesatana asked me to marry. I tried to escape but it was impossible because I had to obey my father and if he told me I was ready to marry, I was married. The girl I took, I didn't know her home or her name and I had not seen her. That was my wife Bizel Fanenalua, from Fulisango in central Kwara'ae. With a traditional marriage, that's how it is; sometimes you cannot choose for yourself and they just ask for her. So when they asked, I was married, in October 1973. Time passed and, as my father had told me, it came to me to provide for the household and not depend on anyone else. Then within two years I had my firstborn son Lawrence Laugere, named after my father's 'father', and I found life more difficult. My father advised me that when a boy is born, that's when you start saving money for when he will marry. You will look stupid if your boy misbehaves by taking some man's daughter and they come to demand and shout at you to no effect. So I began to save and when Lawrence was married I was able to pay his brideprice for him.[7] As for the girls, I looked for good girls to marry my sons. Like my family, the girl should be schooled in religion, she should not drink beer or eat betelnut or smoke cigarettes. She should not do anything which makes her a loose woman. My sons should not make them pregnant before I have paid for them, and I don't want them to run away with the girls.⁸ No, I must go to ask the fathers so that we can have a good relationship to help my family.

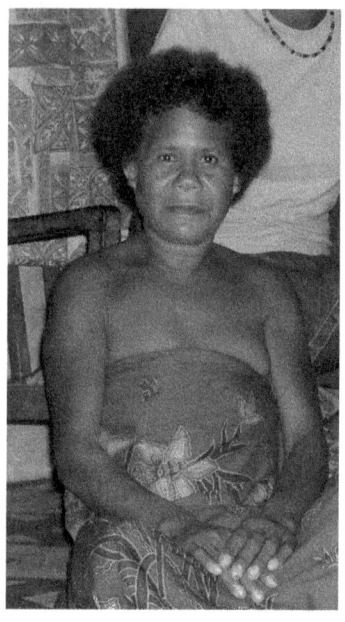

Bizel Fanenalua in 2004. (Ben Burt photo)

When Lawrence was small, my discipline was tough. I would stare into his eyes, tell him he must not do some things, then strike his hand or his bottom. After that I would pray with him and instruct him so he would understand that I was not his enemy but his teacher. Lawrence was to set an example in the family. I taught him to work in the garden and everything, not to smoke, drink alcohol or sleep anywhere else but stay in the house from six o'clock in the evening. I appreciated how

Lawrence had fully obeyed me, and eventually I paid for a girl for him. The father of this girl and the mother, who was a 'sister' of mine, could also see that Lawrence was well behaved, so they had taken him to work in their store. They persuaded Lawrence; it was: 'Money money money. There's a big house for both of you, and a car.' Instead of me going to ask for the girl, the mother came to ask me. I told her, 'Sister, this is wrong by tradition. Why are you asking me? I should ask you.' She said, 'Oh, Lawrence doesn't sleep here; he sleeps in our store to guard it.' Then she said, 'By tradition we must look after our daughter's interests too. If we like a man, we must say so.' I said, 'Oh, that's true', but I didn't know the girl's background. Ben Burt was staying with me, so we both went to pay for her. I gave five red moneys, he helped with five hundred dollars, and after he had returned to London I spent another three thousand dollars for five pigs, rice, local food and transport.

I could see that Lawrence was mature enough to look after himself and care for a family, so I advised him to marry. But that marriage came to nothing, because his wife opposed tradition. In only twenty-four hours she went down to a nightclub and took up with a cousin of Lawrence's, born of a 'sister' of mine, and two other boys in a car. They asked each other where they were from and my nephew, the driver, lied: 'Oh, I'm from Isabel', but he was her tabu in-law![9] So they took two cases of beer down to the Boha River, by the sea, drank it and came back, beeping the car horn in front of our house. I went down and he said, 'Hey, my tabu in-law is down there with a case of beer, drinking with the others.' That same morning my wife and I went and I stepped up to her father's door and said, 'Come and bring everything back. This dog of yours doesn't understand tradition; you haven't taught her. She has rebelled against my family and hurt my son.' I went on until about three o'clock, and they brought back three red moneys, but the rest was lost. Lawrence had also been married in church, but when the marriage broke down I wrote a letter to the president of the South Sea Evangelical Church to explain. They said, 'Oh no, in that case we will pray to annul it as not a legal marriage. The woman spoiled it, and in the Bible the Lord says that fornication destroys marriage.' They just released him.

So I told Lawrence, 'Wait; Willie, the second-born, will marry now.' Everything I tried had gone wrong because I wanted the firstborn to marry, then the second, and the third. So Lawrence had to wait for Willie to marry, and to my son Haman I said, 'Be patient.' Willie had made friends with Ethel at her house at Windy Ridge, Tenaru. He had left his job as a plasterer to work on a big project at Tenaru with Maetala, a Lau man out there. He would sleep at his 'grandfather's', my in-law Gali, at Windy Ridge. Because he made friends with her first and didn't take her in secret, Ethel's mother and father accepted him and he could walk out with her. Ethel worked in town and the two of them would go down every morning and sometimes come back so that Ethel could sleep at Kobito. So three of her 'brothers' hid by the road and attacked Willie. Willie fought back, and Ethel did too, until Willie escaped and reached home. He said, 'Eh, father, they attacked me because of the friend I've taken and I was fortunate to fight them off and escape.' Then I had a shock when five of them came after him. 'Alright Michael, that son of yours is up to something with our sister. Twenty *bani'au* shell-moneys and five thousand.' I thought, 'That's a lot,' then I said to them, 'Are you taking this back to the father to speak about? Because if it's you and me, that's not tradition, it's just a demand. If I had it and I gave it, I wouldn't be sure if it was to pay for the girl, or just to give it and later you'll take the girl back. So take this back to the father.' They wanted to strike me, but I said, 'No.' They were not born of her father but of 'brothers' and I didn't know their relationship with her father. Two of them said, 'Ethel is born of one, Alfred, and we are born of another.' I said, 'I know, I'm well aware. But leave it to the fathers according to tradition. I will talk father to father; that will sort it out, and then you can collect the money.' If they had used force, the boys would have heard and come running from Kobito with axes and knives. They were guarding the road, so I said, 'Oh, go down this way,' and they ran off.

So I said, 'I'll go after them in the morning.' I went straight to Windy Ridge, by myself, and I was not afraid because it was the right thing for my son to marry. I reached old man Alfred Loke and his wife Lilly and told them. They said, 'Oh, just five red moneys and two thousand dollars. Don't listen to those boys.' But Alfred was from Kwaio and his wife was from To'abaita, so of the five it was three Kwaio *bani'au* and two northern ten-strings, and two thousand dollars. They specified that the three Kwaio ones must be what is called a *bani'au* of seven, with each string measuring seven lengths from thumb to collarbone, with red *safi* beads at the top of each string. That cost me a lot. When I found it and changed the money it took a ten-string and two hundred dollars for one as long as that. I exchanged ten-strings for *bani'au* and paid a Kwaio man to come and join them together, with the help of my 'brother' Wilson Folimaete'e. The standard measure in Kwaio is *lausu'u*, from thumb to above the elbow, but this was extra, to the opposite collarbone. I don't know the name for that length.[10] Then with that there was a ten-string with a net in the middle,[11] a nine-foot ten-string, and the two thousand dollars. For the brideprice ceremony I went to their house at the time arranged, then the girl's side all gathered and two or three of us set out the moneys. When they saw them they were pleased, they hung them from a pole and checked they were the right length, and they took them.

Michael Kwa'ioloa discussing ten-string moneys offered for a brideprice in 1999. (Ben Burt photo)

Then we arranged a time for the feast. 'Oh, so next Saturday we'll come back with two or three fish to eat.' That's the traditional way to talk, but as a surprise my sons and their cousins gathered leaf, oven-stones, firewood and everything, and I bought two great big pigs, one for a ten-string and three hundred. We came with the two pigs in a truck, with bags of sweet potatoes and rice, and took everything to the house of the girl's side. To do it properly they should also bring some pigs, but I just wanted to do it because I knew that group didn't have any pigs. They just worked for Levers and everything seemed hard, so I did it to make friends with them.[12] There were maybe ten of us on our side; just my sons, their 'father' Haniel Bubufera, and the chiefs Benjamin Ramo, David Kwa'ite'e, Nathaniel Sele'au and the other traditional leaders. On their side it was the whole village, and it was they who ate what I brought. They brought a pig and some fish, and that was right because I was paying for the girl. There was singing in the church, as they arranged for the two of them to be legally married. We baked the pigs and that night the young people played music and sang until morning, and sang as they marched the pair to be married.

After the wedding ceremony my 'brother' Haniel Bubufera, Sele'au and chief Michael Ngidu'i shared it out. They just cut up the pigs, counted the people and shared it, but the right way for a wedding feast would have been to give according to how each had contributed. The tradition is that if a man gives a red money we give him a whole pig, legs and all. For the man who gives some cash there is a piece of pig according to the value of what he gave, so if he gives something like thirty dollars it is enough for just him to eat.[13] I just shared it all out and fed everyone, as no-one had helped me and I had paid for everything myself. For me, anyone who came could take something away. At the same time, they ornamented Ethel. They dressed her in a blue skirt and bra, as they do in To'abaita, and they hung a ten-string crossing her breasts and around her naked body. They made a kind of crown of coconut-frond for her head and put banknotes around it. That was her gift, with her box and mattress and other belongings and some bags of rice, which they gave for the two of them to start a home.

So I took the two of them back, but in To'abaita they follow our tradition that everyone has to go back with those who have paid for the girl. They will cut things down and make a mess to give the girl work to do. So they cut all my pawpaw trees and put them in the house until it was full up and surrounded. I was certainly angry with that tradition, and with my relatives; my 'brother' Nathaniel Sele'au, and David Kwa'ite'e and all of them. When we arrived the house was full of my pawpaw trees, which I was marketing, and I said, 'That's a useless tradition.' When I reached the front of the house, someone had been inside, taken my bags of nails, my bedsheets and towels and knives and everything. It was like stealing, but we don't call it theft at that time, because they are being happy. There is nothing like that in tradition; we would just make a mess, but you can't complain because it's the practice at a happy time. The two came to live in my house and I wouldn't allow them to stay elsewhere, because I was worried in case Willie might mistrust his wife or behave selfishly or jealously. He was in my hands and we were there to look after him.

Although Lawrence's first marriage had failed, he was patient and kept up the Lord's work and his job until Willie was married. But, as a man whom the girls wanted to marry, he made friends with a girl and made her pregnant, then another one, while still friends with the first. What happened was that I was at home one evening and the father of one of the girls came around. He sat down and sighed rather than tell me, because he was also a tabu in-law of mine, married to my cousin Emily. He wouldn't say, but I could see that something was going on, because it was the first time he had come. I spoke according to tradition: 'You haven't been here before. It's good that you've come to the house.' 'Ah, no no no, it's . . .' So I brought some fish, he ate and then: 'Oh, now I'm going.' As he went I said, 'Oh tabu, come here.' He came and said, 'Eh, I did come to say something, but I'm a bit embarrassed by you, tabu.' I said, 'What is it?' 'Well, our son, my nephew, has made pregnant his cousin-sister Rosie.' I said, 'Oh dear. Now, we have three types of marriage, and that's one of them. The second is to ask. The third is to run away with her. But if we pay for her, it's still a marriage.' When I spoke like this he said, 'That's good.' Then what I did was bring an eight-foot ten-string and give it to him. 'This could be one of two things. One, if he doesn't want her, there will be another four red moneys, with this as the fifth, as restitution, as our traditional law says. But if he wants her, I want you to tell me clearly how much I will have to pay for her.' He said, 'Because he has done everything wrong; ten, and two thousand.' 'Well, when he comes you can ask him. Because, if it's not his choice and he is forced, he'll refuse.'

So I waited for Lawrence to arrive. Lawrence said, 'Father, if you bring her you'll be paying for nothing, because I won't stay with her.' I said, 'Why, why?' and spoke forcefully to him, and he said, 'Because I've got another one as well.' Then I said, 'Oh, does anyone know?' 'The children.' Then I said, 'Oh, I'm going for our firstborn son, Sam Maesatana.'[14] Sam said, 'I know; when I drove Lawrence down to the wharf there were two girls standing there. They didn't know each other, but Lawrence knew both of them.' That's why I gave the five red moneys. I asked them to come, according to tradition, and I held the five moneys as my wife cried over them, but I gave them. She cried, 'If the money goes, a person should stay. A woman should be living in our home. That's our wealth, it's crazy.' We gave it and talked peaceably, because tradition had been broken; 'Take these five.' If you pay for a girl like this, when the child is born you can take it, but I was sorry for the girl because the boy had forsaken her. I was born with him, so I said, 'You take our grandchild, don't bring him here. Let your daughter be a little happy.' Later the girl married someone else.

After Willie was married I waited a short time and looked for more money, reaching eight shell-moneys and five thousand dollars, and then Lawrence went walking with his girlfriend Mercy Elia down from Kola'a Ridge to the graveyard. On the way one of Mercy's 'fathers' passed them in a taxi and saw them. He was a good man and didn't speak to them, but went to tell his younger brother Stephen Elia: 'Eh, our daughter is with Michael's son.' The couple came down from Kola'a Ridge to Number Nine hospital[15] and he said, 'Oh, that was a shock; I'll go and tell him.' Rather than steal her and pay loads of money, Lawrence should have informed me so I could ask Mercy's father, so he wouldn't be angry and there could be a proper marriage. I took chief Benjamin Ramo with me and my 'son' Sam Maesatana, and we went to ask. They said, 'Alright, that's good, the girl is ready to marry. But your son has taken the girl himself like that, so seven red moneys and five thousand. And we specify that every one of the seven must be nine feet; not eight, seven or six, but nine.' That was a big amount. I said, 'Give me one month' and I gave them one nine-foot money to show that they were now engaged.

By doing that, she was tabu for any man to chat with, as I had 'set the brideprice'.[16] That gave Lawrence the right to visit the girl's house, and her to visit him, to sit together and chat. I could take them some fish and other food, and they could bring me some fish, to open up friendship and link the two families together. If we were in the house they could sit down together, to prepare food and eat together, and he could bring his clothes for her to wash. That's what we call being friends; allowed to visit but not to take her in secret or sleep with her, until the brideprice is paid and the marriage feast held.

I had to give another six at nine feet. The five moneys I already had were a standard eight feet, so to exchange them I would take an eight-foot to a man who had a nine-foot and give him two hundred dollars on top. Then I bought another one and I had them all, without needing to ask my relatives. I didn't want to owe them, but they spoke to me, and they were angry: 'What's this we hear? Did you call for help with the girl? You must be a rich man.' My 'sisters' were angry: 'All of us here have to arrange for the money before paying. But you, you sit on that grassy hill by yourself and do all this.'[17] I said, 'No, it's alright. If you all wait, the time will come when I don't have anything and you can help me.' But this was money I had exchanged for cash saved from my police salary and from contract jobs, because I knew that if my children caused any problems I could suffer if people came to make demands and criticise me. So I went and gave six of nine feet, with the first one of eight feet, and of the five thousand I gave only three thousand eight hundred, as I had paid for Mercy's food since she left her father's house. They could choose whether to accept it or not, but Sam, the chief, said, 'My father has done this by himself.

Not even I helped him. I have come to present it to show that Kwa'ioloa had a senior brother, but I haven't helped with even ten cents, and he paid for me when I was married.' So they felt sorry for me and took them. They didn't hang them up, but laid them on the floor of the house to look at them and give them out. Then I said, 'Alright, on Saturday next week we'll come and take Mercy.' I bought three pigs and fertiliser bags of cassava and sweet potatoes and we carried them down, before we brought back the girl's mattress and the belongings they had given her, plus a very large pig. They also ornamented her in red money, because they were To'abaita people who followed the Malaita tradition.

Michael Kwa'ioloa in police uniform with his grandson in 1999. (Ben Burt photo)

Lawrence looked after his wife well and he begot his first child, but I wouldn't let any of them move from the house as I wanted them to save money and not get used to eating by themselves and become selfish and tired of all my 'brothers' and 'sons' and 'nephews'. Because I kept an open house and I wanted their wives to unite with us, do the Lord's work and abide strictly by my rules, according to my father's teaching.

So later on I was expecting it to be my son Haman, but he seemed to be staying with me, and eventually it was young Michael junior Lilifafia who took Solo's daughter from a house nearby. He chatted with her in secret and on the night they found out Solo came and shouted at me. I said, 'Eh, don't shout at night.' He said, 'You're in the police; arrest me.' I said, 'I won't arrest you, but just say it, don't shout. Even if you shout, if I don't have something I can't give it.' He said, 'In my tradition, with something like this he marries her whether you pay for her or not.' 'Oh, thank you for that. It's the same for us; if a man takes a girl, he has taken her. Say what you want. I don't have it, but say it. That's tradition.' 'Six red moneys. A seventh as restitution because he chatted secretly with her in our house while we were away.' I said, 'Alright, alright. If so, come back tomorrow morning.' He started to cool down, as he was a good man. 'Yes, but I thought you would ignore me.' 'Eh, traditionally, if you come to talk, or even if you strike me or swear at me, if my son does something wrong, I can't say anything. That's tradition.' 'Eh, it's the same with us.'

This girl came of three languages; her mother was from Fataleka, her father from Baegu, and her grandfather from Lau. So they said, 'Six red moneys, but they have to be nine or eight feet, not seven or less, with two thousand dollars.' They came back the next day and I gave them two. 'Alright, this one will be restitution for the house, and this one towards the brideprice.' This 'restitution for the house',[18] for the man chatting secretly with his daughter in their house, was wrong unless he refused to marry her, so I think they should have forgotten about it. But I didn't know the tradition of these people, so I took the two ten-strings and gave them that morning. The man said, 'Oh, in-law, let's shake hands. Everything is fine. Alright, I'll give you three months to get the rest.' I already had moneys, but very long ones gave me problems since I would have to get them by exchange.

When I gave the money they arranged it differently, so that the feast happened at the same time, with singing by a girl's marching band[19] to celebrate during the night, while I provided food. A tabu in-law of mine, Barnabas Bosokuru, who was married to the daughter of my 'elder brother' Gua, heard about it and said, 'Oh, let's help Michael junior,' and he brought a young pig. They said, 'We won't give anything much, just some fish and tea,' so we bought all kinds of cake and things, sugar, tea, bread and fish, then baked the pig first, without them knowing. When the singing finished they were ready for some tea and fish but what a surprise, it was the full works. 'Hey, what's this? What's going on? And a pig too?' I said, 'No, in our tradition it's a big thing to pay for a person and take her for the family. So I have to do a bit.' Then we shared out the pig, everyone there ate and celebrated through the night, then in the morning was the legal holy marriage. Then they ornamented Evelyn and we brought her home. They didn't ornament her with traditional money, but with dolphin teeth – a strap of one thousand teeth. This was what they sent her with,

Marriages and brideprice

and taking her bed, they brought her to us. But their tradition was a bit unusual, because when they arrived they took back the one thousand dolphin teeth. I didn't understand them and, as I told my son, we should have kept it. 'Eh, father, they've taken it back.' 'Oh, that's it then.' It was supposed to belong to the girl, so that she brought some wealth with her to the house. Even the cups and plates which they had collected while she

A Kwara'ae girl dressed for her wedding, with money-bead bandoliers and pattern-strap armbands, a dolphin-teeth headband and old-fashioned skirt.

was joining in the singing during the night, which they had wanted to give to her, they held back. Another thing was that when they arrived her father came and said, 'Our tradition is that when my firstborn girl marries, I won't receive any of the money. Her grandparents take it all. So you should give one more ten-string, for me to take for my daughter, because after I took the moneys on Saturday a father came and took them all away, back home.' I nearly said something but I couldn't, so I went into my room, brought out an eight-foot ten-string and gave it to him for nothing. Now I had given eight red moneys, including this last one and the one for restitution, and two thousand dollars. No-one had helped me, and it really brought me down, but I did it by myself, except for some money from my 'brother' Ben Burt.

Then Haman Namusia made his future wife Margaret Kakabi pregnant. When they called I went down to White River, but they were very good; five red shell-moneys and two thousand. So I took five bags of rice, four large fish, sugar, biscuits, bread and a carton of tinned fish; me and my wife celebrated with them that night and in the morning we took Haman's wife Margaret back to the house. That one was very simple, with no problems, and I didn't buy a pig either, because the mother said, 'You are a brother of mine, by lineage. Bring whatever you can bring and we'll just make an oven-feast, we here.' Because with us, pregnancy is also marriage, as long as you settle it, and if you don't we'll call you arrogant.[20] That's how Haman was married.

Marriage is not something to play around with. It means making a home, which is why I'm concerned that when my sons marry, they will settle too. I want them to separate into their own houses so I can see how they live when they leave the family. Because I am still their father and to keep them from harm they must do what their father and mother say. When a man is married, he should have his own house and his own plates, spoons and forks, saucepans and everything. That was a problem for me. For example, with Haman, when I came to his house he said, 'Oh father, you haven't brought anything. Start your new family off by giving us some plates.' What could I do? I left him the food-safe, chairs, and kept nothing back, because: 'Oh, we haven't got these things yet.'

I concealed the marriages of my sons and their brideprice because if I had announced them people would have come from all over to help me. But their help, although they say I don't have to return it, the way it goes is that if their sons marry I must give a gift back, the same amount and a bit extra to help them, or I am in debt.[21] They won't ask, because a leader's way is to help others, but those who are not wealthy, if their sons marry and they think it will cost too much, will come and share this with a leader. 'Oh, your son, or your grandson, has set his brideprice for such and such a day.' He doesn't have to say, 'Help me,' although sometimes he may do so if he knows it is too much for him. When you hear that, it's: 'Oh, my brother is going to die,' meaning that giving all that money will exhaust him. We say that humorously, 'Eh, let's go and see them kill our brother,' meaning he will give out all his money until he hangs up maybe thirty red moneys. But if someone says, 'Help me', that becomes a debt.

I have helped many men, but I'll give an example within my own family. Wilson Gua Folimaete'e is born of one man and I of another, but he is senior by birth, and a chief. When my son William Maelaua married I asked him to speak on my behalf and arrange things as an 'elder brother', even if he did not give anything. It would look like, 'The big man is coming. Kwa'ioloa is only junior.' Seniority is something we respect as very important in leadership. So I called on him, 'Oh Wilson Gua, our son wants this girl; will you come with me to ask for her?' Because he looked old, and when they saw him they would respect him and not charge so much. Maybe his talk would carry more weight and he would convince them, and when they discussed it they would say, 'We did say ten, but from talking with you, we like your background so just give six.' That's what a senior old man can do to negotiate such things. So we asked and they said, 'Fifteen shell-moneys and three thousand dollars.' He went to talk about it at Fulisango, their home outside Honiara, and they said, 'No deal.' But our son wanted this girl so much that we made an agreement. 'I'll give one ten-string money to put it on hold[22] for a month, so I can find the money they want, and they should buy a mattress and bring pigs.' If you ask someone to do something, you have to be prepared too. If there is a wedding-feast,[23] there should be five pigs for five shell-moneys, although in Honiara it may be just one pig from the man's side and one from the girl's side, we make a meal and that's all.

But with Wilson Gua it was I who began the help with traditional money between our families. When his son Laugere, namesake of my own firstborn son Lawrence, was married, even though he had not given any money for Lawrence Laugere's marriage, or for Lili's or Maelaua's or Namusia's marriages, he came to me. 'Sorry brother, that I didn't help you with our sons' marriages, but they want six red moneys from our son. They are coming tomorrow for payment for the girl. He has made her pregnant and they are saying six red moneys and a thousand dollars.' I didn't say, 'But when all my sons were married you didn't pay for them.' No, by tradition you don't talk like that: it is tabu, because he is your elder brother. He went back and I said, 'Oh leave it with me, brother. When is the payment?' 'Oh, on Saturday.' But he came on the Wednesday. That's our tradition too; even if I am rich and have lots of red shell-money, I can't say, 'Here it is.' No, first I say, 'You go to pay at that time, and I'll let you know what I can do. I'll have to go around and find out if I have it.'

So he went and I got my wife and children to sit down to share with them their 'father's' needs. They said, 'Eh, some would have contributed a bit of support to our father when we were married . . .' I said, 'No, no. Maybe your father didn't have anything at the time.' I had to explain to my sons that Wilson Gua did not work, but he was senior among us, as an 'elder brother'. I told them, 'Oh sons, your father is a man too. If he had something he would have given it, but it's because he has arranged things for us; giving the money, finding the pigs . . .' Michael junior said, 'But he only went to talk about it, and it's you who'll give the money.' I said, 'Tradition. It was he who spoke, and they listened and gave a discount. The pig we are giving should have been a ten-string and a thousand dollars, but by talking personally with the man he knocked off the ten-string. Once he talked to the man whose daughter was to be married and we just gave a bit of cash, and they brought the pigs. That's what I owe him. It's not for nothing; it saved money.' That's how I explained it, and my sons Lawrence and Willie were no problem, but the two Michaels, Lili and Maeisua, and Algen Afutana were more difficult: 'Leave him to himself. I can't see anyone else giving. Sometimes you have to keep away.' I said, 'You must come, or you'll set a bad example to your sons, born of your brothers.' So they sat down again and I explained: 'Talk is important. When he talks he brings down the prices. They can see he is a serious senior man and if we go with him people will respect him. That is why the day after tomorrow at the brideprice, you Lawrence will take an eight-foot ten-string and give it to your father to pay for your namesake Laugere junior, Gua's son.' (It was my father who named him.) So with that they agreed: 'Alright, bring it out. Mother, go and open the trunk.' Then mother brought the money and we all examined our family's wealth, and they said, 'That's the one we'll give him.' Then we took it to the marriage. Because Lawrence gave it, Gua was in debt and a bit embarrassed. He would go home and talk to his wife and sons and say, 'Did you see? We haven't helped them, but I saw your father send money.' So from then on he was always kind to my family and would come to watch movies and stay at the house.[24]

Not long after that, Michael junior Maeisua was married. Gua continued to talk about it, with another 'brother', Nathaniel Sele'au, until they said, 'If it's like that, we'll give Michael Kwa'ioloa another month,' so I had more time to find the money. If he had not spoken well, it would have been, 'Give it next week.' My word, they were calling me rubbish for not giving it and shaming me. Asking someone else to help me would have shamed me more, but that's the way of marriage, asking your 'brother' to give you something on account. That's what made Gua and Sele'au go and make them give me another month. So I went and changed some money and so did one of my sons, and I laid it upon them. 'You, Lawrence, such an amount of cash. The same for Willie and Haman and the two Michaels; I'll arrange for you four to change the money. And Sam Maesatana, cash from you, and traditional money too, because you are the head of the family.' So I did very well, and all my sons helped me. I wanted them to do it, not me, to make them practise so that if I die they can do it themselves. They knew this and said, 'Let's help our father so everything will go well for us; our younger brother will be married and they won't speak badly of us.' Sam Maesatana, Wilson Gua, Ukumani, Eddie Rua, Willie Anute'e, John Maetoto and everyone came. If a son of mine marries, all the senior men must come, even if they give only fifty or a hundred dollars, out of respect for my leadership. They didn't expect me to have all the money, and that morning when I brought out the bag and laid out all the money on the floor, they said, 'Michael, you've got the money, you've been pretending all the time.' That's our way. 'Oh, what a man you are.' They thought I didn't have it, that I was poor and they had to help me, but when they came the money was already there. Then they were proud of me: 'Eh, that's good. You are a wealthy man Michael; you are a leader and it suits you.'

So we brought fifteen red moneys, Ben Burt sent some money, and there was the three thousand dollars too. Then Gua's daughter was married at that time, so he had money from that and he brought an eight-foot ten-string in return for the other one, and a seven-foot one as well. He came himself and said, 'I'll give two. I'm helping my needy son with one, because he helped his brother, and another I'll give you on account.' We gave the brideprice and then when the other group saw the twelve-foot ten-strings, with the net in the middle, they said, 'No, take two back. We will just take twelve, because these are too big. There could be two or three moneys in each. Take two back; Kwa'ioloa is overdoing it.' So they took out the two moneys, and then Sam Maesatana said, 'In that case, you can exchange those red moneys for five hundred dollars each, so that's a thousand dollars, and then we just give another two thousand.' They replied, 'If it was just us men it would be alright, but the woman who bore this girl demands it. If not, she won't let go of the girl.' It was the mother-in-law, whose son had begotten the girl, who was charging the three thousand dollars. The girl's grandfather said, 'If it were just me, it would be alright, but the girl's mother wants it to be three thousand.'[25] So I said, 'I'll give the three thousand for her and we'll take the two moneys.'

A large brideprice presentation of about twenty ten-string moneys given by Langalanga people in the 2000s.

Well, after only one week, another of Gua's sons was married. He came up again and said, 'Oh, that affliction has come again.' I said, 'How's that?' 'Eh, another one has made another girl pregnant.' My word! 'How much are they saying?' 'Seven.' I just said, 'Oh, there are two here with me.' Well, those were the two I had in reserve, which I had got back from him. One was on account but he wasn't expecting it back, as he'd said, 'I'm helping Michael even more because when his sons were married I didn't help him, so now I'm giving two.' He was surprised at the brideprice presentation when I came with another two as well. 'Hey, what are you doing to me? Are you trying to give me a shock? You didn't let me know.' I said, 'Even if you have more than enough, leave yours. These are coming because you helped me the last time and lightened my brideprice burden.'

So that's how we become wealthy. We had one money in credit with Wilson Gua, and if our boy Alden Afutana were to marry, Wilson Gua would have to bring one, and if he had more he would 'make a pathway'[26] between us. It means clearing a path which was blocked and making it hard for people to reach you. The more you give and exchange, the clearer the way, so that if anything happens they will come. That's our traditional way. But if Gua had no traditional money, he could give fifteen or twenty dollars as what we call 'entering into a gift',[27] meaning that the money is still there between us and he acknowledges it by giving a part. Whenever another son is married he just comes and, 'Oh, here is that traditional money. Last time I just entered into the gift.' Entering into the gift keeps the pathway open so we don't miss him out during a brideprice: 'Oh, that man will come.' If he doesn't, people will say, 'That man, if someone helps him he does almost nothing.' The 'pathway is blocked'[28] again. That's the tradition.

My sons still depend on me, even though they work. They eat at my house and the grandchildren come to eat. For example, I should say, 'Eh, we'll go to your father, because when you sleep with us you pee in my bed,' but I love my grandchildren too much. It's good for them to relate to their grandparents and get to know them, because a grandfather can teach them and pray for them better than a father.

When my eldest daughter married it was a new thing for me and my family. She is Annie Maranabua, namesake of my mother's mother. Annie married Martin, a boy from Talakali in Langalanga, Malaita, son of Harold Walesidele of Rafea. He chatted with her in secret and my sons heard, and their cousins from Kobito. My sons were alright, but the sons of my 'brother', who lived the kind of life where they drink beer, they actually stopped the bus he was driving, with a rock. When they reached his house, they demanded four thousand dollars in restitution, because the boy had taken Annie in secret, against our tradition. They broke down the door of Martin's father's house and damaged things inside, so Sam Maesatana came and quietened them down. He said the man should give just one thousand dollars, because it was a young boy and girl, although it was wrong for him to take her in secret. Because of that they stopped them but eventually, two years later when Annie was sixteen, she got back in contact with Martin. One of my tabu in-laws, Margaret, the wife of Haman Namu, heard and went to tell Martin's father, because she was related to them too. 'Eh, if you want Annie for your son, just go and ask my in-law directly. He's a good man and it will be alright.'

So then Martin's father sent a message to me. His eldest son stood in the road and said, 'My father would very much like to see you and your wife.' I went to him because his leg had been cut off in an operation and he couldn't come up the hill to me, so I humbled myself and came down. He asked me, 'Oh, as Martin has contacted Annie again, I want to pay for her. How about it?' I said, 'If so, seven red moneys and two thousand. That is to reimburse me for all the money I have paid out, brother.' Martin's father accepted. Later on he sent me another message, 'Oh, I was afraid to tell Michael that my son has already made his girl pregnant.' I heard and went back to him and said, 'Oh, that is wrong. The first time we forgave you all, the second time he took her in secret and you called me, but I was wrong to come because he had already taken her, and now she's pregnant. So you will give ten red moneys and two thousand dollars. Of the ten red moneys, three will be twelve-foot ten-strings with a net in the middle, and one eight-foot. I'll take the eight-foot now.' Then he said, 'If so, I'll have to make more shell-money. I can make money, no problem, but you must give me time.'[29] So I said, 'I'll give you three months, or whenever you are ready,' and he was happy: 'Eh, thanks very much, Mike.'

They made all the money and then called me, and I called Ben Burt in England for help with some cash to buy food for Annie's wedding. I bought thirteen bags of rice, two cartons of Taiyo tinned fish, a bag of sugar, two cartons of noodles and some fish, and we went down to take the money. That was not part of the wedding feast, but because Martin's relatives lived at home on Malaita I knew that if they came, when they returned they should take some rice. They didn't expect it, but when

A family from Langalanga, the community which produces most of Malaita's shell-money, making money in Honiara. The woman is shaping shell disks with a hammer and anvil before drilling them with the wheel-brace. In the background, the man is grinding a string of beads smooth on a plank. (Michael Kwa'ioloa photo)

they saw us coming that evening to take the brideprice, they were so happy. 'Hey Michael, what are you doing now?' I said, 'Nothing, brothers-in-law. It's so when they return each one can take some rice back, and two or three tins of Taiyo and some noodles.' That was to set an example. But I still didn't send Annie yet. For that I would make a big party, with fish, pigs and things, then Martin's and Annie's brothers and sisters would come to contribute things to take home. I gave her a mattress and a box, cups, dishes, even chairs, for her to make a home. I prepared for that, and when I did it showed off our tradition of unity, respecting Martin's family because his father had given me a very good brideprice. When I took it I was laughing so much with happiness.

With the money I helped two men to marry; my son Michael junior Maeisua and three 'brothers'' sons, and that was my new link with others again. If any son of mine marries, they will give something back to me. One twelve-foot ten-string was a small present to Ben Burt and his wife for their help with my sons' marriages. Others I gave to chiefs. When my second-born William Maelaua was married, my 'brother', chief Michael Ngidu'i came and said, 'Oh, I want to help you. I hear you need a ten-string with a net in the middle, and I have one, eight foot long.' Later on, when Lawrence was married for the second time, he gave a nine-foot ten-string. Because of that I gave him a thousand dollars for the net-money and then a nine-foot ten-string for his son's marriage. That made him very happy, that we had helped each other. Then Sam Maesatana took a twelve-foot one with a net in the middle, and his younger brother took a nine-foot. That was because their father had paid the brideprice when we were married and Annie was born, so we gave the money to these two fatherless sons of my dead brother John Maesatana to show them respect. When my 'son' Sam Maesatana was married I helped him with five red moneys, because it was twenty-five red moneys and three thousand eight hundred; a great amount. And when Kwasi was married I gave eight hundred dollars, because they demanded one thousand five hundred dollars and four red moneys, and as Willie and Lawrence had also exchanged a money from 'Are'are for four hundred dollars, I met almost half the cost of Kwasi's marriage. Kwasi and Sam treated me as their 'father' so I had to pay for them, and then give them the money from Annie's marriage out of respect as their 'father'.

A wedding photo of Kwa'ioloa's daughter Fasti Lekafa'iramo with her mother Bizel Fanenalua, her husband Felix Oro of 'Ere'ere, East Kwara'ae, and his mother, in 2009.

Marriage is the first thing which gathers people together, and the second one, the only other thing which unites people, is the bad one; death. When a person dies we treat it as very important in the community and everyone is sorry. In Honiara especially, whether a person is from Lau or To'abaita or Kwaio, it's, 'Eh, don't play loud music; a neighbour of ours has died. We'll stop our ceremony and postpone it; someone has died.' If anyone seems happy, people may say that he had something to do with the death, perhaps by sorcery. So when someone dies everyone comes and sits down together to mourn. Friends come with bags of rice, cartons of biscuits, sugar, tins of meat; not for the dead person's family, but to cook. It's not the same as the former tradition, but we do it because the people who come will be hungry when we sit all night and all day to mourn with the dead body and encourage people: 'Eh, don't worry brother; death comes to us all, but sorry to lose this man.' All night people come and go, including different groups and languages related to us by marriage: 'Oh, my in-law, his son is dead, he's dead.' When people come they go round with plates of food as they sit under the trees. Some don't eat but just go to encourage people, and leaders, if they have already eaten, may just hold a piece of sweet potato and pretend to eat. A man who doesn't show his face when someone of ours dies, when one of his dies no-one will come either. That's why both these things are important; death and marriage both gather people together.

---

1 *Omea*, which refers here to the marriage ceremonies as a whole.
2 'Village' and 'community' both translate *fanoa*, which has the general meaning of 'home'.
3 *Ara'inga'a*, from *ara'ai* or 'married man'.
4 *Daura'ia*; 'hanging up' the shell-moneys from a beam to display them as they are presented.
5 *Kwatea fāfia*.
6 This is speaking figuratively: no-one who wants to maintain a relationship would expect immediate repayment.
7 'Saving' here implies gaining credit by helping others who will one day help your son in return.
8 Making a girl pregnant or eloping with her may be treated as 'stealing', leading to conflict and a punitively high brideprice.
9 Brothers- and sisters-in-law are especially tabu to each other because of the risk of sexual impropriety, hence often referred to as 'tabu'.
10 In fact, this is not a conventional Kwaio unit for measuring *bani'au* or other shell valuables.
11 The 'net' pattern of interwoven strings, usually in deep red *romu* beads, adds to the value of the ten-string.
12 As the convention is for the woman's family to provide the wedding feast, such a gesture would be very much to the credit of the man's side.
13 Conventionally, this is how the woman's family would share out the food when giving a traditional wedding feast or *tolonga*, according to the man's side's brideprice contributions.

14 As the son of Kwa'ioloa's deceased elder brother John Maesatana, Sam Maesatana is senior by birth in their family.
15 The Central Referral Hospital.
16 *'Olea daurai'ia.*
17 The exchange system requires people to accept contributions as well as to give them, so Kwa'ioloa's relatives were voicing the normal expectation that he should accept obligations to them.
18 *Fa'aābua luma*, or 'make the house tabu (again)'.
19 A church group who sing choruses as they march to and fro.
20 *Naunau* or 'me-me'.
21 Kwa'ioloa's reluctance to incur debts by accepting brideprice contributions is a candid admission of tensions in the exchange system. People need to receive gifts as well as to give them in order to create the relationships on which leadership depends, but this does mean being put under obligations. The cash economy of Honiara, by enabling people to gain wealth independently of the exchange system, can encourage generosity (*alafe'anga*) at the expense of reciprocity (*kwaima'anga*).
22 *Fa'ababato'o* or 'make it stay quiet'.
23 *Tolonga.*
24 This incident reaffirms the contradictions in the exchange system, in that Kwa'ioloa has to argue for the morality of giving to those who have been unable to make the appropriate contributions themselves.
25 Contrary to the common assumption of opponents of brideprice, women often share their menfolk's approval of high brideprice as raising the status of their daughters.
26 *Kwa'i tala.*
27 *Ru'ufikwate.*
28 *Tala buru.*
29 Being from Langalanga, he belonged to the community who make most of the shell-money used by Malaitans.

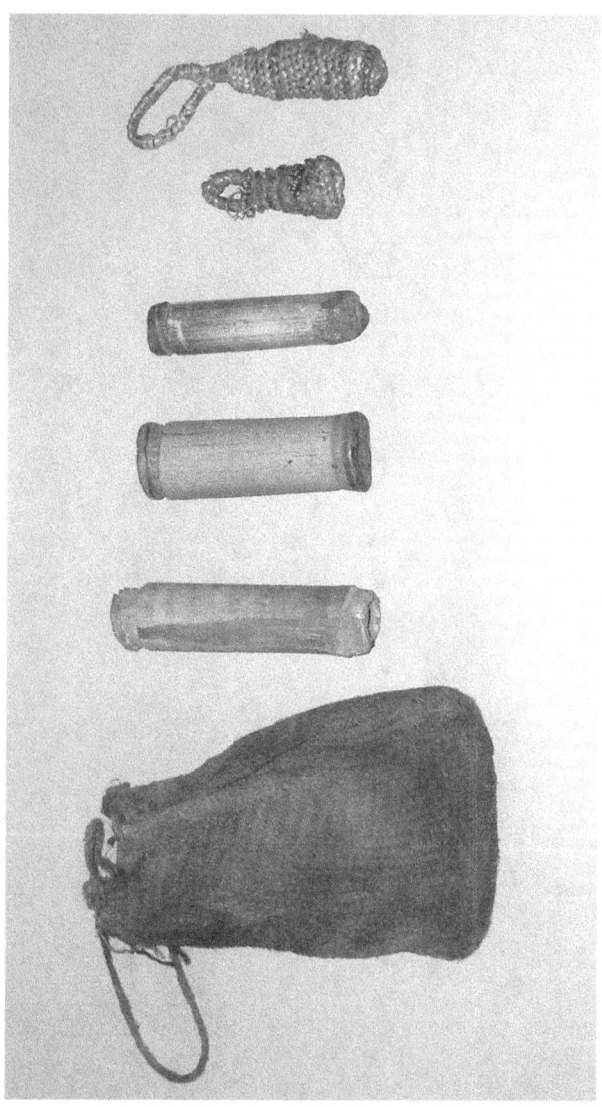

A *vele* sorcerer's kit from the early 20th century in the British Museum, with two charms for the finger and three flasks of magical materials, all kept in a bag. (BM Oc1944,02.1351)

5
DEALING WITH SORCERY

My home area in Malaita is very bad for sorcery,[1] and it is the same in Honiara. The reason is because people are jealous of those who have a few good things; there is nothing more to it than that. If they see you building a good house, they'll sorcerise you and you'll die. It's because they don't want you living well with your family; you have to be poor like them. At home some men are jealous too. When people have money coming into their bank account, some say, 'How does that man do it?' and that causes problems at home, in my experience. There is sorcery because of jealousy when a man goes home with the money he has gained and spends it on materials to build another five-bedroom house at home. In my own family, no-one at home will kill us because we take the role of leadership and are kind to people, making them obligated by giving back more than we need. So in my family we are not afraid to go back home. It appears that sorcery affects a man who talks big, who is proud, and things like that, but who has no land. We have land, we keep everyone on our land, and they also reserve it for us: 'Oh, you can't do that; Michael Kwa'ioloa will come. That's his place.' You see, instead of thinking to sorcerise us, they help my family. But some men will do it, and I won't give examples, but that's their way, as I have seen. My 'younger brother' Thompson Atoa, he was not proud at all, but someone killed him because they were jealous. He ran a passenger truck and was doing well at home, but in 2004 they sorcerised him and he died. I don't know who did it, but someone knows.

Thompson Atoa in his truck, with Adriel Rofate'e, in 1987. (Ben Burt photo)

They have different sorceries. One way is when they see you go and they put it to wait for you to return, so you step over it. Another way is to throw it at you and when it hits you, you're finished. Ulawa do this, and Malaita too, and they call it 'promising with a wild yam'.[2] They take this wild yam and pray with this sorcery, then throw it at you and you fall down and die on the spot. There is another from Langalanga, which Mark Li'iga, Folota and others bought to kill one another, until none of them were left. This is 'pointing',[3] which means the man points at you and you fall down and die. Guadalcanal people have warned me of the power of the *vele* man. You cannot see him for he has a magic packet[4] and if you meet him he'll cut open a tree or a rock and hide inside it while you pass. The *vele* knows you are coming and he will make his magic kill you. There is a powerful sorcery from Ulawa and from To'abaita in north Malaita, called *aru'a* (sorry to say, and without wanting to accuse our 'brothers'). There was Dori, son of my senior 'brother' chief Bugua Folimaete'e, who suffered for three years and then died in 2003. He was a handsome boy who didn't smoke, drink beer or chew betelnut and he did church work in our evangelical team, which went to Makira. A man sorcerised him and his arm swelled up. It was Ulawa, because an Ulawa man came and treated him just at the time he died. They can treat it and kill with it at the same time. I don't know how he did it. The Kwara'ae buy sorcery and adopt it, like the sorcery at Uka in East Kwara'ae, which is a special snake in a hole. If your shadow goes over it, you die, and it can work with the remains of a person's food. This is called *aru'a* and it means that someone will pick up food remains which a person has thrown away and give it to the snake, and the person dies. But

Kwara'ae didn't have this; they must have bought it from the north.[5]

In Talakali in east Fataleka they have a 'flare' for tracing a man who has caused another man's death through sorcery. People pay for it and tell them that all they want is the man's name. They don't know where he lives and they don't care; they just want his name, and they know the only way is to 'launch a flare'.[6] Sosoke and others paid for it when they believed someone had sorcerised a relative of theirs at their home in Taba'akwaru in East Kwara'ae. They sent for it and eventually it came and landed near their home. It was like a flaming light in the air, a magic which comes and knows the name of the man who has sorcery, and lands on his house. It doesn't kill him, but it's a sign to them that this is the man, and then maybe they will kill him, or discuss death-compensation.[7] When Sosoke and the others paid for it, they saw it come like a fire in the sky. It missed the home and landed in the forest, but they saw it with their own eyes, and that proved it was indeed true.

Another thing which deals with sorcery is the spiritual power of the Melanesian Brothers, the *tasiu*.[8] I was brought up in the Church of Melanesia before I eventually ended up in the South Sea Evangelical Church, and I saw this when I was small. Some of the Brothers at Gwaunamanu went to look for eels in the river, with a torch at night, but instead they saw a snake. Their leader, a Papua New Guinea man called Wenceslas, said, 'Oh God has given this to us,' pointed at it with his staff, and the snake died. They prayed over it and ate it, as Paul did in the Bible. The staff showed them the snake but God gave it to them, so they came to no harm and did not die. That proved the Brothers' staffs, when I was small. They wore a uniform with a white sash and belt over it, and when they came we weren't afraid but said, 'Oh, the holy men.' We were told when we were small, 'That staff is a miracle staff. If they point it at something, that's it.' The bishops dedicated the staffs for clearing places where there was magic and ghosts. So when someone dies from sorcery, everyone says, 'Let's bring in the *tasiu*.' The church leaders and chiefs come together and get the man who they say has killed someone; not just on suspicion but because of a sign.

This happened to Masing Rul,[9] an important man of Taba'angwao near 'Atori in East Kwara'ae. They said he had killed a man and the chiefs gathered, they brought in the *tasiu* with their staffs and discussed it and eventually said, 'Now we'll prove it. If you have sorcery and you killed the man, when you hold this staff you'll fall down, then we'll pray for you and you'll get up again.' Masing Rul told me this himself. He said, 'They did this, I was proud to go and hold it, and I didn't faint.' Then the *tasiu* said, 'Oh, this man doesn't have it.' But, Masing Rul said, that day some others held it and they did fall down. They had to pay death-compensation of ten red moneys, because they had actually killed the man by sorcery. They do this in Honiara too. There is an ex-Brother near us at Gilbert Camp who can tell if you have sorcery. He also has a staff and when he uses it we chiefs judge by it. It is hard to judge an angry man because he'll look for something to kill someone else, but the ex-Brother can tell you, 'Oh, you did it, it's you who killed the man.' If you did it he will just show it straight away, then pray for you and you'll fall down.

I'll explain about sorcery and the spiritual power to stop it. My father had this power. Back in the 1960s, when I was a child, my father came to Honiara and an Anglican bishop living at Fera'uai in west Guadalcanal showed it to him, when he was working on the Lever's plantation. I don't know who this bishop was but at that time they were all Whitemen sent from England. My father's 'younger brother' Tolia was killed at Ruafatu in East Guadalcanal by a *vele*, a Guadalcanal sorcerer, who was looking for my father to kill him too. So my father fled from Ruafatu and went to stay in west Guadalcanal, at Lafuro in Lambi Bay. He was a churchgoer and he said to the bishop, 'I'm afraid that the same ghost which killed my brother will kill me too.' That was when he showed my father a tree and said, 'When you approach this tree, bow down and pray to the tree and then cut a diamond-shape from the bark on the side where the sun rises, saying, "I'm taking this for protection." Peel off the piece of bark, scrape off the outer part and cut the inner part in pieces and put it to dry. That's what you will eat and then, whether it's ghosts or sorcerers, they won't be able to kill you.' My father said, 'This *vele* who is looking for me has promised to kill me,' and he said, 'Alright, I'll pray for three days and you will meet this *vele* and kill him. But you must eat this tree-bark first, and go late in the evening when everyone has come back, then go to the paddock and pick up all the coconuts to break ready for making your copra next morning. At dusk or dawn while it's dark, the *vele* will come as he has told you.' My father did all this and on the third evening the *vele* came, put his small basket on his little finger, made a zzz sound and turned it round. When you see him do that, your eyes go round and he will kill you with a small long-handled tomahawk. He always cuts a man in the belly. The *vele* came and said, 'It's me; I've already killed your brother at Ruafatu. You fled and

I'll kill you too.' But my father had already blessed the tree-bark and eaten it, so his eyes were not affected. When he slashed violently at my father's belly with the tomahawk, my father took it by the handle and cut him in the belly, just as he was turning the small basket for the *vele* to come out. Then he took the basket, put it where it could do no harm, and fled.

That showed the protective power of the tree-bark, which the bishop had blessed, and we live by it. I keep it with me, and so do my children. Ben Burtte'e and Rosie always have it because there are school students who attack them. Maniramo is our main supplier from home. He prays to the tree and to God the Father, Son and Holy Spirit and makes the mark of the cross, then cuts it and the power is in it. There are three different kinds my father gave me; one you burn and the smoke drives off the sorcery. They are very useful and I have saved lots of people with them who almost died. Biblically, Jesus did the same when a man whose eyes were blind since birth came and said, 'I want to be made whole.' So Jesus took some clay, spat on it and rubbed it on the man's eyes and said, 'Go and wash your eyes in the pool at Siloam,' and when he did so he received his sight, with eyes brown, bright and clear.[10] That proves that Jesus used nature to heal, and that makes me believe that what my father told me works and keeps us safe. The White Dog of A'arai in East Kwara'ae, which my father formerly sacrificed to, whose spirit will kill a man; if we eat that tree-bark when we go there it's quite impossible for it to kill us.[11] There was one time in 2000 when I was in charge of the police in Honiara Central Market, keeping the peace and preventing the young boys from troubling the women and taking their money, produce and betelnut. A woman fell down because a man gave her a peanut, and then another one, which he had put magic on. She just ate it, fell down and screamed as if she was dying. They ran to see her, so I came running with the tree-bark, opened her mouth and put it in, and it cured her straight away.

Lots of people have sorcerised me to try to kill me, from jealousy over land and the success of my work. Honiara is very dangerous, more than Malaita. I'll give an example. In 2000 there were four men staying at 'A'ekafo whom we knew to have sorcery, and one person died one week, another the next, and the next. I dealt with the case for the chiefs, with Bamae, son of the late paramount chief Sangafanoa, and we charged one of these men, a cousin of mine, for killing Alex Rukia's brother Sukulu. But when we went to speak to him a sorcery bird called a *ka'ura* cried out from the front of the house, and he said, 'That's something from our past crying out.' Then 'Au'au, the paramount chief who had taken over from Sangafanoa, said, 'You say that, and Kwa'ioloa will give the judgement because we have been looking for evidence, but this *ka'ura* bird has come and shown it was you, from how you spoke out.' It was very arrogant of the sorcerer to say that. He said to 'Au'au, 'But that's our bird from the central inland come to cry. The *ka'ura* way is to come and cry, and a man's life is over. In three days he'll die. Day one, two, three, and you're dead.' Sorcery is very dangerous.

Then I said, 'Alright, you don't have sorcery, as the chiefs have no evidence to prove conclusively that you killed, but on the evidence that you danced and talked boastfully when the man died, you must give a traditional red money, because all the signs look as if it was you who killed him. Not ten red moneys for killing, since you say you don't have sorcery, but because when the man died you rejoiced[12] and said things which showed you were pleased. So the House of Chiefs still says you have the signs of sorcery. The chiefs charge you to give one ten-string to Sukulu's people, to clear their minds and reconcile them with you.' So, acknowledging he had sorcery, he said, 'I agree to give it, but which of you will hold the ten-string?' He meant that he would sorcerise the ten-string so that if you held it you would die straight away. He brought a red money: 'Who will take it? Who will take it?' He spoke so proudly. It was an eight-foot ten-string. Then chief Ramo stood up and said, 'Put it on this chair' and he said, 'No, I want one of you to take it, to see you touch it.' Kiloko's son Jimmy, who had arranged the meeting, was afraid to take it. 'Eh, father, I can't take it. If I take it I'll die.' Ramo said, 'Never mind, I'll take it, don't worry.'

I was a pastor at the time and I held that piece of tree-bark, I prayed for it, then I ate it. The powerful tree-bark, which the Anglican bishop had explained to my father and he had passed on to me, was my weapon at that time. When I went to take the money I said, 'Does anyone have some betelnut?' They said, 'You're chewing betelnut? A pastor? That worries us.'[13] I said, 'It's bitter, and in any case if I eat it by itself, it won't do anything. It's not that I want to chew betelnut; it's for protection from this man killing me, because it's just me who will hold the money.' It was so we could deflect and smooth the sorcery so it was not powerful but normal. I spat it on my hand[14] and said, 'Alright, show me the money. You hold the end so I can see that it is eight foot long.' He held it and I said, 'No, hold it by both ends and if it falls down so far, it's eight feet. Lower your right hand, lower the other hand more' and so on. My father told me to do this, so that it would make the man chase out the sorcery by holding every part of it. So he held the ends level and it reached his navel, meaning it was eight foot. 'Alright, I approve it, cousin. I'm very pleased that you have obeyed the talk of the chiefs. Hold the two ends together; hold that part; hold it like that again; let it go and coil it up. Oh, it's really eight foot.' He put it away and said, 'Why are you treating me like this, cousin? You have really spoiled my plans.' I said, 'Alright, now go.' By saying this, he had confessed. 'You Tolingas,[15] I don't accept Tolinga authority. Thank you brother; I'm going. Take it.' It was my father's knowledge which protected me at that time. So Ramo held the money and when I held it something passed through my hand and then reached my head and affected me so that I almost fell down. So I spat some more and I gave it to Jimmy, because they had killed his brother, and that maintained the peace.

My actions proved that this man was a sorcerer and had killed people. So everyone from 'A'ekafo and Namoliki came and set fire to his house and beat him up because their men had died. His relatives escaped with him and took him to hospital, but his body was swollen from the wounds. After two or three days he and his brother-in-law came to the Central Police Station to report the incident, but I had already written a circular to all the police stations, with the authority of the chiefs: 'Even if they beat up this man, and this one and this one, take no notice. These men finished off 'A'ekafo, one man dying after another.' So the police took no action, because of the authority of the chiefs.

When the two of them came they saw me sitting under the trees by the police barracks, opposite the Hibiscus Hotel,[16] and the sorcerer came up and said, 'Brother,' and touched me on the shoulder. This was when my son Wilson Maelaua was to be married, and when I almost died. That evening, when I should have taken the moneys to pay for Willie's wife, I was unable to go. With the things they use to kill people, everyone has to leave you and the sorcery chases them off so you die by yourself. Its way is to tell everyone to go away: 'Oh Michael, stay here. Father, stay here. Let's all go, we're going to pay for Willie.' They were going to Windy Ridge, far away in the Tenaru area. Not long after they had taken the brideprice away, chief David Kwa'ite'e came to check, as he was to be the main spokesman. He saw me but didn't worry: 'Hey, namesake!' 'Oh, your sister-in-law and our children have already gone and taken the bag of money.' He wasn't worried about me either. He said, 'Your eyes are going round, what's up with you? Oh, I'll follow them.' That's the way of such a person, making everyone leave you before you die. 'I must go, to speak about the brideprice, so they won't argue about it. I must go because you can't and I'm the elder brother.'

That's when I thought I was about to die, and I saw how spirit-possession[17] by sorcery will kill a person. I didn't see with my eyes, but I saw this man in my mind, with my feelings, and he was laughing at me. He said, 'Now you'll die.' I was sick and as I looked at the sun it turned green, then I counted the rafters and it looked as if everything was going round. Then I thought of that tree-bark, and only Ben Burtte'e was there with me. My whole body was done for, I was so weak. So what I did was unfasten my belt and move my lavalava up to my chest so I could breathe, and I said, 'Eh, Ben, go and bring the jar from up on the table in the room. It has the tree-bark in it.' At that time he was very small, about five years old, but he understood enough so that when he saw me he nearly cried: 'Father, what's happening to you?' I said, 'No, don't worry, bring the tree-bark I put there.'

He gave it to me and I said to Kwa'ite'e, 'Do you have any betelnut?' He said, 'No.' 'What about in your mortar, is there a little in there?' He said, 'Yes, it's full.' I said, 'Bring it so I can eat it.' 'Hey, you're a pastor, and you're eating betelnut?' I said, 'I must eat betelnut with this because it's really bitter.' If they sorcerise you and you want to eat it, your eyes will be sore and if it's even near your mouth it feels like your head will come off, because it won't let you eat it. Your body rejects it because if you swallow it you will be healed, so it makes you vomit it up. So I told Kwa'ite'e this and he got the betelnut, which was ground up in the mortar. Then I took it and put it on some paper and said, 'Ben Burt, bring the tree-bark.' I tried holding it to my eyes but my eyes went out, and so did my head. I said, 'Ben Burt, bring the kettle from the tea they were drinking.' The kettle was heavy so I said, 'Pour a little and bring that, enough for a cup.' 'Eh, I might spoil the mat.' 'Pour it; pour it and bring it here! Bring a cup with tea leaves in it, four big spoonfuls.' 'It's quite cold, Father.' I said, 'Now stir it, quick, quick, quick!' So I took it and said, 'Bring the tree-bark.' All three at once, I took them, put them in the paper, and told Ben Burt to pound them with a hammer. Then I ate them all at once with the mortar of betelnut. It was hard to swallow and my eyes and my whole body seemed to boil. Then I took the cup of tea with sugar and swallowed it and I fell down and slept, from four o'clock to six o'clock in the evening. The sun was going down and I woke with a start when Ben Burt said, 'Father, wake up, the sun's shining on you.' I moved and lay down again. I was healed and the sorcery had fled. It had happened the same day he sorcerised me and it wasn't an illness so the treatment had to be traditional. I treated myself and it was cured.

Two or three years later chief Benjamin Ramo and his wife, who were staying down in Kwaio Valley, saw this sorcerer early one morning coming up the path to my house, at the junction coming from Gilbert Camp. He looked around, dug a hole and put the sorcery in it, to wait for me. Ramo and his wife called out, 'So and so, why are you digging? What are you hiding?' and he ran away. What it meant was that if I went by when the sun came up in the east, my shadow would cover the sorcery he had buried and I would die; either me or my children. It's like the snake hole in the shrine at Anomula, which they must cover with a leaf before they go into the most tabu place where they kill the pigs, in case their shadow goes into the hole and they die. As Christians, we prayed a lot about this, so Ramo warned us and watched until noon so that no-one would walk past along that path. The Lord took pity on us, and we went a different way to work or school. Ramo had the same power but it was dedicated to healing, so he cleansed it by prayer and made it normal again, then called for me and explained it all.

Solomon Islanders live between two worlds; their original society and its modern transformation. Sorcery afflicts in particular the people who raise their standard of living and work hard to develop the country. People use it to break down businesses so everyone will live as poorly as themselves. The use of such evil power must be punished to stop it. We chiefs have drafted by-laws for Honiara City Council, including laws to make those who buy or use sorcery give restitution payments, as high as those paid for direct killing, and these laws should be sent to parliament to be incorporated in the common law of the country.[18]

---

[1] 'Sorcery' translates *kelema*, a general term for various kinds of harmful magic, known in Pijin as *poison*.
[2] *Alangani 'ania fa'i da'u.*
[3] *Sususu.*
[4] A small basketry container of magical materials with a loop to hold it by the little finger, as illustrated on page 118.
[5] Although people tend to attribute sorcery to foreign origins, several histories relate how sorcerers from Uka in East Kwara'ae killed people by this method in former times.
[6] This practice, *labua unu*, is from north Malaita and the Kwara'ae import it as necessary. See Burt & Kwa'ioloa 2000:100-101 for details.
[7] *Toto'a*, as distinct from restitution (*fa'aābu'a*).
[8] The Melanesian Brotherhood is an Anglican religious order which played an important mediating role in the conflict, *tasiu* being their Mota name (see Macdonald Milne 2003).
[9] So named because he was born during the Maasina Rul movement after the Second World War.
[10] John 9:6-11.
[11] This ghost dog, whose relic was kept in one of Kwa'ioloa's clan shrines (see Burt & Kwa'ioloa 2001:84-5), would kill passers-by.
[12] *Aola.*
[13] The evangelical churches forbid betelnut, as well as alcohol and tobacco.
[14] Chewing something and spitting it over a person or thing is a way of spreading its power, in this case 'making it smooth' (*fa'adadā*) and 'ordinary' (*mola*) as distinct from threatening and dangerous.
[15] Kwa'ioloa's clan.
[16] The former name, which some still use, for the King Solomon Hotel.
[17] *Ta'elia*, experienced as being overcome by emotion, as when possessed by a ghost or by the Holy Spirit.
[18] There have been laws against sorcery in Solomon Islands since the colonial period, but Kwa'ioloa is proposing that these conform to the principles of tradition.

An East Kwara'ae landscape in 1984, looking over Latea towards the offshore islands, with Gwaufala village on the hill to the right.
(Ben Burt photo)

6
OUR CLAIMS TO ANCESTRAL LANDS

Although we stay in Honiara we still have a claim on our home area, for when we will return to it. We stay in Honiara just to work, to pay school fees for the education of our children. At home there is no money; not because we are lazy, but because when we make big gardens and everyone brings along sweet potatoes and taro and nuts to market, who will buy them? Sometimes we have to give them to the sea people on the coast because it's too hard to carry them back.[1] A great heap of taro and sweet potato for only one dollar! I tried this for nine years, but it was too hard, so I stay in Honiara to get employment. We have gained some education for our children, and I have also attended classes to gain the little knowledge I have by expanding my education. That's why we stay in Honiara, but it doesn't mean we lose our families at home. We have to go back to claim our original home, where we can return to permanently to live in the future. Even if we die in Honiara, there are our children. We have to maintain our connections with our 'brothers' at home so that even if my son arrives they will say, 'Oh, it's Lawrence Laugere, he's the firstborn son of Kwa'ioloa and when Kwa'ioloa died he became senior for our land.' That is so the sons of Tisa and of Toto'o and Aburofou, such as Nelson Kona, Nelson Berote'e, and the sons of Maelekisi and of Ta'efa'i and of Manibili, Fa'abasua and Haniel Bubufera, will respect Lawrence as senior for the land. They stay at home, but when they deal with any land issue they have to call me, because they lost in the dispute between my father Alasa'a and Ramo'itolo in a court case in 1965.[2]

So while we stay in Honiara, it doesn't mean we don't worry about the land at home. No, we must go back, as I did one time when those at home called by radio: 'Hey, come quickly. Our opponents' group wants to take over the land. The other groups are saying in meeting after meeting that our family will cease to be. So come quickly, in case they take away our land.' My reply was to say to my elder brother Sylvanus Maniramo and my 'younger brother' Rex Manilofea Di'au at home, 'Why do you bother with somebody else's meetings? They'll have you hanging around and you'll get upset. Wait; leave it to me to arrange a meeting and they will have to come to it. It's not for us to attend their meetings, because their land boundary was settled when Fairu land was won back by our father.' I was referring to the conflict with the Latea group, when my father won that dispute with Ramo'itolo and they divided the land, in 1965. That was a government legal ruling in court with the district commissioner, while we were still under colonial rule. So I said, 'Don't worry too much, because for something like that they will have to appeal.' When I went home they gave up and So'ai, Ramo'itolo's son, came running to say, 'It was such-and-such a man from your group; I was angry and I did so-and-so, but if it had been you it wouldn't have been anything.' So'ai was born of Siumalefo, sister of my father Alasa'a, both born of one man and one woman. The two shared the land between them. That's why I claim this land as the winner, because about ten men had already lost in court to Ramo'itolo before my father appealed and won it back.

My father won leadership of the land, then it came to my elder brother John Maesatana and then after he died, to me. My other elder brother Maniramo is a quiet man and unsuitable as a spokesman. Although he stays at home, he is not educated and when people say, 'Let's do this' he would just jump in, so he authorises me to take the leadership for all of us. Maniramo's speciality is his memory. I am good at book reading but I have to refer back to what Ben Burt and I have written in *A Solomon Islands Chronicle*.[3] Maniramo holds all our genealogies in his mind and can speak without looking at a book. I know what is in our land because we all went around with father when we lived at home, but Maniramo is the main repository of knowledge for all our family and knows all the histories.[4] He stays at home and always reports to me. If anything is wrong he radios and says, 'Michael, come here,' and I have to leave my work and go without delay to keep things in order.

That being so, I don't reject them or say, 'All the land is no longer yours, because you have already lost it.' No, I believe that one man alone cannot claim land. It must belong to the clan, particularly land given to a woman, as Ben Burt and I wrote in *The Tradition of Land in Kwara'ae*. That's the book which explained things so well that the chief justice has used it to block appeals from the Customary Land Appeals Court to the High Court. I have enough of my father's spirit with me to love everybody and tell them, 'Even though you lost, the piece of land which was given to you still belongs to you.' The lands given to the women I am born from within Fairu are mine, but still I won't take them for myself because they belong to all of us. Even so, anyone who wants to do something in the land must let me know, because I am the man in charge, even though I stay in Honiara. If anything is to happen in the land it must be me who initiates it. If not, I will object to it, even if it would benefit the district of East Kwara'ae or Malaita, because I am senior.[5]

It's like this. If a man arrives and an elder says, 'Because you did this for me, I'll give you a small block of land for your help',[6] he has the right to claim it. This still happens today, but now we do it wrong. In the past we would not sell land unless we had a special reason. If we were sorry for a man who had no land when he had been staying with us for a long time, we would say, 'Purchase a bit of land with pigs or shell-money, because you have been helping us.' For example, we of Fairu sold land to the Silua clan, Alasi and others, at Mamulele, because they had lived there for ages, with the church. Then our clansmen, Auluta and others from west Kwara'ae, came back and pleaded for land for themselves, so we sold the land, including the area where they lived around the church: 'You have been living there, and the main thing for all of us is God's work, so take it.'

On the other hand, my 'son' Sam Maesatana went to the opening of a church at Faubaba at Christmas 2005, and the Funilofo people said we should sell the piece of land between Funilofo and Fairu for a group from the Church of Melanesia to take for a secondary school, and they notified the bishop to pay for it. When the opening ceremony was finished, Sam came back by plane the day after, reached me, and we both went back by plane the next day. When we reached home we had a meeting and went straight to Siru'aba'aba, my 'brother', the man in charge of Funilofo land: 'Eh, I hear you want to sell this piece of land, and we haven't yet straightened out whether it belongs to you or me. So don't do it yet.' Then he said, 'Ah, it's because another group who lost are insisting that it doesn't belong to me; that's why I want to sell it. But your coming like this makes it better for both of us. Anything to do with it is between you and me, brother.' He said that, and then there was no more to it; we forgot our difference and then withheld the sale from the bishop. I am related to Siru'aba'aba because our fathers were relatives, and Funilofo formerly belonged to our 'brothers' who worshipped the same ghosts and helped each other to hold festivals. Our fathers always came together and agreed on land without fighting, setting an example for our children not to fight in the future and settling things in ways which would benefit us all.

But with the young men who grew up after us, some said, 'No, this land must belong completely to us.' Then the Fairu side also said, 'This land belongs completely to us.' Because formerly the A'arai river came out to the sea in one place and the Funilofos said their boundary followed the river, but then the river shifted towards Funilofo and so we say now that part belongs to us. But it came out to the sea there long ago, in the lifetime of our elders, so they traced the boundary to follow the river where it is at present. That's why my father won it; because Stephen Sipolo, an elder from the offshore island, now dead, was my father's witness. He said, 'Starting from where the A'arai is now as far as 'Adako'a, if we of the islands of Ngongosila and Kwai needed building materials or somewhere to plant swamp taro, we had to ask Alasa'a. We had to ask Fairu before we did anything there.' Sipolo was an important government

The Kwara'ae clan lands and other places mentioned in this chapter.

man formerly, a policeman and a chief in Masing Rul. Then Fiukwadi said, 'We 'Ere'eres came and cut the thick forest there and planted our coconuts and swamp taro. We asked Alasa'a, and although the elders of Funilofo were still living, including Lalanga, Siu'aba'aba's father, they didn't question it.' That's why the district commissioner said it belonged to us.[7]

The English word 'precedent' conveys how, if they have used the land since long ago until the present, they can claim the land. It is really in our blood. Descent from someone proves that the land belongs to us, and a sacrificial shrine within it is the place which the divine God mentions, saying, 'Remove not the landmark which God has given to your descendants since the foundation of the world.'[8] What God speaks of, I have seen evidence of between Fairu and Funilofo, in a big rock which is divided into the sacrificial places of Gwau'ulu of we of Fairu, and No'onge'e of Siru'aba'aba's side of Funilofo. That really proves what I say: 'God sees it.' So although we argue whether Funilofo covers Fairu, that sacrificial shrine or tabu-sanctum shows it does not. Our priests or tabu-speakers continued until the death of Sausaungia, the last ghost-priest of Fairu to offer sacrifices at this shrine, and then no-one maintained it any more.[9] Lalanga and others of Funilofo were still alive and still pagan but they didn't maintain it because it wasn't their land. That's why, before they died, Kalakini and Sausaungia, the last two priests of Fairu, with whom my father himself offered sacrifices, took all the bones and skulls back to Fairu, to Fiu near U'ata'e, where my 'father' Peter Fini'a and Atoa and his brothers used to live. They took them wrapped in tree-bark and put them there for safety, because Gwau'ulu was an accessible place close to a pathway, where people could damage things.[10] So we claim that land as belonging to us.

Then on the other side is Latea, where the court ruled on the part which belonged to Ramo'itolo and the part belonging to my father Alasa'a. We both agreed with that, but more recently we have seen how Nongwae's Fuliba'e clan wants to overrule it and say that it belonged not to So'ai, Ramo'itolo's son, but to them. Fuliba'e derives from Atōbi in the inland, where they say they came down from. As far as we are concerned, Ramo'itolo arrived at 'Eda'eda in the person of 'Aba'au, who came down from Faureba, which is part of Gwauna'ongi. He settled in Latea when Nongwae was still unknown there, and from the first it was Ramo'itolo who held the priesthood in Latea land and had his ghosts there.[11] That's what Rocky Tisa and the others disputed, claiming that Nongwae's group arrived first and that Nongwae was senior for Latea land. But Latea is in a different place from Nongwae's land, and it appears that Nongwae had only a sacrificial shrine but Ramo'itolo was senior for Latea land. That's something else they dispute. They claim the land, but it was So'ai who benefited when Ramo'itolo and his eldest son Takangwane sold land in Latea. They sold land to Kailiu, Rocky Tisa's father, at Abuna'ai and at Fangidua, which is why, as the dispute went on, Rocky Tisa and others set fire to the houses at Fangidua. So they appear to be claiming that So'ai, that is his brother Takangwane, elder son of Ramo'itolo, had the legal right to sell land to Kailiu, father of Rocky Tisa. If the land it truly yours, you don't pay for it, which proves that the land belongs to So'ai, who already had a court ruling with my father.

But in 1999 we found out that Rocky Tisa, representing Nongwae's group, had taken the skulls and bones from Fiu and

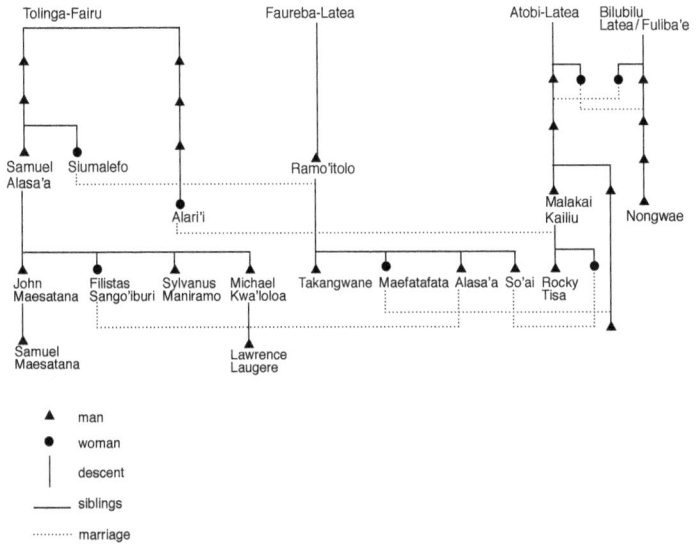

Some relationships referred to in this chapter between clans of Latea and Fairu.

put them in a shrine in Latea called Tako'asai. It was to make people go and look. 'Oh, these are our ghosts,' even though they had no skulls or bones there. That would also mean that we would speak without being able to show the bones of our forefathers as evidence. I have proof that the shrines had those bones in the plan which we put in my father's book *A Solomon Islands Chronicle*,[12] but when I and my 'elder brothers' Wilson Gua and Maniramo, and our 'sons' Sareto'ona, Kamusute'e, Liu, Haman Namusia and others went to survey the ghost's skulls, and when I pointed the camera to photograph them, they were no longer there. That was very discouraging for us; Rocky had taken everything, with my cousin Sina, Nongwaete'e Dolaikafo and others.

When they went to steal them, in the night a ghost showed Maega'asia, the son of Maelekisi, that they were taking the bones. Maega'asia said, 'Make them come,' and when he went down to Anofiu in the morning, Rocky Tisa came walking and Maega'asia cut him up with a knife. The sons of Atoa's elder brother Suda were there and held him back, otherwise Rocky would have been dead, because the ghost had given him to Maega'asia. This power is something we are good at; because they stole their bones, the ghost said, 'Alright, I give him into your hands to kill.' That morning Maega'asia was so stirred up in his mind by emotion that the same ghost came of his own accord to kill him. Rocky ended up in 'Ato'ifi hospital and recovered. My cousin Nelson Konai and others charged Rocky five shell-moneys for stealing the bones.

Rocky Tisa wanted me to lose Fairu land because of business. He wanted all his cattle and all his coconut plantations to take up so many acres that he would deny even me, his own uncle.[13] He had said as much before, when the chiefs said that Billy Farobo of Kwai Island should lose the place at 'Adako'a, which he had purchased from Ramo'itolo's son Takangwane. He said that the hermit-crab was beginning to crawl; it was already beyond 'Adako'a and would go beyond Fairu.[14] Nongwae would win the place in Latea where they had divided it for Ramo'itolo, and then come on to me at Kerete. That was him; business had made him greedy and selfish. But he was born of Alari'i and I of Alasa'a, and Alari'i was the daughter of Sareto'ona, who was Alasa'a's 'brother', so he really is my nephew. After Maega'asia wounded him, he changed his ways and stopped troubling us, but he still said Fuliba'e was in charge of the land belonging to Ramo'itolo, where So'ai has the rights.

The group which replaced Nongwae after he died, led by Rocky Tisa, sent me a letter saying that Latea-Fuliba'e had a

Rocky Tisa with his cattle in Latea in 1999. (Ben Burt photo)

customary land trust board and if anything happened in Latea they had to be consulted first. Because in 2006 So'ai had signed a document allowing for a wharf at his side of the boundary which our fathers had disputed and settled. That is at the District Headquarters at Faumamanu on the coast, where we hold the market between the inland people and the sea people of Ngongosila and Kwai islands. I had already allowed the market to stay on my side of the boundary, on the initiative of my then member of parliament Alfred Maetia, and Joses Sanga, his successor, agreed for So'ai to initiate the wharf on the Latea side. But Rocky Tisa and the others disputed So'ai's right to sign for it. A cousin of mine reported that they had assembled to meet A'ao, an assistant administration officer for the province, to sign for this wharf on my side instead, to make it join up with the market, going down to the women's toilet area. You only have to go out a little there and the sea becomes deep enough for ships to lie. My cousin said, 'Eh, I didn't see the men who should have signed for it. It was those who lost to Ramo'itolo who decided, and the man who signed was Tisa Manibili, son of Taemana, who lives at Kerete Faumamanu, near the market. If I had objected, that good development would not happen, so I said "Let Kwa'ioloa sign it, because he has the legal document to prove that the land at the market belongs to him."' He said I would have told A'ao to hold things back, but they signed it anyway.

The point is that while we stay in Honiara we have a relationship with our home for speaking about our land. This is very important, and it concerns us a lot. The longer I stay in Honiara, the more this relationship does indeed connect me with home. We maintain our tradition wherever we stay, and we do so in Honiara. Once there was a doctor belonging to the Seventh Day Adventists who said during a health awareness programme that anyone who wants to hold on to tradition should go back to Malaita. This was at the market by the police station on the border of Honiara, and I spoke up and said, 'Excuse me brother, I want to say something. You may be a great preacher in the SDA, but Jesus told us in the Bible that wherever you live, there will your heart be also. As we chiefs interpret it, anywhere you live, your tradition will be there too. It doesn't mean I have to go back home. Let me ask you, if you stay in Honiara and someone asks your wife to misbehave with him, is that alright by you? No. I say there will your heart be also and your tradition will be also. If I live in a foreign country overseas, it doesn't mean I will sell my wife for food or money, because my tradition is there too. It is in my blood.'

There are some who speak ill of people: 'Eh, home is too

local.¹⁵ They are really poor.' When there is a problem and they reach home, they are rejected: 'Eh, the woman says we are nothing; poor people.' Then some open court cases against the people at home, claiming they are senior by birth for that land, according to our descent system on Malaita. But when they take them to court they receive no support from the elders, so they lose completely. They fail because they don't know their tradition well, so they lose their land. Sometimes it really is their land, because the other people arrived generations ago but stayed on the land with their ancestors who were already there. But this may not be enough to claim the land when, in everyone's view, the later arrival is entitled because he has stayed on the land generation after generation and been adopted there. His claim is, 'Oh, I was there when certain things happened to the ancestors, and I alone helped them in feuds and feasts and things like that.' That is not actually important, as it is the man who has seniority by birth who has the rights, but those who are angry with such a man may know and not help him. 'Teach him a lesson, leave him to it. The man shows off too much. It's his problem.' This is wrong, and we community leaders should deal with it, but it can happen to someone who doesn't know his own tradition.

That doctor was such a person. When they are small they go to school until they won't listen to their own grandparents and their fathers, or live with them, then they take higher education overseas for many years, and when they come back they have no interest in home. Then they think life will be the same everywhere. The big test of this was during the ethnic tension between the Malaita and Guadalcanal rebels, when people fled back home. When they reached home they went straight to the place which they thought was their land, but people there didn't want them to stay because, they said, 'You left a long time ago.' A man who is not connected to his home is a nobody. He is no longer a person. In To'abaita in the north they cut up my friend Babati who had gone back to stay on land which others disputed. He was senior by birth for that land and he made a claim in court and won. At the very time he won, he came down and they cut him to pieces, like fried chicken, and he died. A man who goes back when he has never been home has problems like that. Some men in Kwara'ae will say, 'It's not your land,' as they have never seen him there. He has tabu sites and ghosts and even genealogical proof, but they don't give him the chance to say anything at all. They just say, 'Go away.' A man must be in regular contact with home and go back to take part in negotiations and discussions and contribute money for fees from Honiara. This makes him part of the group and even if he dies his son has those rights.

I left home too, but when we are ready to return people will want us because we go back regularly to do things at home. If anything big happens, like someone dying or getting married, or a big feast at the end of the year, we have to go home. We continue to harvest our groves of nuts at home and if anyone wants to take nuts from my nut grove they must seek my permission from Honiara. They send a letter or send word with an important man to come and say, 'Eh, your brother, or your father, so-and-so, wants to climb a nut tree in your grove.' I must know what kind of nut it is; some are named after our ancestors and some are specially important because formerly people fought over the nuts when they killed someone for taking them. We reserve those to eat ourselves, to remember what happened in former times. Other nuts we forbid because they are so easy to break that you can bite them open. They will say, 'When you let me get those nice nuts of yours, I'll bring two or three bamboos-full for you, for us to share.' I'll say, 'Oh, in that case I'll allow it.' Then he will climb, break the nuts, put them in bamboos and send some to Honiara, with some taro to make a nice pudding. They ask me at the nut harvest every year, from the places where we formerly lived, or they ask my brother Maniramo who lives at home, and he goes with them.

All this demonstrates that although we stay in Honiara, we are there only temporarily. We came to work for money and when, for instance, they prepare for a marriage, they will bring pigs they have raised and local food, and we will bring rice. 'Oh, I'm purchasing ten bags of rice to give away with our girl, according to tradition.' Our clans are established permanently at home, but while we are here we are still part of them. They know that and call: 'Hey, it's all arranged, they will pay for the girl at such-and-such a time.' Then a representative of the family will arrive and they will give him a share of the traditional money, according to blood. That's how we treat our home, as more important than any place we stay, in our country or overseas. It unites us as a single group, from which we can come and go.

Since 2004 we have had the Fairu Land Trust Board. Our member of parliament Joses Waiwari met the expenses for me and my brother's son Sam Maesatana to go home and hold meetings at U'ata'e for two days at a time. The day after we arrived we would meet all day, and the next day, going on until ten or twelve at night. I organised the meetings, because if those at home were left to themselves there would be no meetings.

They included everyone who had pieces of land which Fairu had given them within the land, such as Maelakisi, Toto and Nelson Konai.[16] There are a lot of them, and our clan is numerous. At our meetings there were thirty or forty of us, because we invited everyone belonging to that land and community. The old women came to contribute, the young men, and we allowed open discussion.

Formerly the elders didn't do this, because they didn't argue over land, and if a man did something they were quite happy: 'Oh, you do that, my brother.' Nowadays it is difficult, and an elder may put a leaf there as a 'block'[17] to forbid it, which spoils things. But we have organised the Fairus who stay in Honiara, and we meet often. The sons of the elders at home are in Honiara and there are many of us, but I picked ten men, the senior sons who represent their clans. We organised as Honiara Fairu and then we formed a board at home called Malaita Fairu. We have a constitution with two executives, one in Malaita and one in Honiara. We plan and if anything happens we hear from the chairman of Malaita Fairu: 'Eh, they are starting trouble at home. A neighbouring clan are doing so-and-so.' He comes from home, we discuss it and he goes back: 'Oh, the message from Honiara is this . . .' They say, 'What Honiara says is important. We won't do anything now. Leave it until Kwa'ioloa comes.' I don't know if other groups do this, but we want to create a model for everyone, and our aim is to welcome development within Fairu.

My family belongs to Fairu because we are born of several Fairu women over several generations, but before that we came from Tolinga in inland Kwara'ae. So I have claims to other lands as well.[18] We of the Tolinga clan also have a connection with north Malaita and the Gao people of Isabel Island. I myself went to link up with our members there, as descendants from Siale in Kwara'ae who settled these places. This was unknown for many years; a hundred and fifty clans came down from there long ago and were lost, but when I took delegations to them, they said, 'You have revealed all our secrets.'

Long ago, a man of ours by the name of Taloafunu went to north Malaita and married a girl of Bita'ama, because he had quarrelled with his brother at Tolinga. The two of them went to buy a ghost from Lobo, at Fiu in West Kwara'ae. One bought a ghost for warfare, one bought a ghost for festivals, for fame.[19] Then when they came to midway along the path to Tolinga the one who had taken the warrior ghost went into the forest to relieve himself. While he was gone his brother said, 'I don't want warfare, I want fame', so he took it and said, 'Eh, brother, you live quietly at Tolinga; you hold on to the one for war and I'll hold on to the one for feasting. So I can go down over there and if you hear me announce that I'm making a bit of a feast, you can bring down some taro and then I'll give you fish and shells.' The other said, 'Oh no, no,' but he was busy relieving himself. The man fled with the festival ghost, reached the house, took his angle-club and all his belongings and fled to the north. He fled to Bita'ama, to the offshore island of Basakana, and stayed there to make festivals, and his brother stayed up there to make war, defending his clan. He married a girl at Bita'ama and claimed a big area of land there, which now belongs to us. He named it 'Afo'a, but the people there don't know what this means. Then he said, 'Look, I'm an inland man; I don't want to be mixed up with these coastal people. I want to stay on that island with nobody else there.' So he was first arrival on Basakana Island and stayed there until he died, which is why I claim Basakana for Tolinga. The tradition of Malaita is that if you arrive first in a place, cut the forest and stay where no-one has yet been, that is your land.

So then, that man Taloafunu begot a son whose name was Gabili and he married into Gao, on Isabel. The tradition of Gao is matrilineal, in which it is the girl who is important, and the girl he married was senior by birth of the clan belonging to a man called 'Ainigao. 'Ainigao came from Siale, although they didn't know that he was the first arrival in Gao and when he had begotten Gao he returned to Siale and died there. That is how we are connected to Gao. Gabili married the girl from Gao and then he settled there and safeguarded[20] Gao, killing the clans which had attacked them. He was a warrior and he told his wife, this important woman, 'Because my ancestors are men of the inland, I want to live on that island, far away where there are no people.' That was Ramos Island, Anogwa'u. It is where the spirits stay, and they also call it Agalusa'o, after a tree with leaves which, they say, turn yellow when someone is about to die and when they fall the person's spirit goes to stay with the dead in Anogwa'u. Then they built a war canoe called Binabina, which is an Isabel word meaning far out to sea, because formerly they would say an island which no-one had reached was at the end of the sea, far away.[21] So they built it and paddled there, and he said, 'I must stay here now.' Gabili's son married another important girl of that clan of Gao and begot eight children; seven were sharks and only one was a man. That's why Gao does not have many people, because one man begot them and the rest were sharks. They guarded the island as tabu to enemies, that is to the wild sharks. If wild sharks came there they cut them to pieces.

When Gabili's son died, his wife told their son, 'Go back to the mainland and stay with your uncles. I'll stay here until I die, with my husband whom I love so much.' She died with her husband and was buried on Ramos Island.

It was my father Alasa'a who told me this history, just before he died. It was because Gabili's son and his wife came to stay in that place, where no-one had been before, that they called it Anogwa'u, Empty-land. The people of Gao and north Malaita asked me, 'What does Anogwa'u mean?' It's a Kwara'ae word, and they were surprised when I explained it was because my ancestor was the first arrival who stayed on the island. In 1997 the Basakanas were searching for whom they were descended from. They came to find us, we didn't find them. 'Eh, we're looking for our man Taloafunu, who was married to us, whom Basakana Island belongs to.' Because they knew that a company which was scanning for resources had found oil under Ramos Island, more than in Kuwait, where they fought over it. They were searching for who had begot them, so that we could settle who was the right clan for the resource-investors to come to and harvest it.

In 1989 a Basakana man by the name of Alik Faubala married into our group at Fauābu in West Kwara'ae. He was searching and while staying with his in-laws he learned about Tolinga from them, so he did some research and called on Johnson Lucas at Kakabona on Guadalcanal, who said, 'We are Tolinga.' Then he asked those in Gao to send a representative, because they knew about each other but not about us of Tolinga, the one root from which both Gao and Basakana descend. They sent a paramount chief, Ben Bola, who stayed for six months and slept in my house. They asked us to hold a meeting in the house of my 'brother' John Lucas and we organised all of us to come together to hear the two other parties. Then they questioned us and I got out the genealogy chart which Ben Burt and I made from what my father knew. When I pinned it to the wall of Johnson's house, Ben Bola said, 'That's where we come from! We are descended from that man Asimaoma!' Then we were surprised: 'Eh, we all have places somewhere in the sea, which our fathers told us about.' 'Yes, we come from him and we are descended from you, but we are looking for who first arrived and begot us.'

To continue the history my father Alasa'a told me, that woman from Gao, wife of Gabili's son, stayed behind until she could die there. Her hair was long, she was dirty and she didn't eat, until she was what we call an ancestor,[22] meaning she was really old and about to die. But still she did not die, because a ghost had taken hold of her. The same ghost inspired my ancestor Asimaoma at Tolinga and told him that the wife of his ancestor, who had died, was still alive but ready to die and had to remain there. Then this man Asimaoma went down to Bina and made a raft and the ghost took him on the raft to Ramos Island. When he arrived he prepared to bite a betelnut for defence from other ghosts who might approach and kill him. Then he saw his in-law sitting with long hair covering her, not noticing him. He thought she had died, so he bit the betelnut and made an invocation, which means using special words to call on the power of a ghost. Then this woman Fakangelea shook and she pushed her hair from her face and stared straight at her in-law. That's why we also call the island Bubumauri; Gazing-alive. It began as Anogwa'u, Empty-land, and ended as Bubumauri, as a result of the discovery by my forefathers. So I told those from Gao that it is not Ramos Island but Ramo, as

Kwara'ae would say, because Gabili and his son were *ramo*, or warriors, who came and killed those who were attacking the people of Isabel at Gao. Now they knew that I was the man to answer their questions.

To clear up Basakana, I took twenty men, including my first son Lawrence Laugere, my third son Haman Namusia and another 'son' Liu Kamusu, and we went down there. We talked for two days, night and day, then they killed four pigs, we brought two thousand dollars-worth of goods, and we celebrated for two days and a night before we returned, uniting as one blood with those of Basakana. Then on 26 and 27 December 2000, we took the delegation to Gao. We prepared by collecting money, and Fairu is very good at giving to support the elders at home in discussions concerning land. We Tolinga people have our land in Honiara and an executive consisting of the sons of our clan who live in Honiara. They listen to me and I facilitate meetings to talk about land, so they contributed three thousand dollars. That was to travel down to Gao and provide food for the chiefs for a week. We brought the Whiteman food and they would provide local food. There were four in our party. I led the Tolinga delegation, with Osi, son of Sango who lived at Saufuru in Tolinga. Representing the Taloafunu clan of Basakana was Jackson Seni, a leader for the land there with his old father Manui, and Peter Seleni Masisi. We were led by Ben Bola of Gao, who had stayed with me for the previous six months.

I remember it was a Monday when we went down to their ship, the *Isabella*. The director of the Isabel shipping company was a relative, Luke Hiro from Gao, so they arranged our travel. The day we arrived to attend the meeting with the Gao chiefs was one I will never forget. The senior chiefs were waiting for us on shore and we were alarmed by what we saw: 'Hey, there are so many people!' Ben Bola said, 'They are waiting for you.' Eh, we were afraid to go down, and the cargo went down first. Then everyone, children, women and all, came with us to Poro village. They followed us, invited us, and took us to stay at their rest-house, which belonged to the Mothers' Union of the Church of Melanesia. Then they led us further along the shore to the home of a former premier of Isabel, Joseph Hiro, brother of Luke Hiro of the Isabel shipping company. They had decorated the place to welcome us, and forty chiefs of Gao were waiting for me and my delegation. The last was Irobaoa, their paramount chief, with Alfred Bogoro, their secretary. The senior chiefs, some white-haired, toothless and blind, awaited us, and Joseph Hiro welcomed us at the gate, which they had decorated, and they came and put flowers on me and then on the others. They marched us in and quickly set out a meal for us with lots of fish and everything on the tables, and we were guests of honour. We prayed and chose the food we wanted, and then I said, 'Chiefs, please eat.' There were bunches of betelnut and pepper-leaf and all kinds of food; taro, kongkong taro, sweet potato, tapioca pudding, and fish. Two months before we arrived they had banned fishing in the harbour to conserve it for the feast. There was the fish we call *bubu*, which is very good to eat, and reef fish, which looked as if eating just one would fill you up. When that was finished, they took us back to Poro again, to the rest house, and they sang for us into the night. The whole village came and we threw out to them the rice and things we had brought and they mixed the local and the Whiteman food to make a great feast, with us as guests of honour. They performed traditional Isabel dancing and Isabel reggae while we sat and talked, until two o'clock, when we slept.

Early in the morning they made food for us again, and at eight o'clock we sat down for a meeting. That was on the Tuesday, and by Thursday when it was question time, the blackboard was full of questions for us. I had told them everything I have mentioned here and they were certainly surprised. They agreed and said, 'Who was our important girl who married your boy?' I said, 'No, first I would like to ask you, where did you get the name Gao from, and what does it mean?' They talked loudly in their own language, and I asked, 'Is there something wrong with my question?' Eventually they said, 'Eh, we don't know. Where does Gao come from?' Then I wrote on the blackboard and asked, 'Do you know a man of ours who came from Siale? That man's name was 'Ainigao.' 'Hey, that's the man who begot us!' I said, 'If so, Ramos Island does not belong to you, it belongs to me, because originally I begot you and then Fa'amaea came after his ancestors who first arrived in Gao, and he left you all there.' Joseph Hiro said, 'Exactly. It's your island, not mine.' I said, 'But yet, what I believe is that you have the claim to the land. I have just come to claim a connection to the island by blood.'

So that day we confirmed that we were all descended from Gao and Siale, Tolinga and Taloafunu, and we joined our three clans together and signed a memorandum of understanding to form a legal entity to speak and be heard by the people and government. We called it Totaga, that is 'to' for Tolinga, 'ta' for Taloafunu, and 'ga' for Gao or Gwabili, and we formed a board of directors. We didn't do this because we knew that investors would come, but to prepare the way ahead by straightening our land issues and combining the three genealogies to prove that we were the people to gain any benefit. Because since those one hundred and fifty clans came from Tolinga, no-one had told them what their real blood connections were, except myself. This was the knowledge my father Samuel Alasa'a passed on to me before he died in 1987. I held it back and told no-one until the two clans from Isabel and north Malaita came searching for who they were descended from. Those who stay by the sea must have descended from the inland,[23] so they traced it until they found it was Tolinga they were descended from. I said, 'Go and bring all your genealogies so we can connect them to Tolinga, and before Tolinga to the main original place. That place is Siale.'

Some men say Tolinga is making itself too high. One man from West Kwara'ae, a paramount chief, heard a service message on the radio from Taloafunu's people at Basakana saying, 'Please send an outboard motor canoe to 'Aoke; Michael Kwa'ioloa is on his way by plane to declare the link between Tolinga and Taloafunu.' He was at 'Aoke and when I went down at the time arranged, he saw me at the market and said, 'Eh, you're quite a man! I heard yesterday how you Tolingas trace descent by blood from that island up north. You are liars!' That's how some people feel about this work, but I stick to what my father told me. But even as we were arguing, the Taloafunu people arrived to take me to Basakana, and that put him to shame.

My father Samuel Alasa'a made it clear to his sons, in tracing the heritage of Tolinga and Fairu, that our ancestors laid a sure foundation so that no other clan can claim our land. We ourselves know definitely where we came from, who we are and what we are, and our relationships to people in other parts of Solomon Islands. If people are confused about what was handed down to them from their fathers, others may take over their land and they become nobodies. But we know that our leadership comes directly from Siale, from the fourth generation after the first arrivals when ancestor-worship began. God dispersed them with a storm and an earthquake, leading to the discovery of our land Tolinga by our ancestor Kwanamalefodoe. Since then, no-one has disputed our claim to Tolinga.

---

1 At the market where the inland people sell vegetables to the sea people, and buy fish from them.
2 See Burt & Kwa'ioloa 2001:81 for details of this court case, which established the seniority of Alasa'a and his descendants over the land also claimed by these men.
3 This book (Burt & Kwa'ioloa 2001) contains all the genealogies recalled by Alasa'a.
4 'A'emae.
5 *Fa'ina'ona'o* or 'the first one'.
6 *Ano ana kwai'afi'anga* or 'land given for help'.
7 The argument goes that since previous generations had treated Alasa'a's Fairu clan as leaders for the land, it did indeed belong to them and their descendants, represented by Alasa'a.
8 Deuteronomy 9:14, Hosea 5:10.
9 Men would only deposit the remains of their ancestors and offer sacrifices to their ghosts in shrines on their own lands, so such histories legitimate their descendants' claims to the land.
10 See Burt & Kwa'ioloa 2001:84-85 for details of this history and of the Fiu shrine.
11 In this account, by convention, the names of recent claimants to the land (such as Ramo'itolo and Nongwae) may stand for the clan ancestors whose history is under dispute.
12 Burt & Kwa'ioloa 2001:85.
13 *Ngwai*, which means both uncle and nephew. Kwa'ioloa and Tisa are actually about the same age.
14 In this metaphor, the hermit-crab is said to 'win' these places (Kwara'ae *tasa*), which can mean success in a contest as well as going beyond, implying that it is taking possession of the land as it crawls past it.

[15] 'Local' is used as a derogatory expression by people who imagine themselves to be more cosmopolitan than the rural majority.
[16] Others included Fa'abasua, Osi'a, Misalo, Ko'orea, Sulusia, Fikumani, and Auluta.
[17] *Gwa'i bu'a*; a prohibition on using the land, shown by placing a frond of leaves.
[18] Full details of these genealogies and lands are given in Burt & Kwa'ioloa 2001.
[19] That is, they bought relics of a ghost giving powers for fighting (*akalo ni ramo'a*) and a ghost giving powers to hold the great feasts which confer fame (*akalo ni talo'a*). For another version of this history, see Burt & Kwa'ioloa 2001:25.
[20] *Tarasina*, meaning to protect from attack with a (metaphorical) fence of thorny rattan.
[21] *Binabina* also means a big canoe, in many Malaitan languages.
[22] *Koko'o* or 'great-grandparent'.
[23] On the principle that Kwara'ae histories trace all coastal clans back to inland sites (as with Siale).

Some of Kwa'ioloa's colleagues in the work for Kwara'ae traditional culture: Paul Daokalia, Alex Rukia, Frank Ete, Rocky Tisa. (Ben Burt photos)

7
WORKING WITH CHIEFS AND POLITICIANS

One thing my family has long been good at is leadership in the community. We have the know-how to straighten things out by talk, and when my father died it was I who took this over. If anything is wrong it is I who have to straighten it out, because many of our people are not in the habit of being conciliatory, or cooling down so that the others will cool down too. No, they just react and keep talking, and enmity develops until someone strikes someone else. That's what is wrong with us, at home as well as in Honiara. Leaders[1] are those with a talent for straightening out things which are wrong between communities, between churches, clans, and families, and between individuals. I am fortunate that my family has taken this leadership role, in that people call on us to bring about conciliation between groups, in both Honiara and Malaita. For some clans it is impossible because they don't have the know-how and reputation.

During my life there have been several occasions when I made serious mistakes with members of my family. I was once in trouble when I was living in Malaita,[2] and another time in Honiara. I don't want to talk about the details, but I did not ask anyone else to straighten things out and I dealt with them myself by restitution, of up to three shell-moneys. When you do that the other side will come to realise, 'Oh, let's not be unreasonably angry with this man, he's acted according to tradition.' The money sorts things out and maintains peace, so then you can send word to the man you caused the problem with, by someone like a pastor: 'Tell him I'm asking for him.' The pastor lets him know, then the man talks with his brothers and sends word, and the pastor tells you that on Sunday you will go to meet the man, and after service you will pray together. That is hard, but I have done it myself. So they arrange it and the families wait, then after service the pastor calls the two of you to sit down to talk and clear up what is causing the friction between you. Then you pray and shake hands and you are able to go to each other's houses. We can share any need, coming together to pay brideprice for a son or sharing in a feast. That is what I have done myself, and, having done so, people will always call on me for help, because I have a talent for straightening things out. It's quite usual for me, in Honiara or Malaita, when two men are having a row, to come and talk and they will calm down. Then I say, 'Alright, you give him money.' He says, 'Oh, it was that man who swore first,' and so on. I do this all the time at Kobito, with the young men when they fight. It was also my job during fourteen years of service with the Royal Solomon Islands Police.

For example, there was a nephew of mine, Ishmael 'Ania,

for whom I paid for the daughter of Jack Kena, a senior chief who also contributed to this work I do. In 2002, when the boy took this girl, named Evelyn, and hid in my house, everyone came to look for her: 'Eh, our girl is missing.' I said, 'Oh, but Ishmael has not come here. They must be in the grass, stealing each other. So you all go back and I'll give one shell-money to hold back your anger, and set a date so that within one month I can pay brideprice for her.' Following tradition, I gave an eight-foot ten-string Langalanga shell-money, and they were quiet. When I gave it, chief David Kwa'ite'e came with them all in the morning. Then I said, 'We will try to arrange payment.' They said, 'Twenty red moneys, and five thousand. That's what our father wants.' With that I said, 'Oh, tradition says that we try to get as much as we can, and her father and I talk. Then they can marry. If we refuse her there will be a fight, because they fled here and you have all become very angry. But tradition has very good ways for us to sort things out, and that's what I'll do.' With that they accepted the shell-money and said, 'Oh, very good. You find them and bring them back to the house, then tell them to look out for the money.' So then I wrote letters and sent Ishmael back home to show them to my sisters and to those whose sons I had paid for at home, and they contributed five shell-moneys. Then, because Ishmael's sister 'Aute'e had married the year before and I knew that the family had no money, I stopped anyone from taking the five red moneys from her brideprice and they had to share them out to be given for his marriage.

So that was fifteen shell-moneys, and we contributed two thousand six hundred dollars, not five thousand. When we had shown them all, Kena said, 'That's alright; I'll hold all the moneys and my daughter can come back. When you have given another five moneys and two thousand six hundred, then I will allow her to go.' What I said was, 'If so, you just hold the five from 'Aute'e's marriage, but the others which were contributed in addition to mine, I'll take back. Because they are not mine. My elder sisters sent them and there is a risk that if you take them, and then later on you won't let your girl come to marry my nephew, I will bear the consequences and I will have exchanged all this money for nothing.' Five had been given to me on credit, five I had exchanged, and five I had withheld from his sister's marriage. That's why it was up to me to talk to that man Jack Kena. 'Look, it's another way of stopping your girl, my sister, from marrying, to charge a high price. Why are you charging so much? You may stop it by making us unable to pay for her. Then nothing will happen. So why are you stopping it? Ishmael is a young boy, Evelyn is a young girl, and she started it with Ishmael. I've given warnings to all my boys not to touch your girl because she is so high-priced. They have married elsewhere, but my nephew acted stupidly because your girl persuaded him. Do you understand my point? Whatever you ask of Ilito'ona, he and his boy only have a thousand dollars. It is I who am paying the rest, with my own cash and my own shell-money arrangements. I will exchange the moneys if the man marries her, but I won't exchange them for nothing. If you won't take that eight-foot ten-string, take back your daughter.' 'Eh, but those two won't give each other up.' I said, 'It doesn't matter, that's your worry. Tradition says if you stop your girl from marrying, we do not give restitution for her. With a young man and a girl, if you stop them there is no restitution; that's for a married woman.' Then he said, 'Ah no, I'll take it.' Because of me, he cut out the other five moneys and two thousand four hundred dollars. So you see, the two of them have made a life and born a child, and Ishmael has now settled down with his wife. That's something I did within my own family, in 2002.

Then later on, in 2005, Ishmael got drunk and swore badly at his in-laws, Kena and his wife Evelyn. It really was a very bad swear, so we pulled him from the new house he was building at 'A'ekafo and brought him to my house at Windy Hill settlement, because I could see the man was not able to stay with his in-laws. He had a bad reputation when he was drunk and when he swore so badly at them, John Fao was looking for him to beat him up. It was I who went to ask them: 'Oh, this is a stupid boy who can't live his life. It was I who paid for the girl for him and it was I who asked for her from you. I'm like a father to him, as his mother is dead and his father Ilito'ona is an old man who stays with us and is a father to us all.' So then my son Haman Namusia stepped in and said, 'If you will all accept it, I will charge him to give traditional money to you.' When it appeared they would agree, Haman told Ishmael, 'You will give one ten-string and two hundred dollars to your father-in-law, whom you spoke to so badly about your wife. You swore at him and your wife, whom he begot. And to all the brothers who you swore should eat bad things, you will give fifty dollars per household. There are four households so I charge you two hundred dollars.' So it was, and when they shook hands they loved each other again.

That is the leadership role of a chief, and I am a chief myself and a co-ordinator of chiefs. The chiefs meet to sort things out and it is the chiefs who implement the law which authorises the work I do. I don't do it for myself, to be paid by the people I do it for. No, I do it because it's the chiefly system, the law and the traditional culture of us chiefs. People who are born into our tradition are usually obedient to us so that things are sorted out. If they won't obey and I can't convince them, they are in real difficulty and eventually there will be killing. That's what happened in 1978 at home in Kwara'ae, when Kafo's son Sale killed 'Aukwai at Talanga'idenge, because of his sister whom Ta'angwane had made pregnant. Bare had come with them, and after they fled Ta'angwane shot and killed him with a gun, so in retaliation for the man who died on Ta'angwane's side, a man also died on Sale's side. Sale got a life sentence for killing 'Aukwai and Ta'angwane got a life sentence for killing Bare. They were let out after ten years for good behaviour, at the end of the governor-general's term in 1986.[3]

In Honiara, although we are not at home, we understand that our tradition stays wherever we stay. If we are without our tradition, everything will be all over the place. People of different languages are involved, because our area of south-east Honiara is one community including Kobito, Kofiloko, Lau Valley, and up to Gilbert Camp. Other areas have other groups. We call this a community,[4] because everyone knows each other. We co-ordinate the chiefs and if there are any problems we deal with them. The chiefs of each place come together and arrange it: 'The meeting will be at our place on Sunday.' That man must come, as at home, and the matter is finally settled with a hearing at a police station.

We also saw, when we first arrived in the 1970s and depended on the police and government to deal with things, that sometimes this did not work. For instance, being in the police, when we arrested a man he would tell me to my face, 'I'm marking you.' So I had the idea that we should form a group. Starting from White River, through the outskirts settlements all the way to Aofiola and Abira'adoa, we selected one man for each settlement and then we came together to form one house of chiefs for Honiara. This was in 1980, and it was I who organised it. Old man Sangafanoa was the president then, the chairman was Edmund Maelegwata, and the secretary was Frank Tafea. The senior chiefs Benjamin Ramo, Ben Bamae, David Kwa'ite'e and Simon Geobota were all involved.[5] As chiefs, their decisions had to be obeyed, and if a man would not comply we passed it on to the Magistrates Court, as advised by the principal of the Public Solicitor's Office.

I organised it according to what my father did. My father was a man who had the powers of a senior chief, which gave him the authority to speak so that people obeyed him. He handed on these powers to me, spiritually, before he died. Because of that I had the power to speak, everyone listened, the important men came together and we dealt with the police and the officers commanding the various stations. They put our recommendations in place: 'If anything is wrong within the community, go to the chiefs first, and only if it becomes difficult and a criminal offence, go to the police.' A policeman had no right to hold discussions; his job was just to arrest someone who disobeyed the law. Accordingly, it was we who had the right to deal with our own families. They told us that the government had no money to pay us: 'What you should do is when anyone wants to bring a case he should pay you a fee.' So for instance, when a woman misbehaved and we told her people to return the brideprice paid for her, they would give five hundred dollars as a fee or wages for the chiefs who discussed and dealt with the return of the five or ten red moneys. This was for expenses and for running around, spending a whole day, and another, and another, negotiating for the return of the moneys. Smaller cases might be fifty or twenty dollars.[6]

Well, when we had set it up we went to see the various authorities. We sent a delegation to Kenneth Brown, a Whiteman from England who was principal public solicitor at the time. We explained everything, until he said, 'Oh Michael, this looks as if you are taking the part of the court, but it's alright because you are not giving decisions.' I said, 'If the court gives a decision, the two parties are still at enmity, but if the chiefs give a decision the two just shake hands, give money, pray and it's finished.' Then he said, 'Maybe we should leave it to the traditional system of the country.' We said, 'Well, will you allow us to have this chamber each Saturday to hold court? Because we have no other place.' So he allowed the paramount chief to sit up there like a magistrate and the opposing parties to stand and lose or win the case, while we chiefs sat down to talk. Eventually Kenneth Brown finished and left, and what happened? Our stupid local people would not let us use the chamber any more.

We worked properly, with the various police stations, bringing people together to sort out problems. If a man who accepted money said, 'The two of us want to pray,' we would arrange for a pastor to come and finish it with prayer and restore peace between them. We had to take them to the police station for security so they would not fight and have a court there so that we would not be holding an unlawful assembly. Our chiefs would ask the two parties to come and bring them in a police truck from their houses to the police station and back again afterwards, so that it was hard for them to refuse. That was how the police worked with us and we settled things without direct police involvement. Also, if the magistrates heard a case they couldn't understand because it was to do with tradition, they would ask us to give a decision in court.

One example is the case of a man called Sau from 'A'ekafo, who swore at his wife and beat her badly. Benjamin Ramo dealt with it and said, 'You'll give one hundred dollars to your wife for beating and swearing at her.' Then Sau said, 'Who cares about the chiefs? Chiefs have no power. I'm going to open a case at the Magistrates Court.' So he went to the Magistrates Court to complain against our decision and the magistrate referred it back to us; 'You must give us information on what you said to him and we will look at it in court.' Sau was taking the chiefs to court, so we took him to court because he had not complied with our decision. I had written down all the statements, set out the exhibits and told him the judgement, and the man had not complied. The Magistrates Court gave him a summons and the chiefs prosecuted him, not the police. We gave all the statements to the court, and the court gave a decision, thus: 'Because you did not comply with the order of the chiefs of the country, by four o'clock today you must add three hundred to the one hundred. The hundred goes to your wife, as decided by the chiefs, and the three hundred to the government. Otherwise you go to prison for six months.' The man quibbled over it: 'Eh, you told me it was a hundred dollars.' Ramo said, 'That's not possible now, because you took the chiefs to court to discredit us but you must understand that the law is part of the tradition of the country.' So then the man gave four hundred dollars, crying to his mother to find the money before he could pay it and be released.

Then there was Selo, who married the daughter of my brother Maesatana. He took another woman as a friend and rejected his wife, our 'daughter'. The chiefs took on his case too and said, 'Oh, give a hundred dollars to your wife Fasti, because you have challenged the confidence between you and you must give restitution to her.' When he said, 'Who cares for the chiefs?' we took him to the magistrates and they said the same thing: 'Add another three hundred to it.' Selo said, 'Hey, the chiefs do have power. I didn't think they had.'

In 2003 the chief magistrate was hearing a case brought by Fa'abasua senior of Mage in West Kwara'ae against his son-in-law Fa'abasua junior of Matariu, Honiara, for not offering him shell-money from the brideprice of his three daughters. The chief magistrate was confused and asked the Kwara'ae chiefs to stand in and hand down a judgement. I invited chiefs David Kwa'ite'e and Michael Ngidu'i, and when they arrived it was, 'Alright, the court has finished; come back at one o'clock to hear the case.' They came back and the chiefs gave a decision. 'The tradition is like this. Fa'abasua, who married the daughter of Fa'abasua senior, if you don't give them money from the marriage of your daughter, you are offending against tradition.' We call it 'the top of the money from the male side',[7] given to the woman's side for the uncles, following the blood. 'You courted a girl and so your daughter was born, so tradition says you must give a share to her side when each of your daughters marry. So give two ten-strings to your father-in-law Fa'abasua senior, for the uncles' side.' In such cases, if a man doesn't give this small share, he can be sued in court and fined. The Magistrates Court signed it off: 'Oh, that's true, because the chiefs know.' They gave him fourteen days to pay two red moneys, that's one thousand dollars, or he would go to prison. So we could see it worked for the magistrates to co-operate with the chiefs.

The biggest case was in 1990, with the family of Ishmael Lema, whose son Jimmy Kwa'i killed a man from Kwaio, as I described in my book *Living Tradition*.[8] All the chiefs of East Kwaio came, then Paramount Chief Adriel Rofate'e and the Kwara'ae chiefs, and they stayed for a week or two to talk about it, until eventually the Kwaio side calmed down. By the time they went back, sixty-seven red moneys were already standing by with us Kwara'ae, and two thousand six hundred dollars in a locked box with the police. That was when I stepped in and started talking to the Kwaio clans and the father of Faeni, the man who was killed. Faeni's brother was a pastor at the outskirts settlement of Feraladoa and I was also a pastor. When we talked we came to a compromise including all the chiefs, and they agreed to accept the money. So the day after, the member of parliament for East Kwara'ae, Alfred Maetia, and I took the money to the recreation hall of our Central Police Station and they accepted it, as a result of my efforts.

We have dealt with other serious cases too. In 1995 the president of the Honiara House of Chiefs, Silas Sangafanoa, was killed in a traffic accident while crossing the main road near Kukum. We chiefs held negotiations between Sangafanoa's family, from Kwara'ae, and the driver's people, from Lau, and they paid ten shell-moneys to settle the matter. In 2006 a Lau man again ran over a Kwara'ae man, who died, at the Lau Fishing Village in Honiara. The House of Chiefs, led by Paramount Chief Ben Ramo and Senior Chief David Kwa'ite'e, arranged for Paramount Chief Jemuel Misialo and his people to receive ten shell-moneys and twenty thousand dollars in compensation.[9]

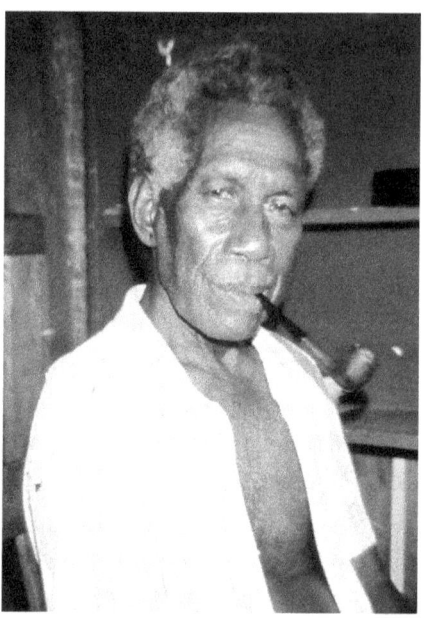

Silas Sangafanoa, paramount chief and president of the Honiara House of Chiefs, in 1987. (Ben Burt photo)

This work is not just restricted to the Malaitans; other people could do it, but they don't, and their chiefs also report to us: 'You come and talk about this case.' The Guadalcanal people have done this, for instance when Daniel Kikile and others from West Guadalcanal expelled those people they had taken in from the Weather Coast in the 1980s. They had grown in numbers, planted more gardens and everything, until they threw them out. The Guadalcanal chiefs tried to deal with it but they fought, so we Malaita chiefs went down to Gorobou to mediate. The Guadalcanal provincial police from Tetere came with us, we asked the provincial authorities to come and the Guadalcanal chiefs came. I went instead of old man Sangafanoa, because although he was president he sometimes talked as though he had missed the point, so I told him to stay behind. Then I divided up their arguments: 'That is your question; that is yours,' to question them and give a decision. 'Who brought this landslide of people from the Weather Coast?' They said, 'Guadalcanal Province.' Provincial representatives were there and admitted, 'We brought them here.' Then we said, 'Kikile, why did you allow them this land to stay on?' 'Because I was sorry for them, as neighbours.' 'If that is so, you must understand that you brought them in tens and you will send them back in thousands. So you must have the money to take them from here back to their own district on the Weather Coast. Why not just increase their land so that there is enough to accommodate them and their gardens and houses?' We went on all day until evening and the decision was to allow them to remain and to extend the land to Araligo, but if they overpopulated that expanded area, then the next generation would have to return to the Weather Coast. Their descendants live at Araligo until today. That was the first such case we Malaita chiefs were authorised to deal with. It is not difficult and we do not force anyone, but the other islands depend on us and come running to us with their own community disputes: 'You are the ones to settle such things.'

The man who leads men does not come from nothing. He comes with the blessing of the ancestors, who make him so because of his kindness and his training in the knowledge of tradition from the teaching of the elders. If he doesn't follow the teachings, he will be selfish. It doesn't mean there is no politics involved, but politics is a thing of the present and in tradition a chief had only leadership. In my view, tradition and politics are two completely different things. The leader is a man who loves everyone and is well educated by his fathers and grandfathers, and he acts it out in a practical way. He will feed many people and work hard, and the more he does it the more blessing he has. 'Blessing'[10] is when everything comes to him and it all succeeds. The benefit is when some woman suddenly brings yams: 'Oh son, these are your yams.' Later someone will bring a pig too: 'Eh, I'm giving you a pig.' Those are the blessings. He doesn't pay because his way is to love people and do good, and they love him back. He receives things from all around the community and doesn't have to make an exchange for them, because they are happy to give, in reciprocity.[11] If his son gets married, they hear and they come with shell-money. That's how it is for me; if my sons marry it's hard for me to announce it, or people will come with lots of red shell-money. I don't have to exchange it, but I must listen for when their sons marry and go with shell-money as a 'return-gift'.[12]

By politics I mean people wanting to run the government. Yes, tradition governed, but that was leadership so not under that name. The elders said that 'politician' meant 'liar' and they didn't know politics, only leadership. Leadership shows decision-making, with people obeying their chiefs or 'head-men'[13] and what they tell them, they do. A head-man had to be a wealthy man, who had big gardens and plenty of pigs, because his kindness made people support him. He was not like a politician, whose house is hard to reach because he wants everything for himself and when we visit for him to feed us he is proud and well-off from his salary and funding but gives us only a small part of his money. Politicians become selfish and people won't listen to them. Head-men govern because the people of the community choose them, because a man has taken the role of a leader. Unlike politics, we don't say a man is good and vote for him; it depends on his lineage, when his father is a leader who dies and he succeeds him. If someone just tries it on he will damage the whole community, because he doesn't have inherent leadership.

When a man takes the role of politician, and especially when he becomes a member of parliament for a constituency in Honiara, he'll be very good to those who approach him, but eventually he will deceive the people. At election time he wants so many people, giving them food and things, but when he wins he no longer wants them. People come and he'll tell them to their face, 'Eh, I don't represent money for us all. The money I have is for my own children.' Ronald Fugu'i once did this when mayor of Honiara. His aunt Bethezel Ngaruru Silida'afi went up to his office and asked him for money directly: 'Oh my son, me and my family voted for you. Can you give me a little for my bus fare, so I can go to market and buy a bundle of greens and a coconut to take back and cook?' He said, 'I don't represent money for you,' and chased her out. You know these old women; they get it wrong, as it's traditional to say he's their 'son'. But he should have realised that he's not the government or a Whiteman (and even some Whitemen can be generous). This shows the thinking of politicians, that once they are in power they will organise things on a community basis in terms of development projects, but the old people think about leadership and say that the man who wins is a 'father' to everyone. As they converse they say, 'Let's go and ask our son to give us a little money to buy some fish.' They think, 'Oh, he's become our leader, he's our father. If not for us, he wouldn't be there. And he's born of that brother of ours. He speaks on our behalf and will get things for us.' The young men say the same: 'Father, just let me have five dollars,' but they chase them out too. They should explain things; 'Oh mother, the money I have is from my salary. You know there are school fees for your grandchildren, and there are so many of them.' Or maybe, 'Your daughter-in-law is feeding so many people who come to the house. I'm very sorry.' He could say, 'Here is just five dollars for your bus fare,' or two dollars. When they give a little something, people are happy and tell everyone: 'My son's alright. I went to see him and he gave me the bus fare.' Many politicians do that, but eventually say, 'Don't come back again,' or 'Come back tomorrow.' They are mean and greedy[14] and think everything will be well for them and they will get away with it.

When Roland Dausabea became a town council member in the 1980s, I campaigned for him. They elected him to the presidency, and he was a good man for helping the people, but he died after four days in office. Someone took him to a party, drank with him and gave him battery acid to drink, as the doctor's report later showed. Two men dropped him off that night at Gilbert Camp AOG Church during evening service, in the sight of my wife and Dausabea's relatives, and he died in his bed that night. We realised there would have to be an election and his elder brother Charles Dausabea had just been released from Rove prison, after four and a half years for stealing more than thirty thousand dollars by forging a cheque from the Port Authority. So, according to the traditional way, it was: 'Oh, we're so sorry for Roland Dausabea, he was a good man. Well, Charles Dausabea can replace him.' You know the elders and chiefs. So I campaigned for Charles Dausabea, for the sympathy vote, and he became a town councillor, and eventually a member of parliament.

That's the politics of Honiara. I don't like to criticise my uncle Charles Dausabea, but he had a group who ruined the people, and when he worked with them he did nothing for others, those of us who later campaigned against him. He treated the constituency development fund selfishly, as if it were his own money, not the community's. Politicians like this really show what people are afraid of. In some polling stations in Honiara only one or two people vote, thinking, 'Even if I do vote, no-one will do anything for me.' That means that the men we want don't stand for election because the people who should support them will not, and others whom we don't want stand instead. The constituency development fund encourages wrongdoing; they keep it, make themselves wealthy, leave their wives who worked to help make them rich, and marry other women. At election time they give away money which no-one else can match, and the man we don't want comes into power again.

Nowadays you have to pay a man before he'll vote for you. In Honiara people say, 'Give me money and I'll be there!' They say, 'Fifty dollars for a ballot paper.' When you go into the room alone with your ballot paper as if to drop it in, you come back with it and a short distance away a man is standing to give you fifty dollars, so you can go and buy a lot of fish or other food for the holiday. Then another man comes, one of the campaign managers, and drops ten or twenty of them when he goes to drop his own in the box.[15] Or they'll stand further away and when anyone passes they'll say, 'Drop it in for this man, vote for him, and your project application is ready.' Sometimes on the night before the election they'll come with the forms: 'Fill them out tonight; tomorrow this man wins and the next day you'll receive your project funding.' When in power he will distribute funds for chicken pens, pig pens and bakeries. These are the things which make people vote for him, and especially food in feasts during the election. He persuades people and robs them, but if he loved them he would do this every day, whether he was standing or not. A lot of people just say, 'Oh, let's vote for this man,' because he says, 'Here's your ten dollars; here's your twenty dollars.'

That is why we established the Solomon Islands Traditional Culture and Environmental Conservation Foundation or SIT-CECF, because we could see that our members of parliament did not remember tradition. Several of us sat down and discussed this, and eventually said, 'We are talking like the elders who used to build a house and talk inside it until it rotted, then built another house, going on until our time but with nothing happening.' So we formed a group which could unify our whole country, including other provincial groups who might feel the same as us. 'Solomon Islands' is our country, 'tradition' is our culture and way of life, 'environment' is our natural resources, and 'conservation' is the sustainability of their use.

It is like this. Church and colonisation came and for better or worse this changed our way of life. What we established was not something we had just thought up; it began in former times. Formerly, as I understand from what my father told me, there was no politics in the ideas of the elders because people did not have a government to deal with. As I understand it, the first time tradition became involved in politics was back in the 1940s with Masing Rul. That was because the elders thought to become government, and maybe also to be freed from England. That was when Nono'ohimae and Nori led our fathers, including my father Alasa'a, and they were arrested because England treated them as rebelling in order to change things. I think that was when tradition became mixed up with politics, because they believed that with Masing Rul they would be independent. This was people like Salana Ga'a, who became first president of the Malaita Council and involved tradition in politics, and Kefo, who also went into politics. These were really senior people, some of whom had formerly worshipped the ghosts. It was not because they wanted to be politicians but rather they wanted to improve the role of leaders in administration, so they would be involved in discussions and people would listen to them, and also use our resources wisely. They worked to uphold tradition and make it strong so that both government and tradition would work. After Masing Rul they went on with various meetings here and there, talking about other matters and building one meeting-house after another. When Salana Ga'a and the others were governing the province from the end of the 1950s and into the 1960s, Ganifiri, Kefo, Rofate'e, Osifera, Maenanai, Daurara and others were holding meetings.[16] In the 1970s we joined in as young men and by the time the elders could no longer work we had ten or twenty years of experience with them. Their skills of talking, organising and governing were injected into our ideas and they taught us as we helped them establish cultural centres at places such as Kwasibu and Taba'a in Kwara'ae.

Politics had over-ruled the rights of the elders and not recognised them, so we came together to form this SITCECF group, through which the chiefs could have a say in government administration. What we did was launch the book *The Tradition of Land in Kwara'ae* in 1994, with the help of Permanent Secretary John Naitoro. Paul Daokalia and I wrote to the permanent secretary and the minister of Home Affairs, saying, 'You both deal with civil society, which the chiefs represent; look at this handbook.' They replied that it was the first handbook of law on land in Solomon Islands: 'Give us an estimate so the ministry can give you what you want.' We estimated the cost of food for fifty people, money for dancers and for chiefs to travel from Malaita and back, and the governor-general, Sir Moses Pitakaka, agreed to launch the book. That was our first public occasion, and it helped to set up SITCECF, because land is a major issue in Malaita and Solomon Islands and we became known for doing such things.

We established SITCECF to give ourselves weight, because as individual chiefs we could do no more than talk a lot. It was to make the government recognise us and support us with money. John Naitoro helped us a lot when he was special secretary in the culture ministry, and Johnson Honimae, who was minister at the time; both men from 'Are'are. Every Saturday when we met, the ministry would provide food. Our idea was to get someone who had experience of government work. Paul Daokalia was secretary to Prime Minister Solomon Mamaloni from the 1980s until Mamaloni died in 2000, so we selected him as president. He was not involved in any government money dealings and was straight in his administrative work.[17] Alex Rukia, the archaeologist and land recorder for

Kwara'ae chiefs at the official launch of the book *The Tradition of Land in Kwara'ae* at the National Museum in Honiara in 1994. They include (left to right), back row: first Rocky Tisa, second Onesmas Omani, last Frank Ete, front row: first Cornelius Kwasi, third Adriel Rofate'e, fourth Richard Folota. (*Solomon Star* photo)

the Ministry of Lands, was technical advisor, Wilson 'Ai'oro, education director for Malaita Province, was secretary-general, Rocky Hardy Tisa, with John Bare, were facilitators, and David Ross who had a sawmill at Bina Harbour, and Frank Ete was the chiefs' advisor. There were former governor-generals George Lepping to represent Western Province and Baddeley Devesi as a paramount chief for Guadalcanal. Joseph Hiro, former premier of Isabel, was assistant president, John Naitoro was technical advisor, Peter Usi from Baelelea, north Malaita, was chairman, Clement Nata'i of Temotu Province was a member, and Benson Hamori of Makira Province, Charles Levi of

Central Province, and Benjamin Ramo of Honiara. That was our executive in the 1990s.

While we were establishing SITCECF in the 1980s, the government was setting up a system for land recording, and we helped. The Ministry of Lands treated this as very important, because land is the main stumbling-block to development, especially in Malaita. The ministry needed a group to straighten out land claims so that when we talk about development we don't have anyone coming to spoil it by saying, 'It's my land, it's my land.' Land recording means gathering all the clan leaders together for discussion and making maps, giving everyone application forms and getting them all to attend a workshop. Alex Rukia, the archaeologist and advisor to SITCECF, co-ordinated this with the land registrar and others from the ministry, who would go to stay with them and explain the meaning of land registration. They would say to the elders, 'Go back and each clan bring your genealogy, discuss it among yourselves and agree what is your land and if we should register it.' They would fill in the forms and write minutes of what they agreed at their meeting, then they could establish themselves as a land trust board.[18]

We also tried politics, and many of us stood for election, but what we were interested in was the community and we were persuaded by people saying, 'Try it.' We started a political party called the Solomon Islands Indigenous People's Cultural Party and launched its constitution and manifesto in a Japanese restaurant in Honiara. When we first started it we called it the Solomon Islands Traditional Culture Party Movement, but we realised while campaigning that people were afraid of the term 'movement' in case it was a movement like Masing Rul, so we amended it.[19] This became the political arm of SITCECF. It was Paul Daokalia and me, Alex Rukia, Wilson 'Ai'oro, Rocky Hardy Tisa, John Bare and Frank Ete who started it, and we had representatives from various provinces of the country.

We decided to start a party because the cries of the people were not being answered or even addressed by parliament, and we were organising the chiefs, from White River in the west to 'Abira'a'ado'a in East Honiara, to raise people up a bit in terms of helping their communities solve their problems. When I say the people's cries were unheard, it was things like our roads being full of potholes, which people would campaign about, saying, 'Vote for me and overnight the roads will be good,' but then when the man came to stand again the roads were still as bad. Students didn't have their own transport to take them to school so they could arrive on time and not be turned away. Another demand not met by those politicians was for clinics to be built in the outskirts settlements. Our community chiefs wanted one clinic at Baranaba on the hill for the Panatina area, and another on a hill at Gilbert Camp, because Naha was too crowded and far away. Something else that we wanted was for the outskirts settlements to become squatters with their own land, which they could use for security for bank loans. People wanted all these things but never saw them. In particular, the constituency development fund was never distributed to projects for the youths to have work. When I campaigned, I said, 'This is not your problem; it's the government's problem.' We were saying this during the 1980s and people didn't listen, but when we campaigned in 1989 everyone supported us. Charles Dausabea had no interest in the people, so we created this big group to oppose him and all those other selfish men who wouldn't give money to help the people. Our candidate was John Maetia and when we campaigned everyone supported us, but Dausabea used the constituency development fund to convince the people. He raised two thousand chickens on land he bought near the airport, to feed the people at election time, and he killed his opponents with food and won for the third time. Charles Dausabea was MP for East Honiara for sixteen years; far too long.

Then I went for the town council. Things like our clinics and feeder roads, transport infrastructure and buses with regular schedules to get students to school and people to work on time; all this I planned to work on. I ran for the town council, Panatina ward twelve, in 1981and lost against Azriel Loaloa by two votes. In 1997 we amended the party and called it the Solomon Islands Indigenous People's Development and Cultural Party. The president was Paul Daokalia, the secretary-general was Wilson 'Ai'oro, I was vice-secretary-general and Alex Rukia was technical advisor. Rocky Hardy Tisa was co-ordinator for Malaita, Paul's brother Ben was treasurer, and David Jack was vice-treasurer. Members included Malison of Western Province and Mata'i from Temotu Province. In the 1997 general election Alex Rukia stood for Central Honiara and Paul Daokalia for West Kwara'ae. There was a meeting at my house at Windy Hill, organised by the chiefs and SITCEFC, with people from Lau, To'abaita, Talakali and everywhere, and they said, 'Let's stand Kwa'ioloa for East Honiara,' and they paid my fee of two thousand dollars. Twenty of us stood in 1997, and we all lost.[20] Then I stood again for the city council in 2000 and the man who won was Ronald Fugu'i. A cousin from Lau, David Maesua, was second, and I was third.

There has been injustice in the country due to the politicians misusing money and making propaganda to denigrate people and gain money for themselves. The worst part of the story is how people have got rich overnight without earning the money, and even killed people, through stupid, illegal plans which take us nowhere, because of lack of leadership for the country by the government of the day. The result was the conflict which began between the peoples of Guadalcanal and Malaita in 1999. This led to hundreds of killings and the displacement of thousands of people from their homes.

---

1 *Fa'ina'ona'o* or 'the one in front'.
2 See Kwa'ioloa & Burt 1997 Ch.8
3 See Kwa'ioloa & Burt 1997:124 for a more detailed account of this incident.
4 *Fanoa* or 'home'.
5 Other chiefs involved included Futal Sanga, John Laetefi, Gu'urau, Fiuga, Kwaomo, Ngidu'i, Dick Maetoa and Irofau.
6 This expectation that people should receive some recompense for public or community service explains the practice of giving a portion from restitution and compensation payments to advocates and mediators in disputes.
7 *Gwaugwau 'i mani 'i bali ngwane.*
8 Kwa'ioloa & Burt 1997:147-155.
9 *Toto'a*, the payment for a killing.
10 *Ngwangwae'anga'a.*
11 *Kwaima'anga*, which Kwara'ae translate as 'love'.
12 *Du'ukwate'a.*
13 *Gwaunga'i ngwae.*
14 *Fangata'a* or 'bad-eating' and *ogaguguta*.
15 Voting procedures have since been reformed to prevent this kind of abuse.
16 For a history of the Maasina Rul and subsequent movements in Kwara'ae, see Burt 1994 Ch. 7 & 8, and for a thorough analysis for the whole of Malaita, see Akin 2013.
17 Solomon Mamaloni was prime minister until 1997, although still influential thereafter. The comment on Daokalia being 'straight' is to disassociate him from the various suspect dealings for which Mamaloni was notorious.
18 Alex Rukia piloted this approach with a workshop at Maoro, Malaita, in 1992.

[19] This seems to reflect the partial success of the colonial government in discrediting Maasina Rul as a reactionary militant 'movement'.
[20] In this election, Kwa'ioloa came sixth out of nine candidates, with 371 votes. Charles Dausabea won the seat with 1014 votes, which was about 20% of the votes cast on a turnout of only 46%. The electoral system of 'first past the post', inherited from Britain, with votes split among numerous candidates, makes such unrepresentative results common in Solomon Islands elections. Alex Rukia came fifth out of eighteen candidates for Central Honiara, and Paul Daokalia was tenth out of twelve for West Kwara'ae.

A view from Mount Austen in 1999 over the Malaitan settlements of East Honiara, the land deforested by years of intensive gardening.
(Ben Burt photo)

8
TROUBLE ON GUADALCANAL

War, as experienced in many continental countries, was unknown in Solomon Islands in the past, but this is no longer true. Formerly conflict was resolved by our traditional chiefs, and feuds between clans and families were fought only with wooden clubs and bows and arrows, not the military weapons used by the two parties in the recent conflict. I will try to explain why our youths so unfortunately struggled against each other and destroyed our standing as 'the peaceful Isles of Solomon', causing us to experience the dark emotions of discouragement, fear and sorrow. I want to get to the root of this conflict. From my own experience, as a Malaita chief and a special constable in the Royal Solomon Islands Police, I can see that the collapse of the country was caused by the government not attending to the advice of its fathers, the chiefs; the custodians and experts in the traditions of the country.

In 1988, as a result of peaceful demonstrations, several meetings were held by provincial leaders over sensitive issues between the peoples of Guadalcanal and Malaita islands. Ten years later, armed groups of Guadalcanal youths, angry at perceived government inaction in addressing their people's grievances, engaged in activities which resulted in the eviction from Guadalcanal of settlers from other islands, and in particular the displacement of maybe twenty-five thousand Malaitans. It was the failure of the government to answer their demands that resulted in the youth of Guadalcanal arming themselves, starting fires, and eventually using firearms to kill the Malaitans who had settled their lands and chased them away. As this continued, the youth of Malaita formed a paramilitary group, the Malaita Eagle Force, and in collaboration with the Police Field Force they opened up the armoury. Then, when Ulufa'alu's government was replaced and first Sogavare and then Kemakeza became prime minister, everything went down and further down, but still they did not appreciate what the problem was and the chiefs were still excluded. Hundreds of thousands of dollars were demanded from the government as restitution or indemnity payments for each person killed or injured, and the cost made the government crawl on its belly. The rebel leader Harold Keke would not surrender and killed those who were sent to the Guadalcanal Weather Coast to deal with him. People were in difficulties over money, the police and teachers were not paid properly, there were no medical services, schools were overgrown with forest, without teachers, books or equipment, and everything collapsed because of the uncaring attitude of the government, who would not bring in the chiefs to co-ordinate things.

As a result of this conflict, people lost confidence in the leadership of government. Our politicians had misused funds, used people to earn money for themselves, become rich overnight, and implemented foolish illegal policies which led us nowhere. Considering all this, the chiefs have concluded that government must be changed, not just by motions of no confidence to replace one government with another, but by changing the leadership as a whole, because our politicians have become blinded by corruption and concern for money. Maybe, if another kind of government came into existence, friendly countries and aid donors would recognise it and provide financial support to revive the economy of this country and help the chiefs to teach the country's leaders about honesty and justice.

There is a very important account in our history, as Malaitans testify, that the Guadalcanal people are descended from Malaitans from Siale in central Kwara'ae who lived in the area of Rere in East Guadalcanal. Guadalcanal people may not agree with this history, but this is what I heard. Rere has an area of thick forest, which nobody has cut, called Rerebonobono, which means in Kwara'ae language that it has been 'closed off' since it was claimed by our first arrivals. One time, when I took a preaching band to evangelise the Marau area, some church leaders and I, accompanied by one or two senior Guadalcanal men, surveyed the area. Jesriel Arukwai was there, Amos Kwa'ite'e, my sons Lawrence Laugere and William Mae, and my 'father' Kona who was living there. We found the land that was first settled by Malaitans, testifying that we have the right to live in Guadalcanal. According to our tradition, when a man was the first to clear thick forest with a stone adze and fire, that area belonged to him. When those people returned to Siale they left a woman on Guadalcanal who died and was buried at a place called Vunuanuli, at Ruafatu. That is why in Guadalcanal the woman is the head of the family or clan, because it was a woman who was left when they returned to Malaita. So this ties us together as relatives by blood.[1]

Then, during the Second World War, it was the Malaitans who assisted the United States military, working as scouts and porters and sometimes even fighting. For instance, when the Japanese set up a gun in the cave at Visale in West Guadalcanal, Solomon Ilala from Tangatalau in central Kwara'ae went down on a rope and threw a hand grenade into the cave, destroying the Japanese and saving American ships and planes. It was through their efforts that the Americans won the battle of Guadalcanal, as the Malaitans showed them how to hide while fighting.[2] Thousands of soldiers and many Malaitan men died during the war and, according to Solomon Islands tradition, when people have shed their blood to rescue or protect a clan or family, if there are no pigs or shell-money they give those people land. This is why we have done no wrong in settling Guadalcanal land, because our fathers and grandfathers were shot dead on the island of Guadalcanal, so that the Guadalcanal people could all remain on their island.

It is also important that the Guadalcanal people appreciate the work done by the Malaitans. With Lever's Pacific Plantations, it was Malaitans who were recruited to clear the forest, without modern tools, for plantations around Guadalcanal, at Rere, Tangarere, Ruafatu where the first ancestors were buried, Lavuro, Tasifa'arongo, Ruaniu, Doma; any plantation you can name was cleared and planted by Malaitans. That is the justifiable reason why Malaitans settled in Guadalcanal, because while working as copra cutters they sought permission from the rightful land-holders to live and garden in Guadalcanal and purchased land to live by businesses such as cattle, piggeries and market gardens. This made the Malaitans prosperous and they even built and upgraded large buildings in parts of Guadalcanal.

Jealousy was one cause of the conflict. People should appreciate that Malaitans were the productive, active people who did everything in Guadalcanal, clearing and planting the thousands of hectares of oil palms for Solomon Islands Plantations Ltd and developing the town of Honiara, which administers the provinces of the country. It was Malaitans who worked for the mining company at Gold Ridge, operating the machines and earning revenue for the government and royalties for the Guadalcanal people from their land. With logging on Guadalcanal, it was Malaitans who were the workers and supervisors for companies such as Foxwood. People flooded into Guadalcanal to seek employment to earn money for school fees, for clothing, for store goods, and for the things that enable people to develop, such as tools and equipment. Malaitans too were the teachers and school principals all over Guadalcanal, teaching the next generation, including Guadalcanal students. It was also Malaitans who ran the construction firms, like J.M. and Brothers Construction, of which I was a manager when we built the Panatina campus of the College of Higher Education. Painting, plumbing, plastering, electrics, telephones; all this was done by Malaitans in Guadalcanal. The government and various companies had staff quarters and labour lines at Kukum to accommodate their employees. These were the people who built Honiara.

When I came to Honiara as a boy at the end of the 1960s, my relatives living in the Kobito and Shahalu Tandai areas had been invited in by the rightful land-holders, Joseph Manimosa and others of the Mount Austen area of Mabulu. They agreed for us to plant gardens in the forest for taro, yam, sweet potato and tapioca, and to cut trees for building materials, to hunt pigs and take anything we needed. These land-holders, by observing the tradition of sharing, showed that they alone could allow our fathers access to this land. Then when the Malaitan Christians at Kobito celebrated their church feasts, they had to invite the rightful land-holders to attend and give them a share of the feast to take home for their families. During national election campaigns they sought the Malaitans' assistance and we co-ordinated the chiefs from the various outlying settlements and ran the campaign all the way from Aruligo down to Selwyn College at Maravovo and White River in East Honiara. In west Guadalcanal when candidates ran in parliamentary elections they also represented Malaitans living in the Gilbert Camp area, who fully supported Guadalcanal province to become a state. I myself was campaign manager for Valeriano Chualu, son of the land-holder Baranaba, when he stood for election. They sought our assistance in everything, co-operating with people from elsewhere who needed their land, until the conflict separated them from us.

Why? Because we were one people, and they were our 'fathers', and as their children we worked co-operatively with the land-holders' children as 'brothers' and shared things between us. What happened was caused by those such as the Weather Coast people, who did not understand the basis on which Malaitans lived on Guadalcanal land. It was a failure of government that such matters were not addressed, and of Guadalcanal Province, which failed to legislate to stop the influx of others into their lands. Besides the settlements around Honiara, there were people from Malaita living all over North Guadalcanal, employed in various areas and settled with the land-holders there, and they invited their relatives to come and live with them. They brought their children, who brought their children, who married and multiplied, so that Malaitans were all over Guadalcanal, in places where they were not accepted as they were in Honiara. This also contributed to the conflict, but those responsible for it should also remember that people from Malaita married women and men from Guadalcanal, building relationships which cannot be disregarded. They should live together as one family and allow people to return to their homes, by arrangement with the government and the province, and settle things properly so a conflict like this cannot happen again. In marriage each party should observe the tradition of the other, so that we are free to reside on either the female or male side,[3] as long as everything goes smoothly and we comply with traditional law and accept sanctions from the rightful land-holders, with whom our fathers established themselves at Guadalcanal.

I remember in 1994 making a phone call to the Minister for Lands in the Mamaloni government, Francis Orodani, an indigenous member of parliament from Guadalcanal. I asked him if I could send my chiefs to show him the history of our 'fathers'' settlement here in the past, on land in Guadalcanal. He agreed, and in June that year we sent two senior chiefs, Benjamin Ramo and Ben Bakoï'a Bamae to call at his office and discuss matters relating to Malaitans dwelling in parts of

Guadalcanal. Orodani asked if we could provide a written history, so I prepared a statement concerning the history of the Malaitans residing in the outlying settlements with the permission of the responsible land-holders of the 1950s, and took this history to his office that same month.

In the 1950s our first relatives to settle approached the rightful land-holders, who had already allowed the government to establish Honiara as the capital here. Their names were Baranaba, Ben Baenosi and Manimosa, Domeniko and Kosi, from Gaobata and Kaokao in the Tandai Shahalu clan lands. Their aim in giving out those areas was to safeguard their customary land against further extension of the town boundary by the government, with the Malaitans there to witness that they were the land-holders. However, as I told Orodani, when more of our relatives flooded into Honiara for employment, instead of consulting the land-holders they called at the Lands Department office for permission to occupy these outlying settlements. Without consulting the land-holders either, the Lands Department automatically issued temporary occupation licences with a yearly rent of five shillings, which rose to ten shillings, then two dollars, rising to thirty dollars by 1994, and now to one hundred dollars.

Because of these increases, we chiefs researched the matter and found that we licensed occupiers should be living under the authority of the land-holders, for it was they that settled our 'fathers' here and had the responsibility for speaking about these pieces of land. As I told the minister, our 'fathers' had co-operated with them so that when gardening or taking building materials and sago-palm leaf, they would seek their permission. Even now, when we need wood from the surrounding area we have to seek permission from these same land-holders, and they charge us a hundred dollars per tree. This proves that we are living on customary land held by the Guadalcanal chiefs and not on alienated or waste land, as claimed by the government. I included a map of the boundary, as it was shifted when our ancestors came to dwell on the land. 'Honourable minister,' I added, 'I am raising this on behalf of the Malaita chiefs and people occupying these areas, as a matter of concern before your ministry makes arrangements for titles to be given to us occupants. This direct approach is for the purpose of representing us to parliament, to serve the people of Solomon Islands with an equitable decision.'

I then identified the first of our relatives to dwell on this land, and their homes, as follows.[4] Moses and Benjamin Ko'oru'u paid for a piece of land at Gilbert Camp, and their children dwell there until the present. Solodia of Fataleka first settled at Kobito One, Laua'a of Baegu'u also settled at Kobito One and he is represented at present by Dongafaka and his son Konongū'i. Maniuri of Fataleka also settled at Kobito One, Kaobata settled at Kobito Two, and I myself Michael Kwa'ioloa represent him today, since the death of my elder brother John Maesatana. Tua settled Mamulele and his grandson Jimmy Ga'ea is there today. Salebanga settled Dukwasi and Benjamin Ramo represents him today. Kamusu settled Adailiua and his son Sareto'ona represents him today, and then later Jack, Deobasi and 'Au from Ata'a arrived and their sons Suxon Talo and Ini represent them today. That is why the Ata'a people as well as the Kwara'ae live at Adailiua. Dioko settled Ferakuisia and chief Michael Ngidui represents him today. Tega and Amagele settled Matariu, and Tega's son Fito'oa and Amagele's son Cedric Kemanu are there at present, and Anthony's son is at Koa Hill at present. Rua and his brother Ramosaea from Fataleka were at White River, and his sons Peter Ramosaea and Ronald Fugu'i are there at present. Lafunua and Oa were at Taba'a, above Bokona, and are still living at present. Then, going up to Koa Hill, a man from Koa in West Kwara'ae sought permission from Baranaba to settle there, and Anthony, whose son now works at the Central Bank represents him today. Then, going up to Gwa'imaoa, the man who originally settled there, John Kuru, is still there.

Houses in Kobito Two in 1991, a Kwara'ae village founded by Kwa'ioloa's clan on the outskirts of Honiara. (Ben Burt photo)

Then there are the new settlements from the 1970s and 1980s. Talo at Namoliki has died but his sons remain, and he is represented at present by Clement Saomae. Kuru at Gwa'imaoa remains at present. Kena Hill is another new settlement, by 'Aitorea, Adam from Kwaio and Dick Maetoea. Lakofi at Feraladoa remains at present and Fulisango was established by Kalaka, who remains at present. These people are a mixture of West Kwara'ae and Kwaio. Coming on up, Kofiloko was founded by Paul Ata, Kasilea and Ben Beuka, who are from East Kwaio. The Lau Valley settlement was established by a chief from Lau and the main person there is Inito'o from Lau, who drained the swampy area of the valley. Maelaua settled at Kaibea, named after a tapioca (*kaibea*) garden, and his sons are there at present. Robert from 'Are'are, south Malaita, settled at 'Ofi'olo and the outlying settlements below, where Ramōgo resides today, and old man Gua settled Abira'ado'e, which he named after his home in Talakali, East Fataleka. These two are different in that they worked for Lever's Pacific Plantations and when they retired they asked permission to settle those areas from Lever's, instead of from the land-holders.

We must also realise that when our 'fathers' sought permission to settle this land they offered gifts of shell-money and pigs to the land-holders, who had to offer sacrifices to their ancestral ghosts to declare everything before anyone settled or cleared an area of land. Otherwise the ghosts would not know those persons and would cause sickness or even death to those settling the land. They also offered the land-holders food such as sugar, tinned meat, biscuits, rice or whatever, and even handed them tools such as machetes, axes, saws, hammers and nails. They provided the land-holders with everything, because they were friends, demonstrating the rights of Solomon Islanders to freedom of movement to settle anywhere as long as we seek permission from the rightful land-holders, avoiding fighting, killing and parting people from their property. This history of how Malaitans settled this land is important. The Guadalcanal people of the present should not have started the conflict with the Malaitans, whether Kwara'ae, 'Are'are, Talakali-Fataleka or Kwaio, because the land was granted by the rightful landholders under the leadership of Baranaba, the head-man of the day, who allowed the capital to move from Tulagi, bombed by the Japanese, to Honiara on Guadalcanal in 1948.[5]

The Guadalcanal people charge some people fifty or sixty dollars rent to work their land, but they don't charge me because I went to court and won land back from a group from Gela and Savo who had won it from them. They went to the high court four times and lost, and I went to court and won. This was in the 1980s, when I was working at Noro[6] and heard on the radio one evening that they had killed some men on Mount Austen, because Joseph Manimosa and the son of Baranaba, land-holders of Honiara, had lost. The Malaitans to whom they had given the land were angry and killed the men who won the land. This was a big problem for my elder brother John Maesatana and for Manimosa. They called me by radio from the Honiara office of John Holland Construction, whom I was working for on a painting contract. I came back straight away, because Maesatana said, 'If you delay they'll kill some more. Come and appeal the land, so that you, as a man who understands the court, will win.' When I arrived we took the lawyer David Campbell as our spokesman and me and my 'brother' Robert Folota paid the fee. I met all the costs; rice and meat and fish, the survey and travel for the survey, fuel, tobacco and betelnut for everyone. This is the land which has Honiara in it, and the Livestock Development Authority, and Kobito and Gilbert Camp, because we were the first to settle this land before anyone else lived there. Joseph Manimosa and others allowed us to work on this land; Chuala's father Baranaba was the spokesman for the land and he let our elders settle there.

That was the history of Malaitan settlement, and then in 1988 a group of Guadalcanal men and women held their peaceful demonstration and marched down to the prime minister's office, and also to the Guadalcanal provincial government headquarters. They wanted to make it clear that they didn't like the influx of other ethnic groups into their island and their customary land and villages in Guadalcanal, and they wanted something done about it. In the view of us chiefs, to avoid something happening between the two island groups the government should have taken measures to stop the influx from other provinces into their island. But nothing happened; they were not a bit concerned and totally ignored it.

In 1998, on 13 March, a big meeting took place at Visale in east Guadalcanal of all the Guadalcanal people settled there. The Guadalcanal premier of the time, Ezekiel Alebua, went down there on the first day, and they celebrated with a feast of pigs and local food. Then next day, at 9.00 a.m. on 14 March, a policeman who was half Langalanga, Malaita, and half Guadalcanal, John Garo, also arrived at Visale. The premier offered prayers and then Garo addressed the meeting, and that was when they selected men as leaders for the group which was born at that very time. They took the B out of BRA, 'Bougainville Revolutionary Army', and put in a G for 'Guadalcanal Revolutionary Army'. It was only later that they changed their name to the Isatabu Freedom Movement (IFM).

That's how it stayed, not yet operational, and then after seven months, in October that year, another meeting took place at Balasuna, east Guadalcanal. There were at least two hundred people at the Visale meeting and twice as many attended this one, with the premier and the same people talking about the same issues. Maybe they were right; they had demonstrated, held meetings and warned all the people from other provinces, not just Malaitans, who had come to live on land belonging to Guadalcanal. They had married there and started businesses, and who knows what agreements were made with Guadalcanal province and the land-holders for business on the land. But the government of the day had failed to address the issues and at that meeting they said, 'Oh, maybe we'll tell these people to go from our land, especially the Malaitans.' For it was the Malaitans who were accused of taking advantage.

It was then that Harold Keke was appointed, and Joseph Sangu, Henry Taupa and George Grey, as supreme commanders. Then they started thinking, 'Oh, we'll tell them to go. If they stay they'll dominate us, maybe they'll contravene our tradition, there will be so many they'll take us over,' and things like that. 'So we'll tell them to go.' But telling a man to go when he has been established in a place and developed it for many years is rather difficult and takes time. They took it seriously enough to confirm during that meeting: 'We'll chase them off, and if they won't go we'll use sticks, stones and clubs, and if that doesn't work we'll use bows and arrows and guns. If that doesn't work we'll burn their houses, and if that doesn't work, we'll kill them.' All this was discussed at this meeting in October 1998, and that's when the conflict was born.

In 1999, before the Malaita Eagle Force (MEF) and the Isatabu Freedom Movement (IFM) of Guadalcanal began their violent action, I led a delegation of fifteen chiefs from the Solomon Islands Traditional Culture and Environmental Conservation Foundation to see the prime minister of the day, Bartholomew Ulufa'alu, and discuss how the chiefs could help minimise conflict between the Malaita and Guadalcanal people. Our co-ordinator Rocky Tisa and myself explained to the prime minister that the row between the two parties could be ended if it was handed back to the chiefs to co-ordinate the relevant authorities in producing a solution to the problem. We assured the prime minister that we had done this successfully in the past. In 1978, when people from Malaita and Western Province were in conflict over an insulting publication about the Western people, it was due to the chiefs' efforts in co-ordinating discussion between the two parties that a solution was found and a peace was signed, with the government paying restitution to Western Province. We did the same with Rennell and Bellona in 1989 after the writing of some bad words in Honiara market, contacting their chiefs and members of parliament, solving the problem and signing a lasting peace with a payment of two hundred thousand dollars to Malaita Province. In another conflict in 1996 between Temotu Province and Malaita, the MPs John Fiisango of Malaita and Michael Maena of Temotu discussed the issue with the chiefs of both sides and Police Commissioner Frederick Soake, agreed reconciliation, and signed a lasting peace. The chiefs charged each side to pay the other ten thousand dollars and the government paid thirty thousand dollars restitution to Malaita Province.[7]

The prime minister replied that the government was doing all this for the two parties, but we emphasised that it was the chiefs who were the most appropriate people, as the fathers of the country. If they could co-ordinate arrangements with the east and west Guadalcanal traditional presidents Samuel Saki and Michael Mulele Chualu, then the message would go down to the militias in the bush and they would back off and sort out the problem. We told him that there are some things politicians cannot do for the people, because they are always in opposition to one another, some losing elections and others winning, with the winners being opposed again by others in parliament. We did not believe that politicians could maintain peace and harmony because they have too many opponents. We told him that we meant to stay and watch what would happen, and that it would be fortunate if things went well, for it was likely to end otherwise.

A few days later they arranged with the leaders of both sides, the MEF and IFM, to gather the people together for a ceremony at the Art Gallery in Honiara on 23 May 1999, at which each side killed fourteen pigs and presented fourteen shell-moneys, all contributed by the government. But the politicians were taking too much upon themselves and were not eligible to handle such matters. It should have been the chiefs, the fathers of the people, who handled it, and then we could have had a resolution of the conflict between the two islands, as in previous cases. They transported several chiefs by patrol boat from Malaita as well as some Guadalcanal chiefs, but invited only our senior chief Benjamin Ramo from Honiara. Even he did not understand why he was there and what they were doing, and nor did Selwyn Saki, the president of the east Guadalcanal chiefs.

What happened was, that very day when they ended the celebration at the Art Gallery, the IFM leader Harold Keke and his gang destroyed the buildings of Tangarare Secondary School in west Guadalcanal and chased away the Malaitan students. That bore out what the chiefs had said in their delegation to Ulufa'alu. As time passed, Keke and his group became ferociously angry and demanded that the government pay 2.5 million dollars for the loss of twenty-five people killed by Malaitans in years past.[8] This was regardless of the fact that those who killed his relatives had been convicted under the law and were serving life sentences, some were dead, and some had paid compensation. Besides, Guadalcanal people had also victimised Malaitans in the past, and the Malaitans had made no attempt to gain compensation in this way. But Ulufa'alu's government can also be blamed because, although they gave them a cheque, there was no money in the account, which annoyed the Guadalcanal people and made things worse.[9] Furthermore, Keke demanded that the government move the capital, Honiara, because the government had not met his requirements. Even so, it was understood that Keke would not enter Honiara but was securing the area which came under Guadalcanal Province, which was indigenous land.

When this started, the Malaitans began to run away, they brought in the people from the outer areas, and the government relocated them in halls at the College of Higher Education, Kukum and Panatina campus, the Rove Police Club, and so on. This was from June and July 1999 to 2000. Then they sent everyone down from the Solomon Islands Plantations oil-palm plantation and they occupied the Roman Catholic hall and everywhere else, and the government fed them. Then they began to fill in rehabilitation forms and received one thousand dollars per head from the government to repatriate to Malaita.

Respecting our tradition

Scenes from the reconciliation ceremony at the Art Gallery on 23 May 1999, with presentations of shell-money and the presiding officials; Premier Alebua of Guadalcanal, Prime Minister Ulufa'alu and Premier Oeta of Malaita. (*Solomon Star* 25-5-1999, 28-5-1999)

Then the government expanded its assistance so that anyone who had lost property could claim payment, then it gave assistance for lost employment so people were paid for time lost, then it gave assistance for loss of business. All this caused problems as the government was unable to fulfil its promises. Loss of property was a problem because, although displaced people were coming through, for some reason the government made Honiara residents eligible as well. Everyone in Honiara filled in the forms, even though some had lost nothing, and they received a lot of money. Those who had come in from outside Honiara, the old people crying, some of them received not a penny.

In 2000 when all the Malaitans fled back home, emptying their houses and gardens until all that was left was bushes, one night my daughter-in-law Evelyn, wife of my fourth son Michael Lilifafia, dreamed that a woman exactly like my younger sister Ivery Arana came crying to the top of the hill. She cried until she reached the house and then said, 'All of you, my children-in-law, you believe my son Kwa'ioloa but he's making you stay among the dead men. You are staying in a home taken over by *oli* vines.' This is a traditional way of saying a village has been deserted. 'Don't believe my son; run away! The GRA will kill you! Run away!' Then Evelyn saw a man come, with his hair parted and oiled, which was my father's style, and a big white scar on his leg. The man didn't say anything, but he sat on the other end of the bench from where the woman was saying, 'You must all go or the Guales will kill you.' As she was describing all this, I said, 'That's my mother you saw, who looked like my younger sister Ivery Arana, and the man you saw, slim like me, with his scar and hairstyle, that's my father Samuel Alasa'a Afutana.' Then Evelyn and everyone just realised: 'That's him. We've seen his photo.' I said, 'Let's pray about this. If it is the will of God our creator to let us go, on Friday we will go, because I believe what my mother says.' But I was sleeping apart in a small house with Ben Burtte'e, and in the night I dreamed that my father came again. He said, 'Kwa'ioloa my son, I have already seen my grandchildren's plans to go home, but I forbid it. You won't die like a *gwali*-lizard here in Honiara. This conflict will end. I'm telling you, if you go now you'll need a lot of money to come back again.' That encouraged me not to leave Honiara, empty my three houses and trouble my children.

I don't always believe dreams, but when I act on them and they work I say, 'Oh, it's true.' I didn't doubt my mother's warning, but women always worry and take more precautions. Men trust themselves to wait until the situation is serious, so I thank my father's ghost that we did not leave our home and property and then have to come back to poverty, as other Malaitans did.

Trouble on Guadalcanal

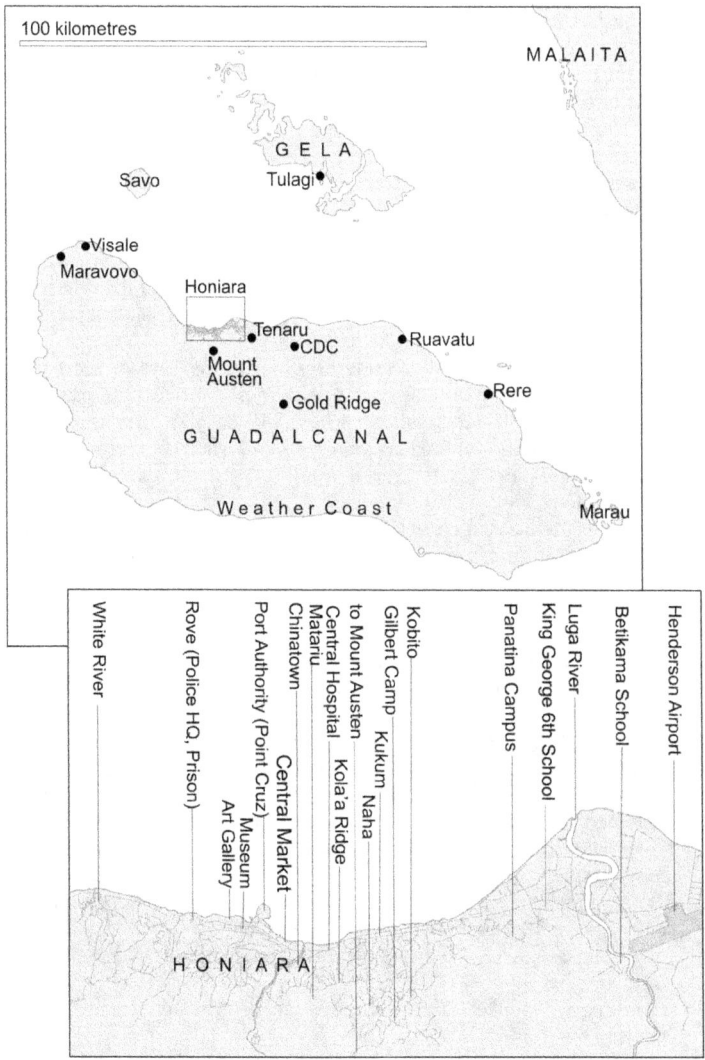

Guadalcanal and Honiara, with some of the places mentioned in the following chapters.

1. While the Kwara'ae trace their origins to ancestors from overseas who founded the shrine of Siale in the Kwara'ae central inland, other peoples of Malaita and Guadalcanal have their own histories. Even people who want to treat each other as blood relatives may find it hard to agree on how they are related, so all these histories are a matter for debate. For further accounts of the Kwara'ae origin history and its role in legitimating their chiefs' movement, see Burt 1994 and Burt & Kwa'ioloa 2001. In accounting for the seniority of the female line in Guadalcanal, Kwa'ioloa is contrasting this with the male seniority of Malaita.
2. Like other participants in this war, Malaitans focus on their own role from a perspective which does not always take account of the others. For Malaitan and other Solomon Islander accounts set in an academic historical context, see White et al. 1988.
3. The seniority of the mother's side on Guadalcanal and of the father's on Malaita gives the children of Malaita men married to Guadalcanal women seniority in land claims on both islands. Kwa'ioloa is affirming the right of children of Guadalcanal men and Malaitan women to have access to their parents' lands, even though they do not have the right to manage them.
4. In naming the first settlers of particular places and then tracing a relationship to the senior son or grandson who now represents him, Kwa'ioloa is following the style of genealogical history used in Malaita, where the living heirs may 'stand for' (*ū fuana*) ancestors up to twenty or more generations before (see Burt & Kwa'ioloa 2001).
5. The consequences of state official ignorance of such land claims include their ambiguity in the eyes of commentators such as Fraenkel (2004:57-59).
6. Noro is the fish-factory port in the western Solomons.
7. Such incidents established the precedent, exploited during the subsequent civil conflict, that the government should be liable for grievances attributed to the agency of the state, including problems of urbanisation. Large factions such as major ethnic groups have claimed restitution or 'compensation' under threat of violent disorder, which, in the Malaita-Temotu incident, was actively incited by certain Malaitan politicians. See Akin (1999) for an analysis of these developments.
8. See Fraenkel (2004:45-47 and Appendix 1) for details of this longstanding complaint.
9. According to Fraenkel (2004:7) this was actually a misunderstanding over access to the money.

The MEF 'joint operation' at the Rove Police Headquarters following the coup on 6 June 2000. (*Solomon Star* 6-6-2000)

9
MALAITA FIGHTS BACK

You have to understand that we had followed the story of Bosnia-Herzegovina, where they put the people aside and just killed thousands of them. The fear was that the IFM planned to invade and destroy Honiara, so when they saw the police were weak and unable to defend the town, the Malaita boys formed the Malaita Eagle Force. Some of the Police Field Force joined with them and their mission was to protect Honiara; the water supply, the power generation plant, the fuel at the wharf, and to protect life. The IFM had raided police armouries at Tulagi, Marau and Russell islands, as they planned ahead and had trained to handle the arms. We were very worried that they would make their way into Honiara to kill the Malaitans living in the urban areas and settlements on the outskirts, as they were angry over land. Whether they were from Langalanga or the north, the south, 'Are'are or Kwara'ae or To'abaita or Kwaio, everyone came together.

The IFM came creeping in, hundreds of them, on Mount Austen. One Saturday afternoon, 30 July 1999, some of our 'brothers' went up in a HiLux truck to the gardens and when they arrived the IFM were there, so they came back. The Police Field Force went up and shot at them and they fled. That's when the MEF set up bunkers along the perimeters, from Alligator Creek, covering the airport, all the way down to White River in the west. The main one was at Gilbert Camp, there was one at Feraladoa on the hill, one further down at Matariu on the hill, one further down at Ko'a Hill at Titige, and one at the Livestock Development Authority guarding the coast. Each bunker had a name – lion, white lion, bear, wolf, tiger – and its own patrol. They were organised by the youths of each settlement, but while everyone was in fear, we chiefs organised them too. We advised the boys not to accept the government call to fight the IFM: 'You look after us and if they creep in, chase them away and call the field force and rapid response unit to expel them. But you must take shifts, day and night, to watch out for us.' We also said, 'You at the Gilbert Camp bunker, each Tuesday come round and we'll give you free food. Whether Chinese or other businesses in this area, when they come, let there be a bit of sugar, and so on. And each Friday, you all come for a little money and refreshments, some noodles or tobacco.' Those at White River did this too and they'd take it to the camp and enjoy themselves, uniting to work together as one band or army.

It was when this had all been set up that it happened. The fighting had been going on for some time when, on the morning of 5 June 2000, the IFM crept in at Alligator Creek in the east and got to Kakabona in the west. At the time there was a meeting of Malaitans in the office of the prime minister, Bart Ulufa'alu, and a West Kwaio man called Robert Sokeni came running in and kicked the chair of one of the government members, saying, 'What are you all up to, playing around here, while my wife and children have been chased out and they're burning the houses at Kakabona!' It was then that the leaders of the MEF met with the leaders of the Police Field Force and the government authorities to agree how they should secure the town, and that was when they formed the paramilitaries.

I want to be clear about the connection between the Malaita Eagle Force and the central government. On the night of the 6 June 2000 the Guadalcanal militants were forcing their way into Honiara. The news had come that Harold Keke and his group were coming to destroy Honiara and burn it, and the government had no way to defend the town. So that night, at ten o'clock, the government brought in Maelanga, Moses Su'u, Jimmy Rasta Lusibaea and all the other militant commanders and discussed how they could defend them. The MEF was already in operation, because they were attacking Malaita people on various parts of Guadalcanal and burning their houses. They had established bunkers but had no good weapons, so that night they talked until the government allowed the MEF to step in before anything could happen and draw upon the armoury at Rove Police Headquarters. Before they did this, Kemakeza, the deputy prime minister, and Sogavare, promised the MEF, 'If you get us into power, we will pay you.' This is something everyone knows.

We chiefs saw this as a big mistake. As I had told them, 'You should just stay in the bunkers and leave Alligator Creek to the Police Field Force, for several reasons. First, if they kill them, they work for the government, which insures their lives. Second, they are legally allowed to bear arms. Third, they must block the place where the IFM came in. Fourth, it's their job. Fifth, they are trained to fight. The rapid response unit of the special constables should man Kakabona, because that's what they signed up for.' I had made a bit of a noise about it, but those involved did not agree. On 6 June they opened up the armoury at Rove and acted just as the police would when taking arms to riots or drill, and so on; they went in, lined up, signed their names and put the registration number of the rifle against the name. Not one of those guns was returned. They armed them that night, then in the morning the MEF called themselves 'special constables', without any authority, endorsement or training. When I went down in the morning, I saw all the trucks full of MEF gunmen. Everywhere in town they were manning road-blocks and wearing uniforms from the police stores. Everyone had this uncaring attitude and they had gone in and looted whatever was left in the stores.

The same night that they formed the paramilitaries, they arrested Prime Minister Ulufa'alu at gunpoint. Through his own ideas and actions he had reaped what he had sown, had ceased to be prime minister, was mistreated and nearly killed. By then I had already taken the delegation to him without response. The people of Guadalcanal had claimed two point five million dollars restitution for the twenty-five people they say the Malaitans had killed and that made it worse. By 1998 and 1999 they were chasing people from the land and burning their houses and it was becoming serious. Things were changing, there was an uncaring attitude, and the people from outside were being crowded into town.

That week at Kongolei in East Guadalcanal, on the border at Kakabona, they really challenged each other, Malaita on one side, IFM on the other, moved towards each other and had a battle. The police radios were open and I could hear them driving the trucks and on the Malaita side, *rrrr rrrr rrrr*, and Guadalcanal just *tk tk tk*. The high-power weapons were held by the Malaitans. 'Oh, they're moving up, the Malaita Eagle Force is on the move, they've come round the hill, they're shooting, they've retaliated.' It was the real thing, in the week between 5 and 10 June 2000. On 7 June the MEF used the police patrol boat, anchored off Alligator Creek, and fired at the IFM. This event seems to have turned the tide of the war, weakening IFM confidence and pushing them to proceed to negotiations when the Australian warships came, where they held the ceasefire discussions.

Members of the MEF at their camp at Kakabona in July 2000. (*Solomon Star* 17-7-2000)

I myself went to visit the MEF militants at Alligator Creek. The bunkers of the MEF and IFM were close, and the camp of the Melanesian Brothers, the *tasiu*, was in between. Both sides respected the *tasiu* because they were neutral, and I saw them carrying messages from one side to the other. Once I went with one of the MEF supreme commanders, and the Guadalcanal militants had sent two sacks full of chickens for the MEF in exchange for two or three sacks of rice, because they had no food and were just eating bananas all the time. They were still fighting but, perhaps because they were hungry, they helped each other. When we arrived they were busy eating, but we said, 'Hey, they may give you so much food that while you're busy they'll just attack.' There were twenty-four of them and twelve should have been giving cover but, you know, an army fights on its stomach. They said, 'No, the *tasiu* are brothers of our Guadalcanal enemies and they said, "Give us rice and we'll give you chickens."' That was the spiritual power of the *tasiu* to halt things.

So then, when we in town and in the settlements on the outskirts saw the influx of people from Guadalcanal leaving their houses, we were living in fear. Over there we saw the big Guadalcanal village at Gilbert Camp burning; the Malaita militants set all the houses alight. They were moving here and there like a mighty rushing wind. Nothing withstood them. Then the two groups came together at Tenaru, the IFM on one side, the MEF on the other, and the *tasiu* of the Melanesian Brotherhood were in the middle trying to restrain them. Night and day they fought, and at Kakabona too. Eventually a 'son' of ours, U'i Maena'a, was captured at Alligator Creek; he was shooting without anyone to cover him, maybe he ran out of bullets, and the IFM took him and cut his throat. Then a 'brother' of mine, William Gua, his son Samuel Fito'o was also killed down at Alligator Creek. As I said, 'If only the field force were at Alligator Creek and the rapid response unit at Kakabona; they've trained to use a rifle, but you lot only know how to hold it, not how to shoot.' So this made us live in fear, our women were really frightened, the schools stopped teaching, the clinics closed, except for the hospital, but the nurses fled. Rifles were everywhere and if any of the wounded were taken to hospital, they shot up the hospital.

The MEF bunker at Alligator Creek as they were abandoning it following the Townsville Peace Agreement in October 2000. (*Solomon Star* 24-10-2000)

The people living in Honiara and Guadalcanal suffered great losses of property; good houses were damaged, long-established businesses were destroyed and burned by the Guadalcanal militants and by the Malaitans too, from Aruligo in the east to CDC Three in the west, and the prosperity of both Guadalcanal and Malaita families was badly affected by the conflict. Residents of Honiara who had spent a lot of money to build themselves big houses fled to the various provinces and people who never worked to earn a penny occupied their houses. When the rightful owners asked to return to their houses, the MEF militants stopped them and they needed police support to get their houses back. Malaitans who fled to their original homes were returning to Honiara because they were lacking money, materials, equipment and their usual foods. Land disputes in Malaita are such a block to economic development that people were just not interested in seeking employment at home, so they began to return to Honiara. But then they found there was no employment here as companies had closed down, gone home or lost interest, because of the conflict between 2000 and 2002.

When the MEF militants took over the armoury at Rove Police Headquarters, they became the boss of the government and the police. They took over businesses without paying a cent, they took company vehicles, and they cheated millions of dollars from the repatriation fund for loss of property, provided by the government of Taiwan for the displaced people from Guadalcanal who fled home to Malaita and elsewhere. In the same way, some government ministers and politicians put themselves first to receive this money, and instead of the victims in various parts of Guadalcanal who had lost their property, these worthless people, who had lost nothing, benefited most. Members of parliament recommended people of their home villages who were unaffected to receive thousands of dollars and militia commanders forced the government to hand over thousands, which went into their own pockets and not to members of the MEF and IFM militias. People pretended to have lost big houses and property so as to receive thousands of dollars.

Worse still, when they organised the public to form committees to control the compensation funds, some greedy leaders of these groups, who lost nothing, received large amounts of money instead of the victims, whose crying was ignored and who received nothing for their losses. The old people, the widows, the handicapped; nobody helped them. The training for overseas students was not funded as agreed, and the students were suspended. Even the rents for overseas high commission offices and residences were not paid and were only settled by the countries concerned.

During the conflict, some of the militias roamed the streets of Honiara, taking cars, housebreaking, shooting, raping and breaking into shops to take goods for themselves and their families. While the MEF were retaliating and people were dying, there did not seem to be this problem. They defended us and we controlled them, and without the bunkers we would have been killed. Our advice had been that we would supply them with food and that they should not look to the politicians, but suddenly there was a certain well-known man, whom I won't name, in a red HiLux with bags of rice, going into Gilbert Camp. The leaders there, Moses Su'u and James Tatau, were defending us and doing nothing wrong. As I see it, the militant commanders didn't intend to steal, because the government had told them to work at saving Honiara from destruction. They maintained strong discipline, saying that the militants mustn't steal. So Su'u shot his brother-in-law Sau in the leg because he stole from the house of Kwan, the member of parliament for Central Honiara. They shot up Kwan's house at Kovale and when they rang for the police I heard the radio message telling them to come quickly, because I was standing in for the sergeant at the desk of the Central Police

Station. Inspector Maelanga went, and they shot him too, their 'brother'. He fell and the police fell down and rolled out. At that time Malaitans of the police and the Field Force had become militants, and Maelanga was also a militant commander. When they shot him I heard the message come back, 'Oh, it's Sau and Ko'olangi and the others.' Su'u was angry, so he ran to the border, because they would escape that way back to their houses, and he met Ko'olangi there. Su'u knocked Ko'olangi down and he ran off, and he shot Sau in the leg. This happened in 2001, after the fighting had finished, when those people came along pretending to be soldiers but stealing.

Sam Maesatana, son of my elder brother John Maesatana, was someone who suggested turning the militants into special constables, when he was chatting with Kemakeza, the deputy prime minister. Kemakeza's house was the militants' house. They would eat there and drink beer with Kemakeza and say they were his 'sons'. When the government found the police were unsuitable, they came to me to look after security, so that's how I know. Some nights Moses Su'u, Toloakalo, Wale and others would sit at the bottom of a mango tree and drink beer and Sam would come by. He talked with Kemakeza, who said that the police had no power, only the militants. Then Sam said, 'What if you turn the criminals into special constables, so that criminals are facing criminals?' Sam was looking ahead, and this was his plan. 'They are restless. What if you give them uniforms and training. That will bring peace and if any militants do something they can be punished and put in prison.' Because when they became an armed force they were disorderly, causing damage, firing off guns and misbehaving. So Kemakeza said, 'Oh, good idea.'

Most of the supreme commanders were honest men, but then somehow some of them began to take advantage. They said, 'This doesn't apply to me,' and those uncaring attitudes caused us big problems. The commanders asked the government for money to pay the militants who were doing the work, as I know because I was working for Kemakeza when he was deputy prime minister. He would give lots of money to Moses Su'u, filling up his bag with fifty-dollar notes, then Su'u would say, 'I'm going to pay the boys,' although he didn't pay anyone. Su'u, Malcolm Lake and Jimmy Rasta took millions of dollars from the government to pay their men, and for themselves, because they had put them in power. At that time anything could be compensation. The government would meet it, so everyone claimed. This was not tradition, but a problem caused by the government itself, because they promised the people and then passed this Sol Law, as they called it, to pay a high compensation of a hundred thousand dollars for anyone who was killed. When we went to the bank we would see them taking out thousands of dollars by cashing cheques signed by government ministers. When I worked on security in the ANZ and Westpac banks I saw this with my own eyes. They would come with big wads of money and I'd ask, 'How about a little for fish and chips, mate?' 'Eh, uncle, this is all budgeted for.' They were lying, but you know these selfish people who think they are somebody. They had bags of fifty-dollar notes, went around with girls, made women pregnant in the hotels, took a new wife, left the old one, took two or three more.[1] Most of the MEF supreme commanders are now remarried.

Elsewhere, as I have seen on television, the president of Yugoslavia did such things during his reign in the 1990s, then when his government fell the man was in a cell and appeared in court with sixty-six counts against him. I told them, 'You can do this now, but law and order will return. Don't act up, you have finished fighting, so stop.' This practice of giving money to everyone was not just because they demanded it, but because the government promised it. If they needed it, the government was there: 'Yes, fill up the bags.' Money, money, money. Kemakeza would go to the bank and there he was with the money. Once my wife saw her 'brother' Toloakalo, a militant commander, taking bundles of fifty-dollar notes, and she asked him, 'Brother, give me a bit for the bus fare.' He just laughed and went, and we had fed him when he was small. He was sick and almost died and I took him in my truck, fed him until he was grown, then I asked for a girl to marry him, made the feast for him, and from the time he was married he didn't come to see me. So when his 'sister' asked him and he took no notice, I was really surprised.

When things became really serious in 2001, there was a time when Robert Folota and I were coming from 'Aoke to Honiara on the Ramos, when suddenly we saw a speed-boat. It was the dinghy of a government patrol boat and they had put a machine-gun on a tripod at the front. They hailed out, 'Stop the ship! Stop the ship!' It was Jimmy Rasta holding the gun, with Malcolm Lake and others, and the men came on board and stopped the ship for two or three hours. We drifted on the sea so they could look for a man who, they said, had set fire to buildings in Honiara. They suspected he was on the ship, but he wasn't there. When I spoke up they almost shot me, as they wouldn't recognise anyone, and I said to one of them, the son of John Fo'ogao, 'Eh, son, why not let the ship go on, for us passengers, and search as we go? The children are crying for food and we are short of time.' But they said, 'Hey, what do you want?' They wanted to shoot me, and Robert Folota said, 'Shoot me, man!' The militants had replaced the police, authorised by the government. They didn't find the man and allowed us to go, but it was night by the time we reached Honiara, with the children crying on the ship. I witnessed this with my own eyes; they held guns, wouldn't listen, and threatened to kill us. It was too much, and it was wrong.

The man they wanted was Samani, who lived at Faugwari in West Kwara'ae near Langalanga, towards the Kwaimanafu River. They suspected it was he who had used petrol to burn the buildings of Abraham Eke and Placemaker's, opposite Honiara Central Market. It was because he didn't like businessmen and he was a delinquent. That's why the militants wanted to catch him, and later on they caught him in Malaita, brought him to Honiara and put him in custody in Rove Prison, then killed him in prison.[2]

Besides working for the chiefs, I was also a long-serving special constable in the Royal Solomon Islands Police, and with this training and experience I set up a contract firm, K.H.M. Risk Professional Security Services. So I witnessed the disorderly behaviour of some of the militants and the way I dealt with them shows the importance of working with our traditional culture. For instance, I was providing security for the directors of AusAid and the Solomon Islands Water Unit, and I taught my sons to guard their places so people wouldn't run away with their cars, damage their houses or threaten them. Then in 2000 Charles Dausabea and others in the government caucus saw that the police were unable to maintain security because the guns were in the hands of the militants. Some Kwaio Malaitans had taken a load of timber from the house of Deputy Prime Minister Kemakeza and emptied the house of all its furniture, in broad daylight. Johnson Koli, Minister of Home Affairs, and Joses Tafua, Minister of Infrastructure, also had their houses robbed. So they took me on to work for them, while things were getting worse with Prime Minister Ulufa'alu under house arrest, because my work for traditional culture gave me a technique to deal with things. If someone approached, I'd go and talk with them to facilitate a meeting: 'Sons, brothers, before you see this man you have to do so and so.' 'Oh, alright, that's good.'

However, there were times when people came to fight. One night six armed Guadalcanal militants came to see Kemakeza to demand money and my son said, 'No, come back in the day, it's too late.' One man swore: 'You're just a little kid,' and wanted to fight but my son raised the alarm, his brothers came and they ran away. Then there were some Guadalcanal chiefs who fled because Harold Keke had issued a decree to kill them for discussing peace in the Marau area, against his wishes. He accused them of betraying him to the police, so they were sheltering in a house provided by their member of parliament, Johnson Koli, Minister of Home Affairs, and I provided security. When a Malaita man with a knife forced his way in, my boys had him arrested. This is where my technique came in, as a chief. Through the Solomon Islands Traditional Culture and Environmental Conservation Foundation I was well known to both the Malaita and Guadalcanal militants and when they came, I talked and they listened. This is how I worked, protecting ministers for more than a year, until peace came. I only stopped in July 2001 after they had not paid me for six months, and the police took over where I left off.

One night towards the end of 2000, while I was working for the police, two trucks of MEF militants, fully armed, attacked the Central Police Station, while my 'brother' Henry Ifu'i and I were there with six others. I jumped in front of them and said, 'Hey, we're all Malaitans here. If you strike us, what are we to do? If you have a complaint, go to the prime minister. We're just doing our job.' They meant to take over the station and I was afraid that, if they did, they'd take over every station in the country; Kukum, Naha and the headquarters at Rove. It was through our tradition that I made the night turn out well. I talked to them in Kwara'ae language, because the dialects of Malaita understand each other. Their commander was a To'abaita man and he said, 'Oh, if you're serious, maybe you lot should get out now. We have to destroy the station, but we won't burn it or kill any police officers or raid the shotguns.' We were worried for Inspector Johnson Taupa because he was from Guadalcanal, so we made him run away and he went to the King Solomon Hotel. Inspector Kabai escaped onto the roof, jumped off and was injured. The rest of us ran away into the night, dropped into the storm drains, and the trucks came past on each side. Eventually we came back, guided by our radios and mobile phones, running and jumping into the drains, until I spoke to the parliament building and all the police came down; Commandant Kalisalo, Inspector Masae and the officers sleeping in the police quarters. We assembled and walked down and the MEF drove off in the trucks, taking out the iron gates of the police compound. Our commandant shouted, 'What's the matter with you?' They just laughed. 'Sorry boss, we're just mad because the government hasn't paid us, and we're playing around with you. We're just showing the prime minister what we think.' We shouted in anger, but they were gone. They had trashed the whole station, the computers and radios, taken our spare uniforms and put all the desks in the middle of the main road. The government agreed to pay all seven of us twenty-five thousand dollars compensation, but we never received it.

During 2001 I was transferred to the Harbourmaster's police post in the Port Authority compound, where we ensured the security of the ships, the traffic and the passengers. Then one day when I was in the office on the 2.00 p.m. shift, someone came running to say that MEF militants had cut the locks of the compound to creep into Port Cruz wharf. We ran to the scene and the trucks had banged open the gates. I saw one of them go to another truck, knock down the owner, take the keys and drive off. I could see they were from north Malaita, but one of the drivers said to me, 'This is Moses Su'u taking his turn.' As I watched, Su'u ordered Special Constable Musia to open the gate and I shouted, 'Don't open the gate! You are the law, outsiders can't order you about!' But the officer, who was also from Kwara'ae, was afraid and started sliding the gate open. This was Su'u's chance, but I stopped him and when he saw me he said, 'Oh, I give up.' Because I am in fact his uncle as well as his cousin and we are of the same place. So Su'u said, 'Oh, let's go, the sheriff's already here.' He drove up to me and said, 'Oh, sorry uncle. I'm just showing my mind because that man Wilfred Akao criticised me on the radio yesterday.' Su'u was operating a security contract for the Y-Sato company for journalists in Honiara, but Akao, the deputy commissioner of police, said he was not authorised. As he drove out I said, 'Su'u, you have to understand, I'm looking after this area and it's an important resource for our development. We want the ships to arrive to pay revenue to the government so the public services can keep going. You climbed to the top of the tree to gather its fruit, but what you have done now is slide right down to the bottom.' If I hadn't been there I can say for sure that the Port Authority would have been another place in Honiara to burn, because they were armed with pump-action guns and other dangerous weapons. That's how I used the power of the chiefs to defuse the kind of incidents which happened at that time.

During the conflict a man counted the time of day and was lucky to live until night; it was a terrible time. There was a dangerous area called the 'borderline', because it bordered all the roads going up to Kobito, Mount Austen, Kola'a Ridge and Gilbert Camp, on the border of town. If a truck came they'd shoot at it, demand money or even kill someone. One night they seized a Guadalcanal man there, took off all his clothes, tied him to a standpipe and beat him up. In the morning people coming to catch the bus released him, took him to hospital and sent him home. This was youths of the MEF living nearby. One night while working at the Port Authority I went off duty at 2.00 a.m. and rang for a police truck to take me home, but the police were afraid of all the arms in the hands of the militants. So I told them to drop me off near the borderline and the boss said, 'These people will kill you,' but I said, 'It's alright, you go back.' So the people came running, to kill me or demand money or something, and I moved boldly towards them, shining my torch at myself. When they saw me they were taken aback: 'Hey, father, don't come like this; if we had shot from a distance you'd be dead.' I said, 'Why would you shoot?

Have you got enemies here? Whoever it was, it wouldn't be an enemy. It's senseless, what you're doing, and quite outside our tradition.' So they just laughed stupidly, I gave them twenty dollars, and they said, 'Oh, maybe we'll just leave you down at the store.' 'Who are you leaving? Go away.' That was their useless way. Because I was recognised at the borderline, I was able to stand up against the criminal behaviour of the former militants by traditional means.

Everyone was affected by the conflict, and it turned 'brother' against 'brother'. One evening in 2002, my son William Maelaua had been to do some work up at CDC in east Guadalcanal, and he came back to his house crying and calling for me. 'When we went down today in the truck, they had a road-block at the Malibu bridge and when the truck stopped I saw that Selwyn Saki was in command. They asked if anyone in the truck was Malaitan and told them they were going to kill them. I was frightened, because there was just me and my brother Michael, and they said "Those two men are Malaitan." When the Guale militants wanted to take us from the truck, Michael jumped down and they chased him and beat him up. But fortunately I stayed in the truck and prayed to Selwyn Saki: "Oh please brother, save me, because I don't know anything about all this." So he gave a word of command and they let go of me, and the truck took me away.' William was badly shaken, because they had pointed guns at him and slapped him.

I knew Selwyn Saki because his father Samuel Saki was president of the chiefs of west Guadalcanal, and I had slept over with him when we were dealing with a marriage case, with our president Silas Sangafanoa. So after the peace agreement, Selwyn Saki approached me in Kukum market and we talked.

I said, 'I want to thank you for saving my boy Michael.' Because Michael had told him he was living with me at Windy Hill, and I was a 'father' of his who had dealt with all the chiefs. So Selwyn Saki told me that the conflict was caused by the people of the Weather Coast. 'It is not us who were expelling you all. We have given you land, you eat here and we work together. But Harold Keke and his group came and expelled and killed you all, and pushed us into it. That's why I'm a commander in the IFM, but I also save Malaitans.'

Not long after I spoke with him, they killed Selwyn Saki at Mount Austen. A group of MEF came in a truck and waited for him at his house, saying they would go together to get money to pay their militias, because this was after the peace, and they were friends. So they took him in the truck and later killed him, at the Japanese war memorial on Mount Austen, and threw him down the hill. The man who they said killed him received a life sentence. He is a cousin of mine and when he was small he once cooked for me and Ben Burt on Malaita.

In my view the conflict was promoted by the politicians. We call it a political issue when we see the prime minister of the day under house arrest and another prime minister coming in. That's the daylight politics, but there was also a plan by politicians who wanted to take over land in Guadalcanal because they thought they could get millions of dollars from developing and investing in it. Both Malaita and Guadalcanal men planned this, together, and the Chinese were involved too. The politicians favour the Asians, allow them to get lots of land, get citizenship before they should, and obtain bank loans. They just have to phone, 'I want so and so.' 'Oh, take it.' 'You approve it?' 'I approve it.' Everyone knows and everyone talks about it.

This is very hard to say, but I know these people well, so I'm only talking in general. It's very bad, 'brothers' ruining 'brothers'. The Guadalcanal rebels were helped by Malaitan politicians who provided things like outboard motors, fibreglass canoes and drums of petrol, for them to use. They wanted the Guadalcanal youths to evict the Malaitans so as to take over the land the Malaitans had been using. I saw this and it was evil; ruining their own relatives and countrymen. Later they came to support the MEF because they knew that they'd be killed too, as Malaitans. They thought they could play with matches, but had a shock when it flared up, then said, 'What about my property, my children?' when it was too late. It was fortunate that the MEF took up position and defended the town, but then the politicians got involved, twisted it and asked them to bring down Ulufa'alu's government.[3]

One reason for this was that Ulufa'alu's government took over all the alienated land which Lever's Pacific Plantations and the missions had occupied on Guadalcanal. From Lambe to Rere, they returned it to the indigenous land-holders, but as they were unsure who held what land, they left it in the hands of Guadalcanal Province to hand it over to the right people. The government also paid Lever's, which was wrong, since Lever's had already used up the wealth of the land. And the government said we were living under temporary occupation licences, although we should be the land-holders ourselves. These things contributed to bringing down the government.

1. Note that extra-marital sex is a cardinal sin in Malaita (*usu'a*, often translated as 'sin'), which discredits a man politically as well as morally.
2. Patteson Saeni, a former police officer, was later convicted of killing Samani (Allen 2013).
3. Allen (2013) summarises allegations that national politicians were complicit in the Guadalcanal uprising and the 2000 coup, in support of vested interests which were threatened by Ulufa'alu's government.

MEF and IFM militants celebrating the Townsville Peace Agreement together in Honiara in October 2000. (*Solomon Star* 24-10-2000)

10
ENDING THE CONFLICT

The first attempt to resolve the conflict was when Rabuka[1] came as an envoy to Solomon Islands in June 1999, and the MEF and IFM both ignored him. Then there was the Balasuna agreement with the inhabitants of Guadalcanal and Malaita, who agreed and signed but did not return their arms. Then there was the Marau agreement in July 1999, and nothing happened. Then the Panatina agreement was signed on 12 August 1999, and the two parties did not respond. Then finally there was the Townsville Peace Agreement on 15 October 2000, when the militant leaders went by plane to Australia but came back and many still kept their guns.

I remember well the peace march celebrations with the two warring parties after the signing of the Townsville Peace Agreement. As they drove up and down in Honiara for about a week, I saw tears drop from the eyes of the leaders as they greeted each other, hopping from one truck to another. People were standing on both sides of the road, from White River to King George Six School, shouting and weeping and happy to be released from fear. Andrew Te'e, a 'brother' of Harold Keke, told me he agreed both sides should give up and co-operate with the government and police to stop us killing each other, because we are one people, one nation, with one God and one country. Moses Su'u said he was no longer interested in fighting the Guadalcanal people, because they had been trying to secure Honiara from destruction by Harold Keke. Keke and his group had no further intention of entering Honiara, although they strictly forbade Malaitans from freely investing in their land, as in the past.

After they returned from Townsville, the leader of a civil society group from England met with the militant supreme commanders and said, 'From tomorrow all of you who joined the police as paramilitaries are suspended. Return your arms tomorrow and then you can re-apply for your positions.' But they wouldn't listen and Kili, who had somehow become a police superintendent, said, 'Who cares for you?' because they had already broken the law, recruited illegally and handed out arms. So I said to some who were 'sons' of mine, 'If that's how it is, go back to the Townsville people. We police can't tell you or you'll kill us.' So they checked with them and a week later they came back and were more humble.

That's when it started to quieten down, we police were back in position and things returned to normal. Restoring law and order was not easy. When the MEF militants were allowed to open up the police armoury by the government and equipped themselves for battle against the IFM, the Police Field Force joined with the MEF, while most of the regular police walked out and Guadalcanal officers were sent to stations in other provinces. Some high-ranking officers went overseas on training courses and the rest were supervising by using police vehicles or remaining in the stations. There were fewer of us special constables because the government had placed us in the front line on a salary of just three hundred and seventy-two dollars per month. Special constables were supposed to be volunteers but their duties were made compulsory, without the necessary equipment such as radios, handcuffs, teargas and transport, or the arms and military training of the Police Field Force. At every post in Honiara it was special constables who were officers in charge, men who were fully trained and of long service. They even gave us the same uniform as the regular police officers.

The problem was when they recruited MEF militants, without training in the law, as special constables. Some of these men had no respect for law and order, just dressing in police uniform and misbehaving, being drunk in uniform, while driving police vehicles and when returning to their stations. When I first became a special constable in the 1980s we were under strict discipline, we had to wear uniform to drive a police vehicle and not smoke, chew betel or sit around while in uniform. But these improperly recruited special constables did not even know basic police procedures such as using a notebook, taking statements, and what section of the law to charge under for the magistrate's court. Now, when we set out to deal with incidents, instead of criminals we would find special constables drinking in public. One so-called sergeant was drinking in the market and when we arrested his countryman he threw a bottle at our heads and the paramilitaries grabbed the culprit, put him in a vehicle and escaped. This kind of thing ruined the reputation we had gained from many years' service. In addition, our leaders took police vehicles for themselves, pretending to have paid for them by sending a few thousand dollars to the ministry. Without vehicles for the police to enforce the law, our work was wrecked and we became demoralised and frustrated, without any support from the government.

As a police officer in the Special Constabulary who came forward to provide security for the country, manning various police posts in Honiara, I saw for myself how, during the conflict, people were living in fear and depending upon the police. During the darkest period of the conflict, I was ordered to the Chinatown police post as officer in charge. One of many incidents I remember was when three To'abaita militants called into a Chinese shop, went behind the counter and took three cartons of beer from the fridge. The Chinese man and wife shouted for police assistance and I rushed to the scene with two of my officers and ordered the militants to return the beer. They responded by pulling out knives, but we applied necessary force to push them to the floor, hit them and kicked them, and returned the beer to the shopkeepers. I contacted our police truck to take them to the referral hospital, they were admitted, and when they were discharged they appeared in court and were sentenced to prison.

Even as a police officer, I tried to use traditional methods. Once in 2002, when a woman special constable, Margaret Siu, and I were approaching Central Market, people shouted to us, 'Police! Police! People are fighting, with knives!' I ordered my colleague to stand at the main road to contact our police truck, while I jumped in among them. They were chasing a Lau man who had asked a married woman for sex and indecently touched her, so I applied necessary force to push down the accused, then stopped a taxi and asked the driver to take him to the Central Police Station. After he had left, I ordered the armed men to stand still and talked with them to quieten their anger, and they listened. When the police truck arrived I took the woman's husband only to the station and settled the matter in the traditional way. The man who had propositioned the woman told the husband he was sorry and I made a decision that he should give restitution to the woman of three hundred dollars. When he gave the money to the husband, they shook hands and I released him from the station.

We had no reason to know that a security force would be coming to the country, but by this time we thought things were returning to normal. Companies were about to resume development of the country, schools, clinics and hospitals were re-opening, and the police were working well. Then on 4 February 2003 the government demobilised eight hundred and thirteen special constables on the grounds that they were involved with the militants in disorderly and criminal conduct. This degraded the name and morale of the police. The foreign ministers of New Zealand and Australia, Bill Gough and Alexander Downer, had both accused the special constables of being involved with criminal elements. It was disgraceful that they should make blanket statements covering everyone in the police without distinguishing those of us who had passed out from the police training school and worked to maintain law and order. This caused great frustration and discouragement to those of us who had spent fifteen to twenty years in the force. The government should have considered how the genuine

Michael Kwa'ioloa shaking hands with MEF militants at their formal withdrawal from the Chinatown police post in November 2000. (*Solomon Star* 6-11-2000)

special constables had acted during the conflict, when they placed them in the front line, at police posts where the regular police seldom showed their faces. Special Constable James Maniteta was shot dead at the Foxwood police post, and Basiota had his jaw shot away when special constables in the rapid response unit manned Gold Ridge to secure the mining company. I myself was officer in charge of the Central Magistrates Court, protecting the legal premises and records against people who wanted to kill us, and at the Chinatown police post, where we had to control the MEF paramilitaries who were extorting goods from the Chinese businesses. Special constables, myself and others, manned police posts at Henderson Airport, the Harbourmaster's, King George Sixth High School, and the Central Market, where we regularly arrested people trying to steal from the sellers and buyers. During that dark and dangerous period from 2000 to 2003, we special constables maintained law and order as well as we could. The government failed to recognise procedures or regulations, so there was some difficulty before the demobilised special constables agreed to accept the conditions and compensation offered by United Nations Development Programme.[2]

The way to solve the problem of law and order would have been to negotiate reconciliation between the families of the militants of Guadalcanal and Malaita. When the special constables were demobilised, we knew that the peace in the country was a result of our hard work during the last two years. The prime minister and his cabinet should simply have come down to negotiate with the militants to find out their demands, treat them as human beings like the rest of us, explain that the government had no money, and look at both sides of the problem. However, it was simpler to arrange to give the militants money, both IFM and MEF, costing millions of dollars. Prime Minister Kemakeza promised to pay the MEF militants one hundred and fifty thousand dollars per head for their hard work, but as time went on there was no sign of this happening. So the militants gathered at the Art Gallery to march to the prime minister's office and demand the promised money. But the night before the march, Kemakeza left for Australia on a Hercules plane sent by the Australian government, and that was when he requested international assistance to maintain law and order.

On the invitation of the Solomon Islands government, a peacekeeping force of both police and army, the Regional Assistance Mission to Solomon Islands (RAMSI), arrived on 24 July 2003, taking over the dangerous duties of us special constables. When the four military planes arrived, people were frightened because they flew in formation and they thought they were going to drop bombs on us. The noise of their engines when they landed at Henderson Airport sounded like a bomb blast. People were amazed to see the soldiers in camouflage uniforms step out smartly, on alert in case the MEF or IFM attacked them, and move into position ready to act. For at least an hour there was silence and then army vehicles drove out full of armed personnel, frightening everyone. Most of them set up tents near the airport, while the rest went to bases and rented accommodation in Honiara. From the next day the military were standing everywhere, fully armed, while their patrol vehicles drove in a long line around every road in town, all for nothing, without arresting anyone. They seemed like tourists, being paid to visit all around Honiara.

People saw all this as very funny, for they should have arrived at the height of the conflict, or earlier to prevent it, while we special constables had been forced to face the consequences and had managed to get everything under control. Often when there was an incident and we called them on their emergency phone, they did not attend. Perhaps they were afraid someone would shoot at them, and if they did manage to attend they would come in large numbers, fully armed in several vehicles. They were unable to remove the criminal elements in Honiara as they would wait an hour or two so the criminals escaped before they arrived. We police would have attended automatically, in force, arrested those who broke the law, and brought them to court for the law to take its course, but they were just marking their hours and waiting for their pay. I can speak from experience because I was co-ordinating security for the RAMSI base at the Guadalcanal Beach Resort, the helicopter base and the police posts for two years until March 2006.

I think the way RAMSI came in was a big mistake. It should have happened straight after the Townsville Peace Agreement, and the government should have had parliamentary approval before forwarding the request to the Australian government, because as one man's decision it degraded the country's democratic system.[3] During the dark and fearful days of the conflict between the MEF and IFM, the government took no such measures to maintain law and order. The police had worked to put an end to the conflict and foreign intervention should not have been necessary. In other parts of the world, peacekeeping takes place in the midst of the conflict, not after an agreement such as Townsville. I cannot support it to disarm the militants, when the prime minister himself asked the Malaitans not to

Michael Kwa'ioloa (on the right) at a vehicle check with an Australian police officer from RAMSI.

give up arms because Keke was threatening the government, and the government had made the mistake of arming the militants in the first place, creating the criminal element which did all manner of evil against the nation.

Worse still, Harold Keke was oppressing and even murdering his own people for months and the government took no action to prevent it. As the government declared, twenty-four men were murdered by Keke's militants, plus ten Kwaio men who went to capture him. The former IFM supreme commander Andrew Te'e says fifty men were murdered by Keke in this area of Guadalcanal. It seems to me that if Keke had come down to negotiate with the government and sort things out, the government could have met his demands. But Keke feared he would be captured, tortured or even shot dead, so he wouldn't give up. He killed his own people who helped the police and used about fifty followers to enforce his will and take the law into his own hands. Keke used the *vele* sorcery of Guadalcanal for security, which was very powerful in those rebel areas where he and his followers were living.

Although the Guadalcanal chiefs, headed by Moro,[4] were negotiating with Keke, they could only have succeeded by working with the Malaita chiefs. Keke was using Malaitans who had married Guadalcanal women to kill Guadalcanal people, because the Guadalcanal men were not fierce enough. If the leaders of the Moro Movement had worked with the Malaita chiefs, they might have convinced the Malaita rebels to withdraw from Keke and return things to normal. I believe that it should have been possible for his commanders to work with the church leaders and houses of chiefs to calm Keke and bring him to the negotiating table. When Harold Keke saw the end approaching he made his own people kneel down on the beach and said that if the troops came for him they'd all be killed with him. He was desperate because the government would not deal with his demands, and his own people fled, their houses were burned, and they came into Honiara for help.

We prayed that Harold Keke would withdraw his rebellion and when he heard that RAMSI was about to arrive, on 5 July 2003 he asked for a ceasefire. Keke was arrested by RAMSI on a visit to the Weather Coast on 13 August and he and his supreme commanders were charged with murder, arms smuggling and transgression of the Townsville Peace Agreement. One of the supreme commanders of the IFM, Joseph Sangu, was arrested for being drunk and disorderly in Honiara market and then, while in police custody, he was charged with several counts of murder. Then later an MEF supreme commander called James Kili, who had been promoted to superintendent in the police after the conflict, was arrested in connection with shooting incidents and other things, including financial matters within the police force. Then a founder of the MEF, Moses Su'u, was arrested on suspicion of murdering the IFM supreme commander Selwyn Saki, but he was found not guilty and released. Other militant leaders remanded in custody include Andrew Te'e, Alex Bartlett and Roland Timo, as well as some high-ranking police officers. Deputy Police Commissioner Alfred 'Akao was sentenced to six years in prison. When other men are brought to trial they may reveal how the leaders of this country were implicated in the creation of the conflict, and I hope they too will face justice.

People also depend on leaders to represent them, and after the Townsville Peace Agreement we chiefs assisted by calling on the MEF commanders to collect arms from their men, with the result that many weapons were destroyed. We also worked through SITCECF to help deal with the problems of the country. In December 2001 the representative of United Nations High Commissioner for Human Rights (UNHCHR) contacted SITCECF to hold a discussion comparing customary laws and human rights law. They took me on as a facilitator and co-ordinator of Solomon Islands culture to bring us together in a convention to work on unwritten tradition, as traditional culture is my speciality. No-one has worked on this for the country in general, but I had done such work with Ben Burt and the East Kwara'ae chiefs and visited other provinces to select traditional dance groups for the twentieth anniversary of independence celebrations in 1998. UNHCHR planned to co-ordinate the provinces, but when they asked me they were surprised to find I already had everyone lined up. We held a series of conferences, workshops and lectures in February and March 2003, bringing together twenty-five chiefs from all provinces. As custodians of tradition, these chiefs contributed what their ancestors had passed on to them, to advise the government on amendments to the law. Gregory Balke, the UNHCHR advisor, and Messach Maebiru, MP for Central Honiara, recommended that traditional law should be written down, so when we conferred I wrote up the conclusions on my office computer, photocopied the documents at the parliamentary Hansard office, and distributed copies to everyone who attended the conference.

Because all the provinces were represented, we were a unifying group. Everyone got to know each other and we really fulfilled our aims in working out plans we had previously been unable to make. At the official opening in the Ministry of Home

Affairs, the ministry told the House of Chiefs that the room and the office were theirs to use every Friday until the end of the year. I was surprised that although they received no money, all the representatives kept on coming of their own accord. They could see how we had been brought to our knees by corruption, which is why SITCECF was recognised and we chiefs came together to fulfil tradition. This promoted our organisation, as it was we who had done the work.

After this, AusAid facilitated another workshop at the Art Gallery, reaching out to all the provinces to share the conclusions agreed by the House of Chiefs in Honiara. We proposed a system of tribunals, selected by local clans, to discuss and resolve land disputes and make decisions on them. Because it is the clans who know the landmarks, signs and boundaries of the land, the genealogies of the ancestral ghosts worshipped there, and the names which identify the land as belonging to a particular clan, family or individual. From there, we commented on parliamentary land law proposals, because the politicians often make drafts for laws which contradict the traditional laws from the past. We had contributed to previous acts of parliament, using our expertise to set things in order, for everyone in the country. If the government would give financial support, we could go further and set up a centre for documenting customary law, as was planned and initiated by UNHCHR. The knowledge of each part of the country would be compiled and published, preserving valuable information from the local experts for present and future generations to learn and use the knowledge of our ancestors.

At the same time we Malaitans formed a new organisation to support our people in Honiara and Malaita, the Malaita Ma'asina

Forum. During September 2003 we heard repeatedly from the chairmen of the Peace Monitoring Council and RAMSI that temporary occupation licence residents should move out from government land. But this affected the people who had come to work and had sought permission from the rightful land-holders in the settlements on the outskirts of Honiara since the 1950s and 1960s. It led Dr John Naitoro and others of us to bring together all the Malaitans in Honiara to discuss the matter at the Art Gallery. Seven hundred people attended that meeting and gave all kinds of views, and when we considered the matter it encouraged us to form a council. We organised people in Honiara from each electoral ward in Malaita to appoint a trustworthy person to the committee and they selected thirty-three persons from the wards throughout Malaita, including myself and John Maetia to represent Ward Sixteen in East Kwara'ae. The representatives chose the name Malaita Ma'asina Forum; Malaita is our people, *ma'asina* means brotherhood, and together as Malaitan 'brothers' our organisation is the forum.[5] We met weekly and called the public forum of Malaitans to explain our plans and hear their views, and then made representations to the government, RAMSI and other sectors. We did not come together to make war, but to settle things among our own people so that they would no longer take things for granted, as in the past. We were trying to organise ways to re-settle our militants in their home areas and create development for them. We wanted to find ways to help not only Malaitans but also the other ethnic groups of the country, so that we might live together without enmity in Honiara. That was the plan, but unfortunately, after the Forum was launched, its four senior officers began to organise things without consulting the rest of us.

One important case which SITCECF had to deal with was the ten Kwaio men killed by Harold Keke, and this is an example of the role of the chiefs in mediating the problems of the country. In June 2002 the government[6] sent ten men from Kwaio to the Weather Coast to assassinate Keke, which the Police Field Force were unable to do. They gave them a million dollars and when they came back they were to receive another million. They took seven high-powered weapons from the police armoury at Rove and a two hundred horsepower boat belonging to Jimmy Rasta which the government hired. I know this from a document which journalists gave to the police. The government believed the Kwaio ghosts were very strong so it would rain when they went at dusk and they would be hidden from Keke, so they could easily get him. That's the kind of spirit they believed the Kwaio had.

Kalisto was a life prisoner who had escaped from Rove prison and hidden in the inland of East Kwaio, and because he was a killer they took him on as leader of the group. His father 'Inisusu was a senior tabu-speaker of Kwaio, so it was he who offered the pig sacrifice. The ghosts said, 'Go, all of you, and you will succeed,' so Susu and his sons came by plane from Atoifi in East Kwaio. But when the Kwaio arrived in Honiara, some of them defiled themselves by going with women and drinking. What kind of ghost would look after men like that?[7] They got drunk and boastful, showing off their money in fifty-dollar notes: 'How much for a betelnut? What kind of money is this?' A chief called Martin Maratino from Kwaio answered, 'Hey, we pay fifty cents for a betelnut. Leave off, we are ashamed of you. Brothers, where did you get these bags of fifty-dollar notes?' Then on Friday 7 June they set out in the boat for the Weather Coast, led by a man from Bougainville. As I understand it he was Harold Keke's man, who had lived on the Weather Coast, and he betrayed them. They were dropped off at Harold Keke's village and taken to be questioned, and Keke identified a man called Padro who had joined the Field Force, because Keke was ex-Field Force too. 'Eh, these men are from Kwaio. The government sent them.' So they questioned them, tortured them, cut their hands off, killed them all and buried them all in one grave.[8]

So then the paramount chief of the Kwaio Fadanga, Maenaa'adi, with his secretary Dick Kolosu and the former member of parliament for West Kwaio, George Luilamo, brought a delegation of thirty-two men from East and West Kwaio to deal with the government sending the men to assassinate Harold Keke. Maenaa'adi came to my house on a Sunday afternoon with two young men: 'Michael, we have come but Prime Minister Kemakeza doesn't want to see us, nor does Ezekiel Alebua. I'm afraid the Kwaio may kidnap the two of them, take them to East Kwaio and kill them.' Then he said, 'For two weeks we have been staying with neighbours and going hungry every day at the Art Gallery, but they refuse to see us. We sent letters in advance to make an appointment, but they won't accept us. Even our members of parliament, John Garo and Alfred Sasako, refuse to help.' So I said, 'In that case I'll come tomorrow and set a time for you to meet them.'

On the Monday morning I brought Rocky Hardy Tisa and senior chief David Kwa'ite'e and went down to the Art Gallery. We talked with them and Luilamo said, 'We've tried everything without success. People are angry. The young men of Kwaio might behave foolishly.' Then I said, 'Who is leading you on the political side?' and he said, 'I am,' and I said, 'Oh, that's why it's not working, because your term has expired. John Garo is the man to lead this because he has replaced you in parliament.' He said he had gone to Alebua by himself and with that I said, 'If so, you stand back. That means all the two of you did was drink beer and he gave you some money. You should have taken a delegation including the paramount chief, the secretary and two or three of the dead men's people if you really meant to do something, but by yourself like this, you are finished. So from now on, you say nothing. Tomorrow I'll send a message to Australia for your East Kwaio MP Sasako to come,[9] and I'll send word home for John Garo to come, then on Wednesday you will see the prime minister, former Guadalcanal premier, Alebua and the present premier, Waeta Ben.'

Then the young men, who were drunk, got angry: 'Hey Kwa'ioloa, how can a man like you say we will see these two? Because for two weeks all the important men have tried and they won't hear us.' I replied, 'You can leave it to the big men, but I'm telling you that they will just cause difficulties.' 'In that case we'll burn the town, catch the two of them and kill them.' Then I said, 'That would be another story. You'll be part of Harold Keke's wrongdoing. You'll be put behind bars for life, and if you resist they'll kill you.' This made them angry. I said, 'You are helping the government.' 'Oh?' 'They want to ignore you all in case you realise it was they who sent them, because they are saying they didn't know about their going.' At the time I had this information about who sent them, but they didn't. They wanted the government to pay for their lives because a law had been passed for a hundred thousand dollars to be paid for those who were killed, and they said the law should include the ten Kwaio men because the government had paid for Malaitans killed in various parts of

Guadalcanal. What I said was, 'Alright, let me try it, but whether they will see you or not, come to the leaf shelter in front of parliament at ten o'clock on Wednesday, the day after tomorrow.' They doubted and criticised me but I said, 'I'm a chief so I'll try it, and we'll find out when we get up there.' Then Maenaa'adi confirmed, 'Kwa'ioloa is the boss. When we worked with the United Nations High Commissioner for Human Rights, it was he who spoke and they listened. He paid our allowances and food and sat with the computer in the room next to the high commissioner while we from the provinces worked with them.' That was what their paramount chief said.

When the talking was over David Kwa'ite'e, Rocky Tisa and I sat down on the concrete beside the Art Gallery and wrote a letter to the prime minister, saying, 'The SITCECF Foundation asks you, please put this demand to rest. If not, I have information that your life and Alebua's are at risk. Whether the government sent them or not, the law is that you must give a hundred thousand dollars per head for them. It is wrong that the government is paying for things that happened during the ethnic tension but not after they signed the Townsville Peace Agreement. So I'm writing to say that whether you agree with this or not, we want you to come and meet them, not to talk with them but to authorise us chiefs to talk with them. Don't be afraid, because you will have police security, but both of you come out at ten o'clock and speak about the following: One, apologise for not receiving the delegation. Two, say how they died and who sent them. Three, say the government has no money. Four, say you will accept that what the chiefs say the government will do. And lastly, that the chiefs should discuss and give a decision. Then go back and don't say more, or something unexpected will happen.

We will deal with it.' Then I went to see Barnabas Kalisalo, commander at the Central Police Station, and said, 'You police and us chiefs have worked together for a long time to deal with community matters, bring reconciliation and maintain the peace. How about writing a letter to support the SITCECF Foundation and say that the PM should see them?' So Kalisalo wrote a letter and that night David Kwa'ite'e handed both letters in at the prime minister's residence.

On the Wednesday we waited outside parliament, with the West Kwaio MP John Garo who had come from home, and the East Kwaio MP Alfred Sasako who had returned from Australia. At ten o'clock the prime minister and Ezekiel Alebua came out, they addressed the meeting and approved everything and quickly went away. Some wanted them to deal with things, but I said, 'No, they said the chiefs will do it on their behalf.' When they had gone we started to talk, and what do you know? They demanded two hundred thousand dollars per head! I said, 'Look, our tradition cannot be altered. I want to explain something. Everything which happened from October 2000 with the Townsville agreement was just wrong. If we place our tradition under the dispensation of that period, we are wrong too.' John Garo and Sasako supported me: 'Oh, what the co-ordinator of SITCECF says is very true, our brothers.' Then John Garo said, 'In our tradition, how much is it for a life?' Kwa'ite'e said, 'Ten red moneys. Their value is five hundred dollars for one red money, so it's only five thousand dollars.'[10] Sasako said, 'In your case it's fifty thousand dollars for all of them, not one at a hundred thousand.' The young relatives of the dead men started to pull off their shirts: 'You are all supporting the government!' Then I said, 'I heard you Sasako, when you said in the media, "A Kwaio man should not join the conflict," and it's true, the Kwaio did not fight, except for two or three fools who took it on themselves. During the conflict you forbade them but when it was over you went off and we had to see this! Okay, we have pushed ourselves into this modern custom, which the government has made into Sol-law.' That's the so-called Solomon Law that the government should pay a hundred thousand dollars per head for those killed. 'It doesn't apply to after the Townsville agreement, but because the High Commissioner for Human Rights authorised me to work on human rights law, I have authority to rule on any kind of traditional law, and I rule that the government must pay the hundred thousand dollars. We'll tell the government to give it, and if they won't we'll take them to court to find out who sent them.' We discussed until they agreed and it was alright.

So with that we handed it over to the chiefs to deal with Kemakeza and with Alebua at his office in the Guadalcanal Province Assembly headquarters. I left this mostly to Kwa'ite'e, but I advised that if we were charging a hundred thousand dollars per head the reasons should be: one, because they were allowed to use ammunition from the government armoury; two, because they had other support from we don't know who (although I had papers saying the government sent them); three, the government had already paid them one hundred thousand dollars each; four, the government arranged their transport, and so on. They argued for a month and eventually Kwa'ite'e said, 'Everyone come down tomorrow for the decision; the government and Guadalcanal Province have agreed.'

When I went down to the Art Gallery, everyone gathered and said, 'We agree to a hundred thousand dollars. The government must give it.' I said, 'No, according to tradition, in general it's not the government who should give it. If a man kills someone, it's he who must give it. Who killed them?' They replied, 'Harold Keke.' 'If so, it's Guadalcanal Province, with the former and present premiers, Alebua and Waita Ben, who will give them a hundred thousand dollars each.' The two of them said, 'We are willing, Michael; our government will give it.' I said, 'No, there are three steps to this case. This is the first, but there are two more before it is finished and then the Kwaio will be happy.' They said, 'If so, what do we do?' 'Your man Harold Keke killed them. That means Guadalcanal Province must pay for the ten lives with a million dollars.' 'But there is no money. Even the workers are not getting paid, or transport or electricity bills; there are power cuts.' I said, 'Okay, leave it for a day,' and we went to talk with the minister for the provinces. 'How much money do you give to pay the expenses of Guadalcanal Province?' 'Five hundred thousand per month. It's called the terminal grant.' So David Kwa'ite'e and I went back to Waeta Ben: 'It's a million dollars for your administration for two months. What if you close your offices for two months, your officers go home and eat tapioca, let the government give you the terminal grant, give it to the Kwaio, then you will be free of threats, kidnapping, and so on.' 'Hey, that's an idea!' So it was agreed, they raised the money, made out the cheque and issued the restitution, in January 2003.

After that the Kwaio took the million dollars, they were happy and it was finished. But they didn't pay me. Kwa'ite'e said, 'Sign an agreement for ten thousand dollars for Michael Kwa'ioloa's office, because he has dealt with all the paperwork and food at his own expense.' When I went to shake hands with

Waeta Ben he said, 'Oh, what you said has made an impression on me Mike, and I appreciate the way SITCECF handled all this. I'm happy with how we dealt with it, and the province has met all the costs.'

Then later on, in 2005, the Kwaio chiefs came again to my office in the National Museum, where Alex Rukia and I had put the SITCECF computer given by the New Zealand High Commission, with permission from Lawrence Foana'ota, the museum director. Six men arrived: 'Eh, you spoke about a second part, for our dead sons. Can you let us see the second part?' I said, 'What's bothering you? I was just speaking in general.' 'No, something has happened. Those six Melanesian Brothers they killed, they have already dug up their remains, as well as other countrymen of theirs who were killed there. But now RAMSI wants to dig up the ten, and they don't have permission from us. We don't want them to be dug up because we are not too unhappy. Leave them there. If they bring their bodies back we will be so sorrowful, unable to forget them. But we want you to explain to RAMSI.' I said, 'Alright. Now the thing is, they work according to their own procedures, and whether you like it or not they have to dig them up, so my advice is to let them. On the positive side, it will make you happy to have your relatives' remains come to you in a box so you can bury them somewhere accessible and take them back home. But we must maintain our tradition, so I'll write a letter to the commander of RAMSI.'

I wrote to tell him, 'You must understand that my tradition is my tradition. When you take those remains without the consent of the relatives you are in the wrong. In my tradition, in the past if I found that you had dug up my man, whether or not you killed him I would say you had killed him. I would whip you with rattan, shut your mouth, tie you up in front of my house, take leaf, stones, firewood and greens, then kill you and bake you and divide your flesh among the family whose man you had killed. So you will have to compensate for each man with five thousand dollars before you dig up their remains, and dig them in their presence.'

I signed and stamped it and told my in-law Tome, 'Go along to the police station there and say you want the Whiteman from England who has come as an advisor.' He went and had just returned when the telephone rang in the museum: 'Kwa'ioloa, telephone for you from RAMSI.' Was it good or bad? The six men all came to watch. 'Oh, hello Michael, good morning. We have only just heard about you and the SITCECF office, and your UN reference shows you are the way to deal with this. We agree, but wait until we have emailed to Canberra; we will have a reply in fifteen or thirty minutes.' I said, 'Don't worry, take your time,' but he said, 'No, this is an emergency, and the first time we have found this in this country.' During the thirty minutes we discussed it, I explained it all to the six of them and then they said, 'We will take one thousand dollars for each of them, but you should receive something too.' I said, 'Just make it five hundred, then you can take four thousand five hundred.' 'Well said!' Then after thirty minutes they rang back: 'Our head office in Canberra agrees for RAMSI to give five thousand dollars per head.' So I said, 'Alright, it's between you and them.' When they received the money they gave it to Sasako to divide up, as if it were pieces of pig-flesh.[11]

But Sasako didn't think of me either and they didn't give me ten cents. I worked so hard for nothing, and I didn't worry because I am a leader. I didn't ask for money, but my own money went on the typing, photocopying, my food and transport and expenses for them. They didn't know, so I said, 'Oh, what of it? Let it go.' David Kwa'ite'e, who had replaced Benjamin Ramo as senior chief, swore an oath that I should not work. He said, 'Alright, from today, because they didn't give even a little money for the first job, and now this one, for my younger brother Michael Kwa'ioloa, my boss on matters of tradition; the women of those who talked about restitution and have taken it twice already will shit on old man David Kwa'ite'e's head before you discuss anything else.' That's a big oath.[12] 'If you want to talk, give me five shell-moneys.' That's because I couldn't cry for myself, for working for nothing. Then my wife got angry with me: 'You make them rich but not yourself. They talk proudly, make chicken pens, get cars, build big houses. They won't look at me. When transport picks me up at the border, I see them and say, "Good morning" and get no "Good morning" back.'

I said, 'Oh, that's fine. When you all come back I won't do it.' Eventually, in November 2005, they came back again; 'Oh, Kwa'ioloa, we haven't heard about the third one yet.' I said, 'But the first time you gave nothing. The second caused a problem when Kwa'ite'e swore by his head. You have to take the women's shit from his head before you talk about it again.' 'Oh, in that case, how much is the restitution?' 'I don't know because it's not us who has a problem with him, but I can't work at present because I'm earning a bit of money for food and school fees for my children. I have spent so much of my time doing your work, you received the money and didn't give me ten cents, so I lost money. So I'm sorry; goodbye.' A woman called Ivery Aruana came crying to me and the next morning three of them came, and the next morning, and the next, all weekend, and I asked Kwa'ite'e to come. We discussed it all night until he agreed: 'So we'll do it.' I said, 'We must act as a model for the country, Kwa'ite'e. Regardless of the money, we must play our part in showing the importance of leadership by the chiefs as fathers of the nation.' Kwa'ite'e agreed: 'They can give restitution. Charge them five red moneys.' They came again in the morning and he told them, 'You must give me five red moneys before my brother writes any bit of a letter for them to talk to him again.' They said, 'How much for one red money?' Kwa'ite'e said, 'Five hundred.' 'Times five?' 'Two thousand five hundred.' They took the money and threw it on my carpet: 'Take it.' I said, 'Let Kwa'ite'e have it. Take the money back. You shouldn't think we want money; leave it.' We argued, they took it back, and next morning they came with money and threw it down again. I said, 'Kwa'ite'e, you have a thousand. Leave the money there. We'll make a start on the work.' Kwa'ite'e took one thousand five hundred for himself and five hundred for the office. I paid for paper and ink for the printer and everything for the computer with four hundred, and the two of us were ready to talk. 'In this document you can see me writing down the five points we must work on with the government. The first is the restitution payment, the second is opening it for me to start writing, the third is my research, the fourth is typing all the documents, and the last is making the submission; then the payment will come.' I said, 'Give me three months to work on this.'

After three months I was finding it difficult and eventually the son of this woman Aruana, Ben, came drunk with two men, wanting to attack me over the money. He said, 'Return it tonight, because three months is up and you haven't done anything.' I said, 'Do you think this is easy? This is a difficult one. The United Nations High Commissioner for Human Rights has already ruled out further payments for things which happened during the ethnic tension. Processing this after they have already signed it, when the men were disobeying the Townsville Peace Agreement; that's another matter.' I had done the writing the first time, and the second, when they took the remains. This was the third time, and when I started work Kwa'ite'e received a thousand dollars and I received five hundred for the office, so I continued. Then they agreed to give ten thousand for my office, because twice they had given nothing. I wanted Sasako to pay this, but he said, 'First give me the document which proves the government sent them.' When Sasako saw it he was angry and said, 'This man is a con-man. He hasn't come to see me during this three months.' Every time I went to his room in the Quality Motel, he was out. So after the three months they wanted to take the money back, but I said, 'I can pay the two thousand five hundred dollars back today, but which is the biggest, two thousand five hundred or a hundred thousand?' They gave in and said, 'Oh, leave it,' but that money was not for work but for cleansing the head of the man they would have defiled. They had to pay me separately for the work, and I told them I had done the work and met all my own costs and expenses. Sasako said he had reported me to RAMSI twice, but I was with RAMSI, had been asked to work with them, advising them and returning guns to them. When Sofu replaced Sasako as MP he told them to leave it to me.

The tradition of Malaita is that if you send someone to

follow your ideas and they kill him, it is you who is responsible. I completed my work on the killing of the ten Kwaio men, consulted with Paramount Chief 'Ubuni of the Kwaio Fadanga, and submitted the claim to the minister of Home Affairs.

---

[1] Siteveni Rabuka, the former coup-leader and prime minister of Fiji.
[2] The decision to disband the special constables as a unit seems to have been a tactical move to avoid the trouble which its militant members might have caused if they had been expelled individually. According to a personal communication from someone acquainted with the committee deciding on the dismissal or retention of the special constables, Kwa'ioloa did not meet educational criteria set for retention. Because of his good service record, he was put forward as a special case and there was a one-hour argument in the committee over whether he should be retained. In the end the criteria were upheld and he was dismissed.
[3] Although the prime minister may have given the impression of acting unilaterally, he was actually authorised by parliament.
[4] Moro was the visionary leader of a longstanding movement to reinstate traditional values in the Weather Coast.
[5] Ma'asina is also a reference to the Maasina Rul movement following the Second World War, although the Forum altered the spelling to another 'Are'are form of the word.
[6] The involvement of 'the government' in this incident should be taken to mean 'someone in the government'. Despite the general suspicion, 'government' complicity has not been conclusively proved.
[7] This is a common kind of explanation for the failure of dangerous enterprises, applied with the benefit of hindsight as in many Kwara'ae and Kwaio histories.
[8] Others say that the men were shot in their boat, which was drifting after the engine failed.
[9] Sasako, a journalist, was living much of the time in Australia.
[10] In fact, the sum of ten red moneys is more a tradition of Kwara'ae and north Malaita than of Kwaio, where payments in their local money may vary according to negotiations under an older Malaita practice.
[11] That is, as if apportioning meat at a feast.
[12] *Talitali*: an injunction meaning 'if you do so-and-so, it's as if you have defiled me in such-and-such a way.'

The Solomon Islands National Parliament building in 2008.
(Clive Moore photo)

11
LEADERSHIP AND POLITICS, TRADITION AND DEVELOPMENT

The relationship between Malaita and Guadalcanal is very special, because whatever development there was on Guadalcanal, Malaitans were involved in the work, and in the Second World War many died supporting the Americans, and when Honiara was developed as the administrative centre for the country, Malaitans were the workers for the building companies. From all this, I see Malaitans as the right arm of the Guadalcanal people. At present, in 2009, there is a struggle for reconciliation between the two groups, but when we chiefs hold meetings throughout the country we can see that a peaceful reconciliation has not happened yet. There has been reconciliation between church and government leaders, but the chiefs have not been involved, to speak and say that it has ended, so I can't see that working. There has been reconciliation between clans on Guadalcanal, which is good, bringing them back together as members of clan lands. But for the true reconciliation which I would like, I will make a few points.

A Malaitan who has paid for land should have proper rights because he spent money on it, so it should still belong to him, or they should make an agreement to repay him for the land. In cases where a Malaitan man has married into a Guadalcanal group who gave him land and he has done something in terms of development for their families, that means he still has the right to claim the land as his. Where they expelled some of these men, they should take them back and make them happy through reconciliation. There are Malaitans who have lived here since the Second World War, for whom going back home seems to have been very bad, whose properties such as cocoa and coconut plantations and farms were taken and are still used by Guadalcanal men. I don't blame those who allowed these people into the land, but do I blame those who came and stirred them up to turn against these people, so they lost all their good things and had to wander around back home without any money.

If we can straighten all this out, there should be a reconciliation to unite the people together, with the two sides killing pigs together, with taro and things to eat and then shaking hands. When this process is finalised, there should be a bylaw to restrict the areas of Guadalcanal where people who have paid can stay on their land or sell it, or whatever. No-one else should come and say, 'Oh, I'm a brother, I've come to live and build my house here.' That causes problems and must stop. And then, when the land is straight, the MEF commanders and Malaita premier and chiefs should go to the Weather Coast to Keke's place and make a big feast there, to thank each other and cry together, as a real reconciliation between us. Then the Guadalcanal side, including Keke even though he is in prison, should go to Malaita and do the same thing, and then all the church leaders of Solomon Islands should come together for us to celebrate the reconciliation. This is the only way, and when the land issues are straightened out and disputes are minimised, the way is clear for economic development and lasting peace.

Government now recognises that the alienated land which was used by Europeans should go back to the original land-holders. People are now applying to take back their lands and we Malaita chiefs are contributing to this because they gave us land and we have lived in it, built and gardened in it, up to the present. If the government wants to do anything with the land, it first has to go back to the land-holders, who can make terms and conditions for our land-holders who are not indigenous to the land. This also acknowledges the word of God: 'Move not the ancient landmark which God has given since the foundation of the world.' Land is the main issue in Solomon Islands and that is what caused the recent conflict.

We have been helping the land-holders of a big clan called Tandei, which includes Honiara, and Kaobata, which includes Kaobao and Suhulu. The way we Malaitans look at the land issue, it was not the people of these clans who expelled the Malaitans, but the people of the Weather Coast, where Harold Keke is from. They are the clans who gave us Malaitans land here, and they are also the rightful land-holders of land used by Lever's Pacific Plantations, which should have gone back to them when the government returned alienated land in 1974. But instead they sold it to Asian businesses, and from Luga to the airport you can now see big stores and restaurants there. In east Guadalcanal, from Rere to Lambi, Lever's returned the land and all the property and equipment on it to the landholders. Those people had no understanding of development and let it go to bush, but that's their problem, and the land belongs to them.

The other thing we need to do is to develop the rural areas in Malaita, so that people can improve their lives while living at home, instead of moving to other islands such as Guadalcanal. That is why we have planned a project at Auluta, near my own home in east Malaita. Frank Lulu Maeaba, a big man in the Ministry of Agriculture, co-ordinated the project and the government of Taiwan provided money for a feasibility study of Auluta and for Alex Rukia to do the land recording at the same time. The first meeting was at Nāfinua and Alex asked me to help him with the maps, and chief Labesau and facilitator Rocky Tisa helped me. They gathered all the chiefs together and I said to Alex, 'I lived a long time in this eastern district, and these people are very hard to deal with. When you speak, if you mention something which supports a particular person, that's the end of it; they won't allow the land. You must be neutral, speak generally and not side with anyone.'

We put forward a system for planning the oil palm. We won't have a big plantation owned by a company like the Commonwealth Development Corporation (CDC) on Guadalcanal. We won't have labour lines and married quarters so that people come and stay on other people's land, gardening everywhere in their area, until ethnic tension occurs again, on Malaita. There will be a company plantation as well as smallholdings further out on people's own land. The company will pay them for harvesting and they will also take their own harvest and sell it to the company. You can have your own block of oil palm and work for the company too. Our aim is for everybody to return to Malaita, because all the Malaitans have trade skills from working for CDC, for the Gold Ridge mine and all the companies in Honiara, so they can hold the same positions in this operation.

I have explained that the conflict was a political matter, caused by politicians destroying our unity, coveting things and destroying one plan after another. I have visited Rove prison to meet MEF commander Moses Su'u and I talked with the IFM commander Andrew Te'e and met Harold Keke. They cried for each other and I could see how, when they met each other personally and promised not to go on, there would be no more conflict between Malaita and Guadalcanal. When they signed the Townsville Peace Agreement they knew it was politics, but we chiefs made them understand the trouble they were involved in and they were sorry it had happened. That is why, when Sogavare's government lost and Snyder Rini was elected prime minister in 2006, the two parties, Malaita and Guadalcanal, came together, and Chinatown burned. When I walked through there early that morning, people were taking everything from the stores, and the young men were saying, 'Look, Mala and Guale have come together! Now you businessmen, beware! Government, beware!'

The point I want to make comes from my talks with the chiefs of Guadalcanal and other provinces, when I co-ordinated the programme for the UN High Commissioner for Human Rights in 2001. I could see that those elders were innocent, and the church leaders, both Guadalcanal and Malaita. That is why, if leadership was in the hands of the elders there might be no problem, but in the hands of the youth it certainly is a problem. So I want us to restore the leadership we have lost, bringing us to this decay. For centuries there was leadership in the various provinces of our country, up to the present, as the Guadalcanal commanders have told me themselves.

On reflection we recognise that there have been errors in the system of central government since independence in 1978, with a prime-ministerial system which was inappropriate for the country. We now know that Solomon Islands gained independence too early, because our leaders encouraged us to admire and respect them and led us into a system which did not serve the needs or interests of the people. This has put us into three categories: the governing group who became rich overnight, the middle group who tried business without much success, and the grassroots who had nothing to develop themselves with. The point is that the rich have got richer and the poor have got poorer, and as a rule a deprived man is an angry man. In his need he will steal and rape, break into houses or even kill, because of lack of support for the grassroots.

In the past we lived under a system of equality of wealth based on exchange. This meant that when someone needed a pig he offered us a garden-plot of taro; when someone on an offshore island needed taro he offered us fish; when someone needed a weapon, he offered home-grown tobacco. When someone's son was married, everyone came together to pay the brideprice, and when someone's daughter was married, everyone came together to receive the shell-money and to contribute things for the marriage feast. When the chief ordered people to clean up the home area, everyone came together to clean it, and if there was a helpless old person in the community, the women of each household would bring food to feed him, even if they were not closely related.

This valuable practice of co-operation has changed since the British colonised the country, and the poor people do not want a system of government which has left them nowhere. In respecting each other we comply with a system which was founded when our first ancestors discovered Solomon Islands, but when we adopt politics and get involved in business it leads us astray so that we do not even love our own 'brothers'. This is what has caused the problem of land disputes. In the past, land was held collectively by the family, but suddenly, due to business interests, one of two 'brothers' would dispute the land for personal gain, using several hectares for cattle or cocoa or coconut plantations to earn money for himself, denying the rights of his 'brother'. Furthermore, Western ideas of economics convinced Solomon Islands overseas students returning to the country to behave foolishly, contradicting the traditional religious and cultural values of co-operation which suit the people of the country best. Then again, overseas investment in harvesting the resources of the country was not properly discussed by the chiefs, because the government neglected to invite them to the negotiations before agreements were signed. If power were vested in the chiefs there would be no disputes over land, for power over land is vested in them as leaders of clans. Community leaders could establish tribunals to settle land issues and clear the way for economic development. Investors would be able to harvest our resources and then everybody could get rich.

Formerly a chief was a big man in the community, and if he said something our ancestors, down to our grandfathers and fathers, obeyed him. He told us to do something and we did it. We didn't say, 'Who is born from you? You didn't beget me!' The chief was also important because he was neutral in handing down decisions, which was why he was the only one we listened to. This is in me, as passed on from my father, and there are many occasions when I have solved problems between people. Then came the government headmen, who were spokesmen because they understood a bit of Pijin or were educated enough to speak English with the Whiteman in court. The district officer from 'Aoke would come to hear court cases and if the case went higher, the district commissioner would come. All those people were very important in those days but some things were still referred back to the chiefs.

Then later on, in 1978, Kenilorea led us as prime minister when we achieved independence, and everything changed in ways which we didn't want and couldn't accept. Prime-ministership suited England because England had money, but by comparison we were very poor. All the money of the country has gone into the pockets of the leaders. The members of parliament have raised their own status through overseas trips, high sitting allowances, and the four million dollars constituency development fund which they have discretion over, for their children's businesses, everyone getting outboard motors, chainsaws, cars and airfares, allowing them to live in luxury. Then everyone else sits there like a big dog while they eat in the house, watching for the bones of the pig he has killed to be thrown out.[1]

I have also been disappointed and frustrated to see the Solomon Islands government recognise and spend millions of dollars from foreign aid donors on new organisations for the women, the youth and the children, providing them with offices, vehicles and salaries. I disagree with the government passing legislation on women's, youth's and children's rights, imposed by human rights organisations. By such actions the government contradicts our real traditional rights and causes pride and disrespect in the community. For instance, it has introduced 'adolescence', allowing young girls and boys to raise their own standing and take a disrespectful attitude to others and pleasing themselves. They gather together in secret, smoking, eating betelnut, and going into the bush to misbehave. They don't settle down with their parents or even seek permission from their mother and father before taking action. In this country, there is no 'right' in the hands of the child, no 'right' in the hands of the woman. Father is the head of the family and even if he is not a chief you should treat him as one, because it was his father who passed to him the knowledge to govern the family. In this country rights are vested in the chiefs as custodians of the original traditions passed on from our ancestors to us in the present.

I suggest that it is not the youth who should be blamed for drinking *kwaso*[2] and smoking marijuana and the girls selling their bodies in town and on the fishing boats. The government is to blame. It should invite more investors and businesses to provide jobs for the youth to receive regular salaries so they can buy beer and cigarettes and not consume illegal *kwaso*, get drunk and cause trouble. The youth of our family have been in this situation, until some sons of mine gave them jobs in their security companies. Once they were busy in their jobs, under strict discipline and control, they became good law-abiding citizens and committed Christians. What I mean is that the various development funds which come through the Ministry of Commerce and Industry should be delivered to the communities for projects such as piggeries, poultry, bakeries, agricultural equipment, reforestation, clinics and cultural centres. On the other hand, the banks would be more open to lending if the MPs supported associations to start businesses. If only the MPs in the government would leave their jealousy, stealing, bribery and greed, and taking up with several women at a time, then householders and their children could become self-employed and prosper. Once again, this means co-operation, as in the original practices of our traditional culture.

Not once do you see the chiefs recognised and supported by the government, yet if trouble occurs in our communities, people run to these chiefs. Chiefs are not even invited to important occasions to speak on behalf of the indigenous people of the nation. This country is the chiefs' country, led in the past by those who cared for the people, looking after the rights of everyone, whoever they were. In Malaita the chiefs have been working to re-establish tradition for many years, and in the 1980s some of us formed the Solomon Islands Traditional Culture and Environmental Conservation Foundation (SITCECF), to achieve a system which would operate to the benefit of the nation and put things into balance. Our organisation has settled conflicts between different ethnic groups, between different languages of Malaita, and between Malaita and Western Province, Rennell-Bellona and Temotu. But the government has never allocated any money to pay for allowances, costs or office facilities for the chiefs to maintain this good work. By fatherly leadership, they continue to serve their communities voluntarily. In the SITCECF executive, when we work we use up our own money to meet the organisation's expenses, stationery and the rest. Government can see that we are reducing the expenses of the police, teaching people and advising them to return to their fathers and pastors so that even the bad ones have become as good as priests.

Furthermore, SITCECF has been organising a programme for various centres in the provinces to teach people about the chiefly system and about their original traditional rights. We have been drifting backwards as money destroys the conscience of the people and blinds them to the value of co-operation and exchange, which in the past brought success and wealth to everyone in society. We plan for a constitution in which we would appoint persons knowledgeable in the wisdom which has been passed down from former times to the present. The fashion since independence in 1978 in no way complies with our way of life from the past, because the rich are rich and the poor are poor, which is bad for everyone. We believe that the country will not have any success until both the government and the chiefs contribute to government policies and strategies. This is important in achieving a system which will operate to the benefit of the nation, to put things into balance. Because, since politics took over with independence in 1978 until the present, everything has become confused by monetary cheating, corruption, misappropriation and conflict and everything attempted has been in error.

In my opinion, it is of paramount importance that the Solomon Islands government should recognise all the houses of chiefs in the country, politically, legally and financially. They should form a council of chiefs, which would become the lower house of the national parliament. When parliament is sitting, members of the lower house would comment on legislation before resolutions are passed and gazetting takes place. Of course, the elected MPs are at the head of the political system adopted from the colonial government, yet some are incapable of leadership and are not involved in community organisations. In the past, senior chiefs worked with the community and leadership was spearheaded by respected persons with traditional skills and knowledge. They arranged for villagers to co-operate and brought people together to settle disputes between them, which is necessary for everyone to become prosperous by allowing land for development. A lower house of chiefs would provide another avenue for government recognition of traditional principles and for traditional law to be used in courts at all levels for the benefit of everyone in the country.

As I said to Prime Minister Bart Ulufa'alu that time we went to see him, you must render everything belonging to Caesar back to Caesar and everything belonging to God back to God, as Jesus said in the Bible. Give everything belonging to the chiefs back to the chiefs, and everything belonging to politics back to politics.

---

[1] This old saying was used of Malaitan relationships with the British colonial government at the time of Maasina Rul.
[2] *Kwaso* is illicit home-brewed alcohol.

BIBLIOGRAPHY

Akin, D. (1999) Compensation and the Melanesian State: Why the Kwaio Keep Claiming. *The Contemporary Pacific* 2:35-67.

Akin, D. (2013) *Colonialism, Maasina Rule, and the Origins of Malaitan Kastom*. University of Hawai'i Press, Honolulu.

Allen, M.G. (2013) *Greed and Grievance: Ex-militants' perspectives on the conflict in Solomon Islands, 1998-2003*. University of Hawai'i Press, Honolulu. (no page references as cited when in press)

Burt, B. (1981) *Solomon Islanders: The Kwara'ae*. British Museum Publications, London.

Burt, B. (1988) Abu'a 'i Kwara'ae: The meaning of tabu in a Solomon Islands society. *Mankind* 18:74–89.

Burt, B. & M. Kwa'ioloa (1992) *Falafala ana Ano 'i Kwara'ae / The Tradition of Land in Kwara'ae*. Institute of Pacific Studies & Honiara Centre, University of the South Pacific.

Burt, B. (1994a) *Tradition and Christianity: The colonial transformation of a Solomon Islands society*. Harwood Academic Publishers, New York.

Burt, B. (1994b) Land In Kwara'ae and Development in Solomon Islands. *Oceania* 64:317–335.

Burt, B. & M. Kwa'ioloa (2001) *A Solomon Islands Chronicle, as told by Samuel Alasa'a*. British Museum Press, London.

Burt, B. (2008) Cultural Research as Exchange. *La Restitution du Patrimoine Material et Immaterial: Regards croises Canada / Melanesia. Les Cahiers du CIÉRA* 2:115-130.

Burt, B. (2009) (ed.) *Ti 'A'emae 'i Kwara'ae / Some Histories of Kwara'ae*. (photocopied booklet)

Fifi'i, J. & R.M. Keesing (1989) *From Pig Theft to Parliament: My life between two worlds*. Solomon Islands College of Higher Education, Honiara, & University of the South Pacific, Suva.

Fraenkel, J. (2004) *The Manipulation of Custom: From uprising to intervention in the Solomon Islands*. Pandanus Books, Canberra.

Keesing, R.M. (1983) *Elota's Story: The life and times of a Solomon Islands big man*. Holt, Rinehart & Winston, New York.

Kenilorea, P. (2008) *Tell It As It Is: Autobiography of Rt. Hon. Sir Peter Kenilorea, KBE, PC, Solomon Islands first prime minister*. Centre for Asia-Pacific Studies, Academic Sinica, Taipei.

Kwa'ioloa, M. & B. Burt (1997) *Living Tradition: A changing life in Solomon Islands*. British Museum Press, London, & University of Hawai'i Press, Honolulu.

Kwa'ioloa, M. & B. Burt (2001) *Na Masu'u kia 'i Kwara'ae:Tualaka 'i Solomon Islands fa'inia logo na rū ne'e bulao saena fanoa kia kī: Our Forest of Kwara'ae: Our life in Solomon Islands and the things which grow in our home*. British Museum Press, London.

Kwa'ioloa, M. & B. Burt (2007) 'The Chiefs' Country': A Malaitan view of the conflict in Solomon Islands. *Oceania* 77:111-127.

Macdonald-Milne, B. (2003) *The True Way of Service: The Pacific Way of the Melanesian Brotherhood, 1925-2000*. Christians Aware, Leicester.

Moore, C. (2004) *Happy Isles in Crisis: The historical causes for a failed state in Solomon Islands, 1998-2004*. Asia Pacific Press, Canberra.

Solomon Islands Parliament (2009) *Commission of Inquiry into the April 2006 Honiara Civil Unrest in Honiara: Recommendations, conclusions and findings*. Paper 13 of 2009. National Parliament, Honiara.

White, G., D. Gegeo, D. Akin & K.A. Watson-Gegeo (1988) (eds & trans.) *The Big Death: Solomon Islanders Remember World War II*. Solomon Islands College of Higher Education & University of the South Pacific, Suva.

INDEX

'A'ekafo, Honiara 68, 126-128, 167, 171
Alasa'a, Samuel 3, 13, 28, 34, 35, 40, 45, 55, 87, 181, 210, 277; his land claims 136-159
alcoholic drink 58, 74, 77, 87, 88, 89, 132, 167, 276, 110, 121, 224, 239, 247, 251, 253, 261, 273, 276
Alebua, Ezekiel 203, 209, 252-257
Allen, Matthew 19, 235, 277
Alligator Creek, Guadalcanal 216, 217, 219-221
ancestral religion and ghosts 3, 11, 17, 26, 31, 35, 56, 123, 124, 132, 139, 141, 142, 148, 151-152, 154, 159, 160, 181, 201, 249; interventions by ghosts 5, 32, 40, 49, 51, 54, 56, 124, 143-144, 154, 210, 251; pig sacrifice 31, 33, 49, 56, 131, 251 (see also priests, sorcery)
anthropological research 5, 23, 39, 48, 57
'Aoke (Auki) 49, 67, 75, 83, 140, 158, 226, 272 (maps x, 140)
'Are'are, Malaita 113, 182, 201, 202, 215, 263 (map x)
Art Gallery 206, 208-209, 243, 249, 250, 252, 254, 256 (map 211)

Auluta Project, Malaita 268 (map 140)
Australia and Australians 49, 57-58, 73, 80, 86, 253, 255, 263; in ethnic conflict 219, 237, 241, 243, 245;
Ausaid 227, 249
Baegu, Malaita 99, 199 (map x)
Baelelea, Malaita 183 (map x)
Basakana, Malaita 140, 151, 153, 155, 158 (map 140)
betelnut 77, 87, 121, 125, 127, 130, 132, 154, 156, 202, 239, 251, 273
bibilical references 34, 47, 90, 122, 125, 141, 146, 276, 267
Bita'ama, Malaita 140, 151 (map 140)
Bougainville 203, 252 (map x)
brideprice – see marriage
British Museum 24, 36, 37, 44, 58, 60, 61, 118
bunkers, militant 216, 217, 219, 221, 223
Burt, Ben 27, 37, 40-55, 57-58
business 6, 59, 67-68, 69, 78, 83, 131, 144, 195, 204, 209, 216, 267, 270, 271, 272, 273, 274; damage from ethnic tension 221, 222, 227, 242, 269 (see also construction work, security companies)

chiefs' organisations 15-16, 40, 41, 181, 265 (see also Maasina Rul, SITCECF, Malaita Ma'asina Forum)
Chinatown 21, 240, 242
Chinese and Asians 75, 83, 216, 233, 240, 242, 267, 269 (see also Taiwan)
Christian church 1, 16, 31, 34, 40, 59, 73, 77, 90, 93, 116, 138, 163 180, 196, 246, 265, 267, 269
Christian denominations; Assemblies of God 178; Church of Melanesia (Anglican) 122, 124, 138, 156 (see also Melanesian Brotherhood); Missionary Baptist Church 74; Roman Catholic Church 207, Seventh Day Adventist Church 60, 146; South Sea Evangelical Church 90, 122
Christian religious practice 34, 100, 121,122-123, 125, 131, 132; 170, 193, 203 (see also biblical references)
class issues 22, 270
Commonwealth Development Corporation (CDC) 221, 232, 268, 269
compensation – see restitution
constituency development fund 16, 179, 185, 186
construction work 6, 18, 64, 70, 72-73, 195, 202, 119, 195, 265
corruption in politics 16, 22, 177-179, 193, 249, 272, 275
coup of 2000 192, 214, 218, 222, 234, 235
courts 15, 38, 42,138, 169, 171, 172, 226, 239, 240, 242, 244, 256, 272, 276; for land 13, 14, 43, 136-138, 142, 147, 148, 159, 202; supporting chiefs 170-173
Daokalia, Paul 162, 182, 185-188
Dausabea, Charles and Roland 178-179, 185-186, 188, 227
development, economic 6, 11, 12, 13, 21, 22, 146, 150, 177, 184, 222, 231, 241, 250, 265-269, 271, 274
dreams and visions 32, 34, 129, 209-210

education, home 59, 76-77, 82, 88, 99, 110, 175
education, schools and teachers 38, 39, 57, 59, 72, 75, 78, 82, 139, 147, 185, 186, 195, 238; school fees 6, 73, 178, 135, 195, 260; affected by ethnic conflict 192, 207, 221, 241
employment and cash earnings 6, 12, 18, 66, 67, 69-73, 75, 76, 86, 135, 195, 198, 209, 222; (see also construction work, gardening, plantations, security businesses, smallholder production)
England and English 39, 40, 41, 44, 111, 124, 141, 170, 181, 238, 259, 272; visits to England 44, 57-59
Ete, Frank Tu'aisalo 41, 42, 43, 53-54, 162, 183, 185
exchange, gifts and reciprocity 9, 47, 48, 66, 68-69, 176, 187, 116, 220, 270, 275 (see also brideprice)
Fairu, Malaita 12, 14, 33, 78, 136-146, 149-150, 155, 158, 159 (map 140)
Fanenalua, Bizel 2, 39, 45, 66, 87, 88, 89, 96, 102, 105, 114, 178, 226, 260
Fataleka, Malaita 86, 99, 122, 199, 200, 201, 202 (maps x, 140)
feasts 147, 148, 151, 156, 160, 164, 180, 196, 203, 263, 267 (see also marriage)
foodstuffs 29, 32, 45, 55, 64, 67, 68, 89, 92-93, 97, 100, 102, 111, 112, 115, 149, 155, 156, 159, 177, 179, 186, 201, 202, 203, 216, 220, 223, 225
Fraenkel, Jon 19, 212
Fugu'i, Ronald 177, 186, 200
funerals 85, 114-115
gardening; Guadalcanal 63, 65, 67, 88, 174-175, 190, 196, 209, 216, 267; Malaita 176, 268, 270; for cash 68-69, 75, 135, 195
Gilbert Camp, Honiara, 66, 69, 123, 131, 168, 178, 185, 196, 199, 202, 216, 220, 231 (map 211)

Gold Ridge 195, 242, 269 (map 211)
governance issues 16-18, 22, 40, 176-177, 187, 191-193, 212, 270-276 (see also Maasina Rul, SITCECF)
Gua, Wilson 29, 100, 103-107, 143
Guadalcanal Province 234, 256-7, 175, 196, 197, 207
guns, of militants 192, 204, 221, 218, 224, 226-227, 228, 229, 231, 232, 237, 251, 262
Henderson Airport 242, 244 (map 211)
house of chiefs 22, 43, 127, 169, 173, 249, 174, 246, 275-276
housing in Honiara 71-75
independence of Solomon Islands 270, 272, 275
Isabel island 14, 58, 89, 183; Malaita links to Gao 151-157 (maps x, 140)
Kakabona, Honiara 153, 216-221
kastom – see tradition
Keesing, Roger 26, 39, 44, 60
Keke, Harold 20, 192, 204, 206-207, 217, 228, 233, 238, 246-247, 251-252, 253, 257, 266-267, 269
Kemakeza, Allan 192, 217, 224-225, 226, 228, 243, 252, 256
Kenilorea, Peter 26, 272
Ko'oliu, Timi 5, 31, 48-49, 51-56, 61
Kobito, Honiara 46, 64, 68, 72, 74, 76, 90, 91, 110, 164, 168, 196, 199, 200, 202, 231 (map 211)
Kwa'ite'e, David 81, 93, 94, 129-130, 165, 169, 172, 173, 193, 252, 254, 255-257, 260-262
Kwaio, Malaita 7, 21, 39, 50, 60, 86, 91, 115, 173, 201, 217, 228; ten Kwaio killed by Keke 20, 246, 251-263 (maps x, 140)
land tenure and claims 12-15, 18, 26, 41-43, 47, 49, 137-138, 141, 147, 148, 193; land disputes 13, 136-146, 149-150, 271; land recording 184, 268 (see also Malaitan settlement of Honiara; Tolinga)

Langalanga, Malaita 7, 108,110, 112, 116, 121, 203, 215 (maps x, 140)
leadership, traditional 2-3, 7, 9-10, 11, 12-17, 20, 22, 31, 34, 35, 46, 81, 86, 103, 104, 107, 115, 116, 119, 137, 147, 159, 163, 167, 176-178, 181, 261, 269-271, 274, 276
Lever's Pacific Plantations 124, 194, 201, 234, 267-268
Lusibaea, Jimmy Rasta 217, 225, 226, 251
Maasina Rul (Masing Rul) 15-16, 17, 141, 181, 184,187-188
Maesatana, John and Samuel 3, 29, 32, 33, 46, 64, 74, 75, 87, 95, 96, 107-108, 110, 113, 116, 137, 138, 143, 149, 172, 199, 202, 224
Maetia, Alfred 41, 42, 145, 173
Maetia, John 186, 250
Malaita Ma'asina Forum 21, 249-250, 263
Malaitans in Guadalcanal; history of migration 193-197, 265; expulsion during ethnic tension 147-148, 207-209, 221-222, 233-244, 266-267; settlement of Honiara 198-203; temporary occupation licences 198, 234, 250
Manimosa, Joseph 196,198, 202-203
Maranda, Pierre 39, 60
Marau, Guadalcanal 193, 215, 228, 237 (map 211)
marriage and brideprice; general principles 7-10, 85-87, 95, 103,109, 115-116, 169, 176, 197, 270; particular cases 27, 55, 86-113, 129, 165-167, 172; marriage feasts 9, 10, 70, 85, 92-93, 97, 100, 102, 104, 111-112, 115, 226, 270
Matariu, Honiara 68, 172, 199, 216 (map 211)
Melanesian Brothers (*tasiu*) 122-123, 132, 220, 258
money, traditional or local – see shell-money

281

Moore, Clive 19, 62, 264
Moro 246, 263
Mount Austen, Guadalcanal 68, 190, 196, 202, 216, 231, 233 (map 211)
Museum of Solomon Islands 183, 258-259
Naitoro, John 42, 182, 183, 250
New Zealand 44, 82, 241, 258
Orodani, Francis 197-198
pastors 23. 30, 32, 33, 74, 164, 170, 173, 275,
pigs 46, 63, 66, 70, 78, 86, 89, 93, 98, 100, 102, 104, 105, 112, 138, 140, 155, 176, 180, 194, 195, 196, 201, 203, 206, 259, 266, 270, 272, 274 (see also ancestral religion)
plantations, commercial 18, 67, 124, 194-195, 201, 207, 234, 267, 268
police 15, 128, 146, 169, 170, 171, 173, 175; civil conflict Chapters 8-10; Field Force 192, 215-219, 222-224, 238, 251, 252; Kwa'ioloa's experience 23, 51, 72, 76, 79, 97, 98, 99, 125, 164, 168; rapid response unit 216, 218, 221, 242; special constables 6, 19, 72, 73, 191, 227, 230, 239, 240, 242
politics, electoral 16, 176-180, 184-186, 188, 196, 206, 250, 269
priests (ancestral, tabu-speakers) 3, 35, 48, 49, 50, 61, 141, 251
prison 50, 171, 173, 178, 224, 227, 240, 247, 251, 267, 269
Ramo, Benjamin 93, 96, 127-128, 131, 154, 169, 171, 173, 184, 197, 199, 206, 260
Ramos island (Anogwa'u) 14, 152-154, 157 (map 140)
RAMSI (Regional Assistance Mission to Solomon Islands) vi, 75, 243-245, 247, 250, 258-259, 262
religion – see ancestral, Christian
Rennell and Bellona islands 205, 274 (map x)

restitution, general principles 9, 15, 40; particular cases 50, 54-55, 95, 99-100, 102, 110, 126-128, 131, 132, 144, 164-168, 170, 173, 205, 241, 260-261; for death of Timi Ko'oliu 49-56; in ethnic conflict 10, 19-21, 192, 206, 212, 218, 225; for ten Kwaio killed by Keke 251-263
Rofate'e, Adriel 37, 41, 43, 49, 50, 52, 53, 120, 173
Ruafatu, Guadalcanal 124, 194 (map 211)
Rukia, Alex 126, 162, 182, 184-186, 187, 188, 258, 268, 268
Saki, Selwyn 206, 232-233, 247
Sangafanoa, Silas 126, 169, 173-174, 175, 232
Sangu, Joseph 204, 247
Sasako, Alfred 252-253, 255-256, 262, 263
Second World War 4, 18, 132, 194, 212, 233, 263, 265, 266
security businesses 6, 19, 73, 75, 224, 225, 227-228, 230, 244, 273
shell-money types 7-8, 60, 84, 91,112 (for shell-money payments see brideprice, restitution)
Siale, Malaita 31, 32, 46, 61, 151, 152, 157-160, 193-194, 212 (map 140)
smallholder production 144, 195, 266, 268-269, 271
Sogavare, Manessa 192, 217, 269
Solomon Islands Traditional Culture and Environmental Conservation Foundation (SITCECF) 16, 20, 21, 42, 82, 180, 182-185, 205, 248-251, 254-255, 258-259, 274-275
sorcery 10-12, 15, 26, 114, Chapter 5, 246
Su'u, Moses 217, 223-224, 225, 230, 238, 247, 269
swearing 99, 164, 167, 171, 228, 260
tabu 9, 17, 51, 54, 89, 95, 97, 100, 105, 110, 115, 116, 131, 148, 152,

Taiwan 222, 268
Te'e, Andrew 246, 269
television and video 6, 76-80, 81, 82, 106, 225
Temotu Province 58, 183, 186, 205, 212, 274 (map x)
Tisa, Rocky Hardy 13, 41, 43, 53, 70, 136, 142-146, 159, 162, 183, 185, 186, 205, 252, 254, 268
To'abaita, Malaita 71, 85, 94, 98, 114, 121, 148, 215, 229, 240 (map x) (see also Basakana, Bita'ama)
Tolinga, Malaita 14, 46, 78, 128, 143; land claims 150-159 (map 140)
Townsville Peace Agreement 221, 236-8, 245, 247, 254 255-256, 262, 269

tradition (*kastom*), concepts of 3-4
Ulufa'alu, Bart 209, 218, 228, 276
United Nations High Commission for Human Rights (UNHCHR) 21, 248-249, 254, 256, 262, 269
Weather Coast, Guadalcanal 174, 175, 192, 196, 233, 247, 251-252, 263, 266, 267 (map 211)
Western Province 58, 183, 186, 205, 212, 274
White River, Honiara 102, 169, 185, 196, 200, 216, 238 (map 211)
World War Two – see Second World War

www.ingramcontent.com/pod-product-compliance
Lightning Source LLC
Chambersburg PA
CBHW071334080526
44587CB00017B/2836